THE CHALLENGE OF SURREALISM

The Challenge of Surrealism

. . . .

The Correspondence of Theodor W. Adorno and Elisabeth Lenk

Edited and Translated by Susan H. Gillespie

Introduction by Rita Bischof

University of Minnesota Press

Minneapolis • London

The translation of this work was supported by a grant from the Goethe-Institut, which is funded by the German Ministry of Foreign Affairs.

Correspondence between Theodor W. Adorno and Elisabeth Lenk was originally published in *Theodor W. Adorno und Elisabeth Lenk: Briefwechsel, 1962–1969,* ed. Elisabeth Lenk (Munich: edition text + kritik, 2001). Copyright 2001 edition text + kritik.

For the full contents of this book, see pages 253–54 for original publication information for previously published material.

Published by the University of Minnesota Press
111 Third Avenue South, Suite 290
Minneapolis, MN 55401–2520
http://www.upress.umn.edu

Library of Congress Cataloging-in-Publication Data
Lenk, Elisabeth.
The challenge of surrealism : the correspondence of Theodor W. Adorno and Elisabeth Lenk / edited and translated by Susan H. Gillespie ; introduction by Rita Bischof.
Includes bibliographical references and index.
ISBN 978-0-8166-5616-5 (hc)—ISBN 978-0-8166-5617-2 (pb)
1. Adorno, Theodor W., 1903–1969—Correspondence. 2. Lenk, Elisabeth— Correspondence. 3. Philosophers, Modern—Germany—Correspondence.
4. Surrealism.
I. Lenk, Elisabeth. II. Gillespie, Susan H., editor. III. Title.
B3199.A34A4 2015
193—dc23   2015023631

Printed in the United States of America on acid-free paper

The University of Minnesota is an equal-opportunity educator and employer.

21 20 19 18 17 16 15   10 9 8 7 6 5 4 3 2 1

Contents

Editor's Note

This book was created to honor the work of one of Germany's most original and interesting woman scholars, Elisabeth Lenk. As first conceived by Robert Hullot-Kentor, the publication of Lenk's correspondence with Theodor W. Adorno gives English-speaking audiences a glimpse of a side of the philosopher that has not received much attention: his generous and forthcoming support of students, especially those he judged very talented. Lenk, who studied philosophy, literature, and sociology in Frankfurt and Paris and later became professor of literature in Hanover, was one of his students. That Adorno's relationship with her reveals an amorous aspect, which was not reciprocated by Lenk, did not lessen the mutual intellectual respect and cordiality in their teacher–student relationship. Adorno supported and critiqued Lenk's work, found a home for it at the University of Frankfurt, and later assisted Lenk in her search for an academic position.

Lenk's interest was surrealism. With Adorno's blessing, she decamped to Paris to write her doctoral thesis on the movement. There she became a regular participant in surrealist meetings and events and an author of significant commentary. Her correspondence with Adorno is one of the few places where the philosopher expressed his attitudes toward this movement. To assert that Adorno was convinced of the sociopolitical import of surrealism would be an exaggeration, but he was open to giving it academic consideration and argued for its legitimacy and relevance as an aesthetic movement worthy of attention in the context of social alienation.

While she was studying with Adorno in Frankfurt, Lenk was a leading member of the Sozialistischer Deutscher Studentenbund (Socialist German Students' Union, SDS). Her political engagement continued in Paris in the form of support for deserters from the war in Algeria. She remained outspoken in her emphasis on the importance of theory, meaning critical theory—a position that among university students was identified with the politically unpopular "Adorno line." At the same time, she was sensitive to surrealism's practical, political energies, which likely accounted for much of its appeal. Writing from Paris, and later from Hanover and Berlin, Lenk came to view surrealism and critical theory as inherently and necessarily complementary. In 1996, in the essay "Critical Theory and Surreal Practice," which is included in this volume, Lenk asked "whether surrealism . . . was and is not precisely the practice that is appropriate to critical theory; and whether . . . critical theory was and is not precisely the theory toward which surreal practice was oriented."

Lenk's question is a serious one. To further deepen and explore its resonances, the present volume includes important essays on surrealism by Frankfurt School critical philosophers Walter Benjamin and Theodor Adorno (here in new translations). Benjamin's foundational essay of 1929 and Adorno's somewhat less well-known writing from 1956 present different, if not wholly antagonistic, perspectives on surrealism. Benjamin's essay, in particular, has helped shape attitudes from the 1960s, when the correspondence between Lenk and Adorno was written, to the present. In spite of her being a student of Adorno, Lenk's own position is closer to that of Benjamin, who saw surrealism as a response to the "crisis of the intelligentsia, more precisely, of the humanist concept of freedom." In bringing together artistic and social practice, personal and political life, surrealism, in this version, has inherently explosive power. Arousing nostalgia for desires and hoped-for futures that have not come to pass, presenting (verbally as well as pictorially) clashing images in ways that defeat ingrained expectations, and revealing the absurdities of the present, surrealist practice might resurrect and even help to bring about a vision of society that is not inimical to human happiness.

In her Introduction to this book, Rita Bischof, Lenk's former student and friend and a leading international scholar of surrealism who has written incisively on Benjamin's idea of the "dialectical image," argues for the "timeliness of a renewed engagement with surrealism." Bischof reminds us that "surrealism itself was a political matter . . . and it remained faithful, to the very end, to the anti-imperialist political intentions it had already manifested at the time of the First World War. The same is true of its uncompromising love for the freedom of all men and women." Her comments provide indispensable background information on the two letter writers and the international intellectual worlds in which they were so fully engaged.

Lenk's own writing, in her essays and critical introductions, draws on philosophy, philology, and political economic theory. In the tradition of antipositivist sociology, it rejects disciplinary specialization and eschews data- or fact-driven discourse, looking to literature and the arts as revelatory of contemporary sociopolitical issues. Lenk's essays on Charles Fourier and Louis Aragon, included in this volume, exemplify her approach, which is driven by an urgency tempered by humor.

In her introduction to her correspondence with Adorno, Lenk expands on the personal and historical context of the seven years (1962–69) during which the two were in epistolary and direct contact. She also links Adorno's response to surrealism to another underappreciated aspect of his work and life: his self-description as a "martyr of happiness" (in Letter 81). The philosopher's lifelong preoccupation with happiness, its exclusion from modern economic life, and its utopian promise figure in his response to surrealism as linked to the attempt to recover experiences of childhood.

The Challenge of Surrealism concludes with a series of short prose pieces that Adorno co-wrote in the early 1930s with Carl Dreyfus, a colleague at the Institute for Social Research. Originally labeled "Surrealistische Lesestücke" (Surrealist Readings), they were published under the amusing pseudonym Castor Zwieback, which obliquely invokes their dual authorship by reference to the twins Castor and Pollux and the twice-baked biscuit known in both German and English as zwieback. That both castor (oil) and zwieback are typically associated with children may be further evidence of a playful mood.[1] Karl Riha, in an introductory editorial note to the complete version he published, suggests that the pieces could be regarded as a kind of "covert sociology," and at the same time as "freestanding experiments" and "the merger of philosophy with sociology and of both with literature." The fact that the *Frankfurter Zeitung*, where the coproductions were first published, festooned the page where they appeared with the well-known surrealist quotation "Frappe à la porte, crie: Entrez, et n'entre pas (André Breton et Paul Eluard)"[2] supports the decision to include them here. The translation includes two pieces ("Harpsichord" and "Funerary Monument") whose German originals ("Cembalo" and "Grabmal") were not included in the standard edition of Adorno's *Gesammelte Werke* and have not been widely available in either German or English.

Thanks are due, first of all, to Elisabeth Lenk for her friendship, patience, and active participation in the shaping and editing of what I will always think of as "her" book. Robert Hullot-Kentor deserves thanks for having inspired this book and for the original selection of material; he was generous with his time and responses to proposed changes and additions.

Rita Bischof, in addition to writing the Introduction, became an invaluable friend, expert, and supporter in the editorial process; I thank her for the suggestion to include two previously little-known "Surrealist Readings" by Adorno and Carl Dreyfus. Finally, Suhrkamp's Petra Hardt has earned our collective gratitude as a most helpful and collegial guide in questions regarding publication and rights of permission.

Departures

Critical Theory and Surrealism

Rita Bischof

THE TIMELINESS of a renewed engagement with surrealism is evidenced not only by Occupy Wall Street, Attac, Anonymous, and similar movements—however unseasoned their actions may appear—but above all by the new forms of political opposition that were shocked into existence by the urgency of oppression in countries with autocratic regimes. Examples include the protest actions of Pussy Riot in Russia or occasionally of the early Arab Spring. Wherever, during recent decades, young artists were interviewed in war and crisis zones, whether Bosnia, Libya, or the Middle East, it didn't take long before they could be heard to proclaim that they were unable to talk about their abstruse political experiences of violence other than by expressing them in surrealistic images.

A similar resurgence of surrealist ideas and procedures had occurred in the period following the Second World War: in Paris in May '68 and in the German student movement (which always had an eye on events on the other side of the Atlantic, in the United States). The roots of this resurgence stretched back even further, to when the nuclear arms race and the Cold War were coming to a head, race riots in the United States were approaching the level of civil war, and France was waging its dirty war in Algeria. These are only a few of the political horrors that, night for night— and this was actually what was new—came flickering across the little screen. In Berlin, a wall had recently been erected, and the social consensus in the Federal Republic of Germany continued to be that it was better to repress the country's Nazi past. Despite these efforts, more and more factual material on the appalling deeds of the Third Reich was coming to light, and it was becoming ever clearer how deeply large segments of the population had been implicated in its crimes. That public pressure continued to mount during the early 1960s is due, in no small part, to that era's critical students, who stubbornly uncovered the almost unbroken presence of this past in their society and put it on public view.

An eloquent example is the exhibition "Action Un-expiated Nazi Justice," which law student Reinhard Strecker organized in 1962, a year before the first Frankfurt Auschwitz trials. In the exhibition, Strecker displayed the prosecutorial and personnel files of 105 legal officials who had been permitted to continue in office under the Federal Republic in utter disregard of their Nazi past. The exhibition created a considerable furor and attracted the bitter opposition of the established political parties, including the Social Democratic Party (SPD), which took the radical step of expelling the Socialist German Students' Union (SDS) based on the latter's support of the exhibition. In October 1962, this led to the refounding of SDS as an independent organization of the student left. Elisabeth Lenk was involved, if only briefly, in the conception of an independent, non-party-affiliated, critical left. She had played a decisive role in its definition in a position paper she delivered at the legendary Seventeenth Representative Conference of SDS. In historical retrospect, it has been said that her aim was to establish SDS on the foundation of critical theory, to ensure its adherence to the "Adorno line," so to speak. That the accent she set did not become dominant is evident from the further development of the organization, and yet at that time many people—not only Adorno's epistolary partner—read Adorno primarily politically. The question that occupied many minds and hearts was how critical theory could be translated into the practice of social change without falling into the trap set by the revolutionary parties. The answer was by changing consciousness.

When Adorno began the correspondence with Lenk, approximately six weeks after the Representative Conference in Frankfurt, changing consciousness soon ceased to be the main focus of concern, and soon a new interest would capture the attention of Adorno's addressee. Elisabeth Lenk, who for some time had been living à cheval between Frankfurt and Paris, moved to Paris at the end of 1962. A few months later, she met André Breton and the surrealist group. That the connection ultimately derived from a political impulse is, after all that has been said, not surprising. In Frankfurt, Lenk had already expressed solidarity with French resistance against the war in Algeria, and in this connection—together with Monika Seifert, a daughter of the famous physician and psychoanalyst Alexander

Mitscherlich[1]—she supported deserters who had taken refuge in Frankfurt and others who were in prison. She established contacts between them and their families, carried messages and, when necessary, writing implements and mimeo machines. It was this active political engagement that ultimately led her to the surrealists. At an event in solidarity with Pierre Hessel, a well-known critic of the war in Algeria and uncompromising draft resister, who was being released from prison, she met José Pierre. Pierre told her about the surrealist group and won her over with the statement, "Politics, with us, happens on a different level."[2] Not until the following night did she learn that she had just met with a representative of the very group whom Walter Benjamin had evoked so enthusiastically at the close of the 1920s. Soon thereafter, José Pierre presented her to André Breton, who, on the spot, invited her to the Café Promenade de Vénus, where the surrealists met every evening. From then on, she was a member of the *groupe surréaliste,* until, a year after Breton's death, she was expelled on grounds of "Situationist deviation."[3]

Surrealism itself was a political matter—anyone who fails to pay attention to this is fooling himself—and it remained faithful, to the very end, to the anti-imperialist political intentions it had already manifested at the time of the First World War. The same is true of its uncompromising love for the freedom of all men and women. Let us not forget that André Breton had been one of the initiators of the *Déclaration des 121 sur le droit à l'insoumission dans la guerre d'Algérie,* which appeared on September 1, 1960, and openly called for desertion from the war in Algeria.

In the mind of the barely twenty-five-year-old Elisabeth Lenk, a connection was forged between critical theory and surreal practice, the title of a much later article of hers.[4] The combination incorporated something new and actually unthinkable, something that would not have been found in this form in Adorno but that his younger readers, in particular, somehow read into his writings. For those who also knew the writings of the surrealists, there could be no question but that between the ideas they were expressing and Adorno's theses there existed an intimate connection. Roberto Calasso was the first to affirm this in an essay,[5] and whenever, later on, surrealist ideas experienced a renaissance, they were seen in relation to ideas of Walter Benjamin and Theodor W. Adorno. That this is still the case today may be seen paradigmatically in the work of Carolyn Christov-Bakargiev, the curator of dOKUMENTA 13, who feels committed to both traditions and expressed this in the exhibition. In an interview, she even spoke of a "surrealist turn" as something happening in the present. This turn, she said, was shown by the fact that in post-Mubarak Egypt she had succeeded in holding a seminar on sleep. Clearer evidence of this turn could be found in Kabul, where according to her the "beating heart" of that year's dOKUMENTA was to be found. Alongside seminars, lectures, and discussions, she had organized a big exhibition there, at whose opening the international military had naturally appeared—among other things for purposes of security. "In the process, finally, a crazy surrealist moment occurred," she said. "The official guests behaved like the bees, wasps, or flies in a Greek tragedy. They came, and when they disappeared again the Afghans remained. Like the Dachau photos that Lee Miller published in *Vogue*,[6] the whole thing had something of a surrealist turn. When reality is the way it is, surrealism is the only way out."[7]

One may hope that this time surrealism is understood in its intentions, in other words, that it achieves a certain broad impact and that perhaps the present volume can contribute to such an understanding. If it succeeds, it will be precisely because it does not present surrealism as something complete in itself and in the past—surrealism, apparently, cannot be historicized—but rather as the object of struggle by diverse intellectuals over its meaning.

The occasion for this book is an exchange of letters that, one may say without exaggeration, is unique in Adorno's correspondence. Not because it was carried on with a student who, in spite of all advances, never abandons that somewhat stiff relationship, and who in the process holds fast, unperturbed, to her standpoint, with the result that the reader sometimes has the impression that the longer the correspondence continues the more the two, with increasing virtuosity, are talking past each other. The correspondence is even more strongly characterized by the fact that, with some exceptions, essential things are omitted, because it is not the letters that matter most but rather the face-to-face conversations to which they refer and from which they derive. Above all, though, this exchange is marked by the discussion, in the background, of a subject that otherwise actually played almost no role in Adorno's thought: surrealism. In the letters, readers may discover a different, lighter, at times even playful and more private Adorno alongside the productive scholar who is tirelessly working on new texts, until, as he likes to say, he has "put them to bed"; or readers may find the hounded figure that he increasingly became under pressure from a more and more radicalized student movement. Beyond such bothersome matters as the applications and recommendations for a fellowship, which weigh it down in the beginning, the correspondence also touches on a whole series of themes that shaped both the life of the new Federal Republic and the workings of the university, which is extraordinarily present in the background of this correspondence. Here, too, politics plays a role, less in the form of a discussion of current events than in gestural descriptions, in the response to moral stances and accepted points of view—discussions that often provide a more telling characterization of the intellectual condition of society than do public pronouncements.

Yet when the correspondence was first published, in 2001,[8] there was already something historical about it. It was therefore accompanied—along with very helpful notes—by an appendix with texts that provided additional references and background. The first of these texts was Elisabeth Lenk's above-mentioned speech on the refounding of SDS. Like that speech, the other texts can hardly be understood otherwise than as political. A second example was a text on Heidegger, entitled *L'Être caché*, written by Lenk and first published in the summer of 1964 in the surrealist journal *La Brèche*. The text was translated into German and included in the volume of correspondence, together with an irritated response by Heidegger's translator, Jean Beaufret, in a letter to André Breton. Even a text like "Mr. Enzensberger's Aporias" ("Die Aporien des Herrn Enzensberger"), which had appeared in the same year in *diskus*, the newspaper of Frankfurt University's student body, is political in the sense of that other concept of politics that also characterizes surrealism in its connection to critical theory—political not *although* but *because* it calls into question the notion of an artistic avant-garde. Surrealism was at the paradigmatic core of this debate, and by this time it had long since formed the secret center of the correspondence.[9]

For this American edition of the correspondence, the editors decided against this selection, partly because the debates were too specialized and would have remained abstract for contemporary readers, especially in the United States. Instead, texts were chosen that play a role in the letters themselves and that are associated with the theme of surrealism. These works, in our view, shed the proper light on what is special about this correspondence. As a result, the emphasis has shifted from the original volume. Essentially, the result only illuminates more sharply the actual, although nonexplicit, core of the dialogue.

The resulting volume explores an earlier response to surrealism—actually several different attempts to contend with surrealist ideas, which occurred in different periods and bore the hallmarks of their eras. Only those texts are included that formed the basis for the rediscovery of surrealism during the 1960s student movement. A key role was played by Walter Benjamin, who very early recognized the significance of surrealism and its political implications, which he expressed in a fulminating essay, "Surrealism: Last Snapshot of the European Intelligentsia." The essay influenced the two otherwise very different correspondence partners in their specific conception of surrealism. That between them there was, nevertheless, a developing lack of consensus may have to do, above all, with the fact that they belonged to different generations.

When, after a certain amount of time has passed, you reread texts that, for you personally, exercised a decisive influence in younger years, it can be a kind of dialectical adventure. You read them anew, yet at the same time the memory of earlier readings rings like a distant echo. This is especially true if you knew the text in question almost by heart and if, for this very reason, you have, for decades, denied yourself permission to reread it. For me, a representative of the generation that did not yet belong to the 68ers but was shaped by them, who read Adorno but no longer had the good fortune to be able to study with him, it would be Walter Benjamin's essay, above all, that without a doubt deserves to be seen as the event that introduced surrealism to the German intellectual public almost simultaneously with the surrealist movement's appearance, thus giving that public a chance to connect with discussions that were then current among the European avant-garde. Only a few years later, a discussion of this kind would have been impossible. For me, as a person who had already discovered surrealist texts very early, reading Benjamin's essay was like a revelation. When I read it again, for this introduction, I quickly succumbed to its seductive power, just as I had the first time. Not only did Benjamin immediately recognize surrealism in its very essence, he also wrote an irritatingly beautiful essay that cannot be understood except as a piece of surrealizing philosophical prose.

Among intellectuals of that era, no one else reacted as enthusiastically to surrealism as Benjamin did, and it is remarkable how quickly he was alerted to the surrealist texts. Sometimes he devoured them almost the instant they appeared. This is true of texts like *Une vague de rêves* (1924), which has been described as Louis Aragon's "surrealist manifesto," and even more true of his *Paysan de Paris* (1926), a book that Benjamin, by his own testimony, read with ecstatic enjoyment. Years later, in a letter to Adorno dated May 31, 1935, he described this experience in an expression that became almost legendary. He says that Aragon stood at the beginning of the idea for the *Arcades Project* and expressly mentions *Paysan de Paris*: "It opens with Aragon—the *Paysan de Paris*. Evenings, lying in bed, I could never read more than two to three pages by him because my heart started to pound so hard that I had to put the book down."[10] Breton's *Nadja* appeared in 1928, and Benjamin began writing his essay in the same year. The essay clearly demonstrates Benjamin's readiness to let himself be inspired by the ideas and perspectives of surrealism. The impact of these ideas and perspectives was already observable in the way that Benjamin, drawing not only on the surrealists' works but also on their demonstrations and their struggle for a new concept of politics, derived elements that he would configure anew in his late work. One would be tempted to speak of a surrealist reorientation of his thinking if he himself had not had in mind something else, which also went back to earlier ideas: a new kind of materialist philosophy of history that would be grounded in concrete, everyday conflicts and events. The medium of this new materialist philosophy of history is images, more precisely dialectical images,[11] whose concept he had introduced at the end of the 1920s and which, in his late philosophy of history, he made a central category. Benjamin calls "dialectical" those images that, like the surrealist ones, spring up in the blink of an eye from the unmediated clash of two heterogeneous levels of reality. In other words, these images are not already contained in their components, but emerge only in the consciousness of the observer. Like surrealist metaphors, dialectical images are meant, above all, as threshold images. They find their precise place on the threshold between sleep and waking, which has been "worn down, within each of them, as if by the tread of the hordes of images coursing back and forth."[12] But there are also distinctions to be made, and the most essential one is that Benjamin transfers the image concept from the realm of the aesthetic to the field of historical experience. In his eyes, dialectical images are characterized above all by the fact that in them two time horizons, the present moment (*Jetztzeit*)[13] and the most ancient time of all, and at the same time two spaces, the space of the body and the image-space, meet in a head-on clash and, in doing so, bring the tension between actuality and eternity to explosion.

Rereading a text can also be vexing, for example, if you no longer find it accessible or if its argumentation more or less clearly misses the point of the subject it is addressing. In such a case, one is especially tempted to reread it. Adorno's brief essay of 1956, "Surrealism Reconsidered" ("Rückblickend auf den Surrealismus"), is such a text. It assembles a variety of arguments without mediating between them. The text already fails to convince by virtue of the fact that it does not engage a single one of the great surrealist works. It also remains abstract due to the fact that it opens with the refutation of an argument that had evidently become the consensus in early 1950s Germany, namely, that surrealism should be seen as a kind of naturalism of the inner life and that this made it possible to file it conveniently away. Adorno is right to reject this: "If surrealism were indeed nothing more than a collection of literary and graphic illustrations of Jung or even Freud, it would not just be replicating unnecessarily what the theory itself already states, without any metaphorical garb, but would be so innocuous as to leave no room for the *scandale*[14] that surrealism intends and that is its vital element."

But Adorno also turned the distance that undoubtedly exists between surrealism and psychoanalysis into a chasm, thus depriving himself of insight into the dialectic that the surrealists created between their notions and Freud's theory. Naturally, surrealist images are not symbols of the unconscious, any more than they reflect the "unconscious per se"[15] of dream worlds. The main reason why this is so is that their works are not about reflection or reproduction at all. On the other hand, the affinity that exists between certain artistic methodologies and the primary psychic processes that Freud described is much too obvious to be neglected. This part of Adorno's thesis is thus no longer compatible with the current state of knowledge, even if we concede that in the early years of the Federal Republic it made political sense to assume a stance that uncompromisingly refused to psychologize surrealism. This misunderstanding—actually I would prefer to talk about *mauvaise foi*—when it came to the surrealists was something one encountered quite frequently among German intellectuals of the period; the Adorno–Lenk correspondence contains hints of it.

That not even Adorno remained free from the influence of this attitude is shown precisely by his surrealism essay. It is an oddly ambivalent text, quite evidently written in the conviction that surrealism was a thing of the past and, as such, of purely historical interest.[16] Adorno wrote a kind of obituary for something that, basically, no one had noticed—including the author, whose standpoint has little if any textual basis. He seems familiar only with the paintings of Max Ernst, from which he derives his thesis. When Adorno believes he grasps the origin of surrealist images in the illustrations of the late nineteenth century, this can only refer to collage-novels like *La femme 100 tête, Une semaine de bonté,* or, in particular, *Le Lion de Belfort,* of which he owned a copy. But even in the case of Max Ernst, Adorno's theory is applicable only to a limited extent. It is even less apt when it comes to the other visual artists among the surrealists and applies least of all to surrealist literature. The notion of "children's images of the modern era" is not convincing, the less so since Adorno, to advance this formulation, overstresses the concept of "illustration" and completely misses the moment that makes this concept interesting from the perspective of the study of media. It is not *what* the photographs of the nineteenth century represent that matters most for the surrealists—in any case the illustrations are mostly woodcuts and lithographs—but *how* the photographs represent it; in other words, not the thing from which the images are derived but what the medium makes of it and how this dialectic can be represented.

It is all the more surprising, immediately following these observations, to encounter Adorno's thesis that the shock of surrealist images is a result of the "tension between schizophrenia and reification," and that this proves, in his eyes, that they are "precisely not psychologically inspired. . . . The dialectical images of surrealism are those of a dialectic of subjective freedom in the state of objective unfreedom."[17] Here, I think, his words have undiminished relevance. Weightier, and more profound, is a further thesis that places surrealism in relationship to Hegel, specifically the Hegel of the *Phenomenology of Spirit,* thus adding to the philosophical characterization of surrealism an essential element that had been almost entirely overlooked until then.[18] Adorno admittedly starts from the—quite unjustified—assumption that one could hardly assume a single surrealist had even a vague knowledge of Hegel.[19] This only proves that Adorno was not familiar with Breton's writings. Consequently, he was not aware that already in the late 1920s Breton had repeatedly referred to Hegel, and that in the 1930s he had attended (albeit irregularly) Alexandre Kojève's legendary lectures on the "Introduction to the *Phenomenology of Spirit.*" Anyone who is relatively familiar with Breton's writings, therefore, will not be astonished to find that Adorno, to explain surrealism, looks back to Hegel, and will be even less astonished given that Adorno's remark comes immediately after a sentence about alienation and reification. There, Adorno had characterized surrealism as the expression of a subjectivity that "in becoming estranged from the world has become estranged from itself." What could have been more natural, in this connection, than to refer to the "language of disruption" *(Sprache der Zerrissenheit)* and "scornful laughter of the spirit" *(Hohngelächter des Geistes)* that Hegel had mentioned in his incomparable chapter "Self-Alienated Spirit: Culture."[20] It would quickly have become clear, as well, that when it comes to the experience of self-alienation of the spirit there is more than a superficial connection between the surrealists and Hegel.

But Adorno mentions this not at all, and the sentence in Hegel that he cites as evidence of the relationship between the latter's philosophy and surrealism can only evoke astonishment. Here it is: "The sole work and deed of universal freedom is thus *death,* a death that has no inner significance or fulfillment."[21] And, as if to confirm this, Adorno's brief text is crammed full of expressions for things that are dead, petrified, and frozen, and that somehow, for Adorno, have become synonymous with surrealism. His Hegel quotation is also taken from the chapter on the self-alienation of the spirit, but from a later section bearing the title "Absolute Freedom and Terror." Still, this statement, which at first glance seems simple, indeed simpler than all the statements we are accustomed to finding in Hegel, doesn't quite make sense, particularly when it comes to surrealism. Nor does the situation improve when Adorno adds "that in it [Hegel's dictum] the Enlightenment destroyed itself with the means of its own realization." This, he opines, is also the case with surrealism, which it is supposedly "not possible to comprehend . . . as a language of immediacy, but as witness to the relapse of abstract freedom into the supremacy of objects and thus into mere nature. Its montages are the real still lives. By rigorously composing out things that are obsolete, they create *nature morte.*"

Adorno cited only the first half of Hegel's sentence, which went on to describe this death as the coldest and meanest imaginable, because "what is negated is the empty point of the absolutely free self." It is, he writes laconically in the *Phenomenology,* a death of "no more significance than cutting off a head of cabbage or swallowing a mouthful of water." Thus, someone might have conceived the notion of seeing, ultimately, an allusion to a possible connection between surrealism and terror—Adorno speaks of "anarchy." Indeed, this conclusion has been drawn again and again, most recently in connection with September 11, 2001, when famous intellectuals managed to ascribe responsibility for this act to surrealism. Adorno himself did not fall into this trap, and never would have done so, but there was another trap waiting for him. At the beginning of the essay in question he remarked that "what is deadly in even philosophically responsible art interpretation is that it is compelled to reduce what is alien and strange to a concept, thus expressing it in terms of the familiar." This is precisely what happened to him, when, at the close of his 1956 text, he draws a parallel between surrealism and the New Objectivity.

With this, Adorno succumbed to a—at least partial—misunderstanding in regard to surrealism. The misunderstanding had already manifested itself at the beginning of the 1930s, when, together with his friend Carl Dreyfus, he composed a number of "Surrealist Readings" ("Surrealistische Lesestücke"), which the two published in the *Frankfurter Zeitung* of November 17, 1931, under the pseudonym Castor Zwieback. The piece was accompanied by the motto "Knock on the door, cry 'Enter!' and don't enter," which was drawn from *L'Immaculée Conception*, a book by André Breton and Paul Éluard that appeared in the same year. Thirty years later, in 1963, Adorno planned to publish an expanded version of the "Readings" in the literary journal *Akzente*, but this time he had a different experience in mind. In a letter to *Akzente* editor Walter Höllerer, he recalled that at the time of writing the pieces he had wanted to express "the feeling that overcomes a person who is climbing a flight of stairs and thinks he has another step ahead of him, when he has already reached the top."[22] Adorno would repeat this sentence almost verbatim in his letter of November 10, 1964, to Elisabeth Lenk, in which he included a copy of *Akzente*. It suggests that he saw the surrealistic aspect of these prose pieces in the impossible attempt to translate a bodily reaction into writing. Yet precisely this slight confusion, mild shock, or happily inconsequential fright is what today's reader will find most lacking in them. The "Surrealist Readings" may defeat our expectations, but they leave behind no sense of irritation. In the presence of this bald prose, shorn of witticisms, which shines a sudden light on the everyday life of contemporary society, one is more inclined to speak of literature of New Objectivity than of surrealist prose, and it is hard to avoid the impression that this very misunderstanding is being defended in the 1956 essay.

In it, surrealism is presented as a corrective to the New Objectivity, and even if Adorno judges surrealism as being far superior to the other—by the way, politically extremely ambivalent—artistic movement, he still fails to do justice to surrealism's significance. He probably sensed this himself. When he sent the brief pieces to Höllerer with his suggestion that they be published, he wrote: "What you see here is an experiment that is perhaps, after all, not uninteresting, from which I would not like to distance myself, although I did not continue the experiment later; certain developments during the past thirty years have shown that the intention was not so beside the point, or rather, that what is beside the point about it is precisely not beside the point.... Certain things have become especially close to my heart in which a possibility is crystallized that afterward, in my own development, never came into its own."[23] At this moment, intrigued by the interests of his correspondence partner, he had just begun to concern himself with surrealist ideas.

But the problem raised by the identification of the Zwieback pieces with surrealism remains. Karl Riha, in the "Editor's Note" to the first and only complete edition of the "Readings,"[24] also saw it this way. Admittedly, he does not succeed in avoiding altogether the adjective "surrealistic," but one can feel how everything in him bridles at it. Instead, he talks about an early form of "cut-up" prose—and in doing so he hits on something essential. What is decisive is precisely when the cut is introduced and what it leaves out. The pieces are no doubt the result, in terms of their form and underlying perception, of an experiment. The coauthorship already speaks for this, as it awakens associations with the primal scene of surrealism, its experiments with automatic writing. The Castor Zwieback texts, though, had nothing in common with automatic writing.

One is tempted, instead, to label this prose "covert sociology," for it is the sociological alertness to the germ cells of social change that is actually what is striking about them. The sociological perspective is further supported by the fact that since 1930 Carl Dreyfus had been Adorno's colleague at the Institute for Social Research, where he was working on a study of white-collar employees.[25] The "Surrealist Readings," which from today's vantage point seem like stenographic records of what was then just emerging—a new social stratum—lead precisely into this world. In this perspective one can identify a link to the New Objectivity but no connection to surrealism. What the "Surrealist Readings" picks up differs from lived surrealism right down to the décor. The prose of Adorno's "Surrealist

Readings" more closely recalls the analyses of Adorno's mentor, Siegfried Kracauer, who had just published a book on white-collar employees *(Die Angestellten)*, than it does the writings of Walter Benjamin, to whom, after all, Adorno owed his acquaintance with surrealism.[26]

Benjamin not only interpreted surrealism dialectically from the very beginning; it is also his achievement to have revealed the dialectical core that unfolded within it. This is shown, among other things, by the concept of "profane epiphany," which he introduced in regard to surrealist experiences. Profane epiphany, for him, is an experience that occurs in the everyday, the terrestrial, and that signifies, within it, the "true, creative overcoming of religious epiphany." According to Benjamin, it is even equivalent to "materialist, anthropological inspiration." In a word, the topic of employees would never have occurred to him. While Adorno actually does talk about the political dimension of surrealism but never says what this is supposed to mean, Benjamin, in his essay, renders it concrete. Benjamin was the first to recognize the significance that must be accorded, in surrealism, to space and the objects that furnish it. His famous theory—later varied by Adorno—is that surrealism was "the first to stumble on the revolutionary energies that manifest in the 'out of date,' in the first iron constructions, the first factory buildings, the earliest photographs, the objects that are beginning to die out. . . . How these things relate to the revolution—no one can have a more accurate concept of this than these authors. How poverty, not just the social kind, but also architectural impoverishment, the misery of interiors, the enslaved and enslaving things, can suddenly turn into revolutionary nihilism—no one had noticed this before these visionaries and soothsayers." In Benjamin's eyes, Nadja and Breton are the lovers who bring the "powerful forces of 'atmosphere' concealed inside these things to explosion."

From the start, Benjamin makes it clear that surrealism has to do with a different concept of politics, one that incorporates a radical concept of freedom, in a way that has not been thought again since Bakunin. The source of this concept of freedom he finds not in party politics but in literature: in Dostoevsky, Lautréamont, and Rimbaud, whom he calls anarchists— anarchists of the spirit—because independently of each other, around 1870, they worked on their "infernal machines," and set them to explode at the same hour, at the time of the First World War. In all of this, Benjamin is not thinking about a politics of poetry but a politics that makes use of the image, not to draw a picture illustrating the promises of politicians but to unmask the moralistic metaphor in politics. Evidence of this can be found not only in what he has to say about the programs of the bourgeois parties and the metaphors they wallow in, which seem to have been taken from bad poems about springtime, but even more explicitly in the link he draws between the surrealist image, which he calls dialectical, and the "realm of political action, the one-hundred-percent image-space." Benjamin imagines a dialectical destruction of the space of political images in the form of an image that blows up this space at its base. According to him, it is not a matter of decorating reality, but of discovering a new world in which the lies of the old one are no longer able to have their effect. The surrealists held a similar view. In a text he wrote in 1925, "Le Maître de l'image," Breton defined the image as the actual "generator" of the world that, "in place of the old one, we want to make ours. Only the image, with everything it contains of the unexpected and the sudden," he writes, "gives me the measure of possible freedom, and this freedom is so complete that it frightens me."[27] In his eyes, the imagination—the capacity to generate images—is not an inborn faculty; it is not given to us but must be conquered and mastered by the subject. Thus, Breton defined it as that active and activating capacity from which, as he writes in the volume of poetry *Clair de Terre* (1923), "the white, curved line on a black ground that we call thinking" is ultimately derived.[28]

That this other concept of politics, as put forward by Benjamin, also played a role in the Adorno–Lenk correspondence is only partly apparent from the letters themselves. Here, one would want to mention the letters from May 1968, although they reflect a more subjective dimension in response to events. The new concept is more clearly present in the accompanying texts. In addition to Benjamin's surrealism essay, it is above all Elisabeth Lenk's introduction to the German translation of Charles Fourier's *Theory of the Four Movements* that sketches it out in its basic contours. This introduction, which was written in 1965–66 and whose creation Adorno followed with great if not passionate engagement, is undoubtedly a high point of the present volume. Its subject, Charles Fourier, attracts the volume's other authors to him and each other like a magnet. This includes Adorno and Breton, each of whom felt a special fondness for this early socialist and, when it came to his fantasies and even fantastical ideas, defended him against those who condemned him as a utopian. Adorno's interest in Fourier can undoubtedly be traced back to Benjamin, who had already drawn attention to Fourier in his exposé *Paris, Capital of the Nineteenth Century,* which he published in 1935, and in connection with which he had thought of the surrealists as possible addressees.[29]

Breton, for his part, engaged seriously with Fourier only toward the end of the Second World War, after coming across the five-volume edition of his works in New York in 1946, in which he discovered the *Theory of the Four Movements.* With Fourier's works as almost his only reading material, he departed in 1945 on a trip out West, visiting Nevada, Arizona, and New Mexico. During this trip, he began to draft his *Ode to Charles Fourier* as a work that would break explicitly with the principles of automatic writing. At a moment when Breton came close to losing hope in the political present, he reverted to a literary form with a very long tradition as a way of recalling the thinker of a universal harmony and, in dialogue with him, rethinking the future of humanity. In this, Breton was inspired by the encounter with a long-lost world, whose inheritors he met in an impressive landscape. As he himself stated, these were the Pueblo Indians, in particular the Hopi and Zuni, with whom he lived for a period of time and in whose customs he found reflected the very same principles that in Fourier regulate the harmonious life in the "phalansteries." "The fate of these human beings and their impressive dignity," he wrote in a letter to his editor Jean Gaulmier, "were in the background of my dreaming thoughts, against which the personality of Charles Fourier was intended to stand out in all its sharp relief."[30]

Already in the book *Arcane 17* (1945), which he also wrote in America and which expressed his state of mind at the time, Breton had made mention of the early French socialists. There, he wrote: "For all their excesses, and for all that originates in their intoxicated imagination, one can't help but concede to the reformist writers of the first half of the nineteenth century, as to primitive artists, by the way, the beneficial effect of a most revitalizing freshness. Today we are especially greedy for this freshness. On the social plane as elsewhere, we may hope that out of the unprecedented ideological confusion that will mark the end of this war will arise a fairly large number of radical propositions formulated *outside the existing framework* and which, resisting accusations of ingenuousness and of gratuitous and inconsequential conjecture, and faced with the temporary bankruptcy of the language of the mind, will make the language of the heart and of the senses heard loud and clear."[31]

Adorno, for his part, felt obliged to defend Fourier against the "dogmaticization of socialist theorems," particularly in the "Eastern sphere of control,"[32] and yet his emphasis was similar. "Among the utopians, the unrevolutionary Fourier occupies an extreme position," he writes in his brief forward to the German translation. "No one is more vulnerable to the accusation of utopianism than he, but also there is no one for whom the susceptibility of the doctrine is so much the result of the will to concretize the representation of a better state."[33] After the sudden death of his colleague Gottfried Salomon-Delatour, who had wanted to write the introduction, Adorno handed this task to Elisabeth Lenk, knowing of her close ties to surrealism. The result seemed to him close to genius,[34] and aroused him to true enthusiasm. Adorno even let himself be so swept away as to write a love letter,[35] the only letter in his own handwriting, which the letter's addressee, since she was not able to read the handwriting,[36] had to decipher with the help of Fritz Meyer, her decades-long partner. She responded not at all, and so "Entirely your Teddie" soon reverted to "Very warmly, your TWA."

Isolated traces of a different concept of politics, which sought a corresponding practice in the 1970s, for example, in the political initiatives of Michel Foucault, can be found in the Aragon essay. But above all, it is Elisabeth Lenk's dissertation—constantly invoked in the letters—in which the correspondence had its raison d'être and that to a certain extent is also its result. The book is addressed to Adorno as its "ideal, certainly not always well-disposed reader."[37]

Surrealism

Last Snapshot of the European Intelligentsia

Walter Benjamin

INTELLECTUAL CURRENTS can plunge precipitously enough for the critic to set up his power station alongside them. For surrealism, the disparity between France and Germany creates such a gradient. What sprang up there in France in the year 1919 among a small circle of literary figures—here we name the most important names: André Breton, Louis Aragon, Philippe Soupault, Robert Desnos, Paul Éluard—may have been a tiny rivulet, fed by the dank boredom of postwar Europe and the last trickles of French *décadence*. The clever heads who have still not managed to see beyond the "authentic origins" of the movement, and even today don't have anything to say about it except that here, once again, a literary clique is mystifying the respectable public, are a bit like the gathering of experts at the source of a river who, after much reflection, conclude that this little stream will never drive any turbines.

The German observer is not at the source. This is his opportunity. He is in the valley. He can gauge the energies of the movement. As a German, who has long been familiar with the crisis of the intelligentsia, more precisely of the humanist concept of freedom, who knows what a frenetic will it engendered to move beyond the stage of endless discussion and come to a decision, at any price, and who has had to experience, in his own person, the intelligentsia's extremely exposed position between anarchist *fronde* and revolutionary discipline—for this observer there is no excuse for considering the movement, as it might appear at first blush, "artistic" or "poetic." While this may have been true initially, Breton also stated right at the outset that he wanted to break with a practice that presents the public with the literary condensates of a particular form of existence and withholds this form of existence itself. More succinctly and dialectically put, this means that here the realm of poetry was exploded from within, as a circle of close associates pushed "poetic life" to the extreme limits of the possible. And one may take them at their word when they claim that Rimbaud's *Season in Hell* held no more secrets for them. For indeed this book is the first document of such a movement (in recent times—earlier precursors will be mentioned below). Is it possible to express the nub of the matter more definitively and incisively than Rimbaud did in his own copy of the book? Where the text says "on the silk of the seas and the Arctic blooms," he later wrote in the margin, "They don't exist."

In his *Wave of Dreams,* Aragon showed just how modest and peripheral the substance was in which the dialectical kernel that would become surrealism was originally embedded, at a time, in 1924, when its development could not be foreseen. Today it can be foreseen. For there is no doubt that the heroic phase, whose catalog of heroes Aragon bequeathed to us in that work, has come to an end. In movements like this there always comes a moment when the original tension of the secret society must either burst into the open in a mundane, profane struggle for power and dominance or disintegrate as a public demonstration and be transformed. This phase of transformation is where surrealism is at this moment. But in 1924, when it broke over its founders in the form of an inspiring dream wave, it seemed to be the most integral, ultimate, and absolute thing. Everything it touched, it integrated. Life only seemed worth living where the threshold that separates waking and sleeping had been worn down, within each of them, as if by the tread of the hordes of images coursing back and forth; language seeming to be itself only where sound and image, image and sound interpenetrated so fortuitously, with such automatic precision, that no slot remained to insert the coin "meaning." Image and language take precedence. Saint-Pol-Roux, as he goes to bed toward morning, hangs a sign on his door: "Poet at work." Breton notes, "Silence. I want to pass where no one has ever gone before, silence!—After you, dearest language." Language takes precedence.

Not only over meaning. Also over the I. In the ordered world, dreams hollow out individuality like the cavity in a tooth. This loosening of the I through intoxication is the very same fruitful, living experience that simultaneously allowed these individuals to step outside the charmed circle of intoxication. This is not the place to describe the surrealist experience in all its detail. But anyone who has recognized that, in the writings of this circle, what is at stake is not literature but something else—demonstration, password, document, bluff, even counterfeit, in any case precisely *not* literature—also knows that this discourse is literally about experiences, not theories, much less phantasms. And these experiences are by no means limited to dreams, to hours of hashish eating or opium smoking. It is such a grievous error to think that the only "surrealist experiences" known to us are the religious ecstasies or the drug-induced ones! Opium for the people is how Lenin described religion, and in doing so brought the two things closer together than the surrealists may have liked. We will come back later to the bitter, passionate revolt against Catholicism within which Rimbaud, Lautréamont, and Apollinaire gave birth to surrealism. But the true, creative overcoming of religious epiphany is plainly not to be found in psychoactive drugs. It is to be found in a *profane epiphany,*[1] a material-ist, anthropological inspiration for which hashish, opium, or whatever else can provide a preparatory training. (But a dangerous one. And the prepa-ratory training of religion is stricter.) This profane epiphany did not always find either the epiphany or surrealism at their best, and precisely those writings that proclaim it most powerfully, Aragon's incomparable *Paris Peasant* and Breton's *Nadja,* show very disturbing signs of lapses. Thus, in *Nadja,* there is an excellent passage about the "entrancing days of Paris looting under the auspices of Sacco and Vanzetti," after which Breton assures us that the Boulevard Bonne-Nouvelle,[2] in those days, fulfilled the revolutionary promise of revolt that its name always already held. But there is also a Madame Sacco, not the wife of Fuller's victim[3] but a seer, a fortuneteller, who lives at 3, rue des Usines, and is able to tell Paul Éluard that, for him, nothing good will come from Nadja. Now, we are prepared to allow surrealism, in its breakneck career over rooftops, lightning rods, gutters, verandas, weather vanes, and stuccowork—for the cat burglar all ornaments have their uses; we are prepared to allow it to reach into the dank back room of spiritualism. But we are not happy to hear it tentatively rapping on the windowpanes to ask what its future holds. Who wouldn't like to see these adoptive children of the revolution quite clearly distin-guished from the gatherings of down-at-the-heel society ladies, retired majors, and émigré grifters?

For the rest, Breton's book seems well suited for describing some basic characteristics of this "profane epiphany." He calls *Nadja* a "livre à porte battante" (a book whose door is banging). (In Moscow I stayed in a hotel in which almost all the rooms were occupied by Tibetan lamas, who had come to Moscow for a world congress of Buddhist churches. I noticed that many doors in the hallways were always left ajar. What at first seemed to be a chance occurrence became uncanny. I discovered that these rooms were occupied by the members of a sect who had sworn never to be in closed rooms. The shock I felt at the time is one the reader of *Nadja* must feel.) Living in a glass house is a revolutionary virtue of the highest order. This, too, is an intoxication, a moral exhibitionism of which we are much in need. Discretion in matters of one's own existence has evolved more and more from an aristocratic virtue into something for petty bourgeois parvenus. *Nadja* has found the true, creative synthesis between the art novel and the roman à clef.

One must only, by the way, take love seriously—and this is also where *Nadja* is heading—in order to see in it, too, a "profane epiphany." "At the same time," says the author (during his relationship with Nadja), "I was much occupied with the epoch of Louis VII, because it was the era of 'courtly love.' And I tried, with great intensity, to imagine how people viewed life at that time." Nowadays, from a new author, we have more accurate knowledge of courtly love in Provence, which brings us surprisingly close to the surrealist conception of love. "All the poets of the *stil nuovo*"—I quote from Erich Auerbach's outstanding *Dante: Poet of the Secular World*—"possessed a mystical beloved; all of them had roughly the same fantastic amorous adventures; the gifts which Love bestowed upon them all (or denied them) have more in common with an epiphany than with sensual pleasure; and all of them belonged to a kind of secret brotherhood which molded their inner lives and perhaps their outer lives as well."[4] The dialectic of intoxication is peculiar. Could it not be that every ecstasy in *one* world is shameful sobriety in its complement? What else could courtly love—and it is this, not passionate love, that binds Breton to the telepathic girl—be aiming at, if not that chastity is also a rapture? Into a world that shares a border not only with tombs of the Sacred Heart and altars to the Holy Virgin, but also with the morning before a battle or after a victory.

The lady, in esoteric love, matters least. So, too, for Breton. He is closer to the things Nadja is close to than to her. What are the things she is close to? Their canon is as revelatory as can be of the world of surrealism. Where to begin? Surrealism can boast of an astonishing discovery. It was the first to stumble on the revolutionary energies that manifest in the "out of date," in the first iron constructions, the first factory buildings, the earliest photographs, the objects that are beginning to die out, the salon pianos, the clothes that were fashionable five years ago, the trendy restaurants when their popularity has begun to wane. How these things relate to the revolution—no one can have a more accurate concept of this than these authors. How poverty, not just the social kind, but also architectural impoverishment, the misery of interiors, the enslaved and enslaving things, can suddenly turn into revolutionary nihilism—no one had noticed this before these visionaries and soothsayers. Not to mention Aragon's "Passage of the Opera": Breton and Nadja are the lovers who convert everything we have experienced—on melancholy train rides (the trains are beginning to age), on godforsaken Sunday afternoons in the proletarian districts of big cities, in the first glance through the rain-streaked window of a new apartment—into revolutionary experience, if not action. They bring the powerful forces of "atmosphere" concealed inside these things to explosion. What do you imagine a life would look like that would allow itself to be determined, at a critical moment, by the latest, most popular hit song?

The trick that gets this object world under control—here it is more appropriate to speak of a trick than a method—consists in replacing the historical gaze at the past with the political one. "Open up, ye graves, ye dead in the picture galleries, corpses behind screens, in palaces, castles, and monasteries, here is the fabulous keeper of the keys, in his hand a key ring to all eras, who knows just where to press the most ingenious of all locks, and who invites you to step right into the world of today, to mingle with the laborers and mechanics ennobled by money, to settle comfortably into their automobiles that are as beautiful as armor from the age of chivalry, to take your places in the international sleeping cars and forge a connection between yourself and all the people who today still take pride in their privileges. But civilization will make short work of them." This speech was attributed by Henri Hertz to his friend Apollinaire, who was the originator of this technique. He applied it with Machiavellian ratiocination in his novel *L'Hérésiarque* in order to detonate Catholicism (to which he remained personally devoted).

At the center of this object world stands the most dreamed-about of all its objects, the city of Paris itself. But only revolt completely reveals its surrealistic face. (Deserted streets where whistles and shots dictate the outcome.) And no face is surrealistic in the same degree as the true face of a city. No painting by Chirico or Max Ernst can match the sharp-edged elevations of its inner fortresses, which we must breach and occupy in order to master its fate and with it the fate of its masses, which is our own. *Nadja* is an exponent of these masses and of all that inspires them to revolution: "Let the great living sonorous unconscious that inspires my only convincing acts in the sense I always want to prove command forever of all that is me."[5] Here one finds the list of these fortifications, from the Place Maubert, where as nowhere else dirt retains its entire symbolic power, to the Théâtre Moderne that I am inconsolable to have missed the opportunity to experience. But in Breton's description of the bar on the second floor ("It is completely dark, tunnel-like bowers that one gets lost in—a salon at the bottom of a lake"), there is something that reminds me of that most misunderstood corner of the former Princess Café. It was the back room on the second floor, with its couples in the blue light. We called it the "Anatomy Theater"; it was the last bar for love. In passages like these, in Breton, photography intrudes in a very particular way. It converts the streets, gates, and squares of the city into illustrations in a trashy novel, taps these centuries-old architectures for their banal evidence, only to turn them, with the most intimate intensity, toward the events that are portrayed within them, which—just as in the old dime novels for maidservants— are bolstered by literal quotations, with page numbers. And all the Parisian sites found here are places where everything that transpires between people spins like a revolving door.

The Paris of the surrealists is also a "miniature universe." This means that in the big universe, things are no different. There, too, are intersections where passing traffic flashes ghostly signals, and unfathomable analogies and overlapping events are a daily occurrence. It is the space of which surrealist lyrics make report. And this must be noted, if only to counter the obligatory misconception of "l'art pour l'art." For l'art pour l'art has almost never been something to be taken literally; it is almost always a flag under which a cargo is sailing that can't be declared because it is still unnamed. This would be the moment to launch a project that, more than any other, would shed light on the crisis of the arts to which we are witness: a history of esoteric poetry. Nor is it by chance that no such thing exists. For if written as it should be written—not as a collected volume to which various "specialists" would each contribute what he considers "most worth knowing" in his particular field, but as the deeply grounded text of a person driven by inner compulsion, who would portray not so much the history of the development of esoteric poetry as its constantly renewed and repeated resurgence—written in this way, it would be one of those scholarly confessions that can be counted in every century. On the last page one would have to find the X-ray of surrealism. In the *Introduction to the Discourse on the Paucity of Reality*, Breton gives a sense of how the philosophical realism of the medieval period underlies poetic experience. But this realism—the belief, as it were, in a real, separate existence of concepts, whether external to things or within them—has always migrated very quickly from the logical realm of concepts to the magical one of words. And magical word experiments, not artistic games, are at the heart of the play of passionate phonetic and graphic transformations that for fifteen years now have permeated the literature of the avant-garde, whether it goes by the name of futurism, Dadaism, or surrealism. The way passwords, magic formulas, and concepts are confounded here is shown by the following comment by Apollinaire, from his last manifesto, *The New Spirit and the Poets* (1918), where he states, "The rapidity and simplicity with which minds have become accustomed to designating by a single word such complex beings as a crowd, a nation, the universe, do not have their counterpart in poetry. Poets are filling the gap, and their synthetic poems are creating new entities which have a plastic value as carefully composed as that of collective terms."[6] But when Apollinaire and Breton push even more energetically in this direction, when they link surrealism to the real world by declaring that the conquests of science owe much more to surrealistic than to logical thinking, when, in other words, they make mystification, whose apogee Breton sees in poetry (this is defensible), the basis of scientific and technical development as well, then this integration is too impulsive. It is very instructive to compare the movement's reckless adoption of the misunderstood technological miracle—"These fables having been even more than realized it is up to the poet to imagine new ones, which inventors in turn realize"[7]—these overheated fantasies, with the well-ventilated utopias of someone like Scheerbart.[8]

"The thought of all human activity makes me laugh." This statement by Aragon shows clearly the road that surrealism had to travel from its origins to its politicization. Pierre Naville, who originally belonged to this group, was right, in his excellent essay "The Revolution and the Intellectuals," to term this development dialectical. In this transformation of an extremely contemplative stance into revolutionary opposition, a key role is played by the bourgeoisie's hostility to every expression of radical intellectual freedom. This hostility drove surrealism left. Political events, above all the war in Morocco, accelerated this development. The manifesto "Intellectuals

against the Moroccan War," which appeared in *L'Humanité,* provided a
platform that was fundamentally different from the one associated with
the famous scandal at the banquet for Saint-Pol-Roux. On that occasion,
shortly after the war, the surrealists, on discovering that the celebration of
a poet they revered had been compromised by the presence of nationalist
elements, had broken out in cries of "Long live Germany!" In doing so,
they remained within the bounds of scandal, against which the bourgeoisie is well known to be as thick-skinned as it is sensitive to every action.
The extent to which, under the influence of this kind of political atmosphere, Apollinaire and Aragon found themselves in agreement concerning the future of poets is remarkable. The chapters "Persecution" and
"Murder" in Apollinaire's *Poète assassiné* contain the famous description of
a pogrom against poets: The publishing houses are stormed, the books of
poetry are hurled into the flames, the poets are slain. And the same scenes
take place everywhere on earth. In Aragon, "imagination," with a presenti-
ment of such horrors, musters its troops for a last crusade.

To understand these prophecies and gain a strategic appreciation of the
line at which surrealism arrived, one must consider the types of attitudes
that are widespread among so-called well-meaning left bourgeois intellectuals. It is obvious enough in the current stance of these circles toward
Russia. We are naturally not talking about Béraud, who paved the way for
the lie about Russia, or Fabre-Luce, who trots down this path after him
like a faithful donkey, his packs crammed full with bourgeois resentments.
But how problematic is even the typical mediating book by Duhamel!
How hard it is to bear the forcedly upright, forcedly sincere and animated
language of the Protestant theologian that permeates it. How exhausted
the method—dictated by muddleheadedness and linguistic ignorance—
of putting everything in some symbolic light or other. How revealing
his conclusion: "The true, more profound revolution that, in a certain
sense, could transform the substance of the Slavic soul itself has not yet
occurred." It is typical of this left French intelligentsia—as of the corresponding Russian one—that its positive function derives entirely from a
sense of obligation not to the revolution but to conventional culture. Its
collective achievement, to the extent that it is positive, approaches that of
conservators. But politically and economically, where they are concerned,
one will always have to reckon with the danger of sabotage.

What is characteristic of this entire left-bourgeois position is its fatal
linkage of idealist morality and political practice. Only by contrasting them

with the hapless compromises of "moral values" can certain key components of surrealism, indeed of the surrealist tradition, be comprehended. Little, until now, has been done to foster such comprehension. It was too tempting to view the Satanism of a Rimbaud or Lautréamont as the counterpart of l'art pour l'art in an inventory of snobbism. But if we decide to unpack this romantic bag of tricks, we will find something serviceable inside. We find the cult of evil as a tool—albeit a romantic one—for disinfecting and isolating politics from all moralizing dilettantism. With this in mind, in Breton, when we come upon the plot of a horror story centered on the rape of a child, we may go back a couple of decades. In the years 1865–1875, completely unaware of each other, a few great anarchists were working on their infernal machines. And the astonishing thing is that, independently of each other, they set the clock to exactly the same hour, and forty years later, in Western Europe, the works of Dostoevsky, Rimbaud, and Lautréamont detonated simultaneously. To be more specific, we could take a passage from Dostoevsky's collected works that was actually published only in 1915. The chapter "Stavrogin's Confession," from *The Possessed*, which is very closely related to the third canto of the *Songs of Maldoror*, contains a justification of evil that expresses certain of surrealism's motifs more powerfully than any of its current spokesmen.[9] For Stavrogin is a surrealist *avant la lettre*. No one has understood as well as he how utterly naïve the opinion is of those Philistines who suppose that good behavior—for all the manly virtue of those who practice it—is inspired by God. But evil, naturally, is entirely spontaneous; when it comes to evil we are autonomous beings and completely sovereign. No one has seen as clearly as Dostoevsky the inspiration in even the most infamous actions, and precisely in them. Thus, he recognized baseness as something preformed in the evolution of the world but also in us—something to which we are disposed, even if it is not imposed as a duty, the way the bourgeois idealist views virtue. Dostoevsky's God created not just heaven and earth, men and beasts, but also meanness, vengefulness, and cruelty. And even here he refused to let the devil meddle in his affairs. That is why, for his God, all the vices are equally pure in origin, maybe not "splendors," but eternally new "as on the first day," and worlds away from the clichés under which the Philistines conceive sin.

How great the tension is that gives the above-mentioned poets their astonishing impact at a distance is demonstrated rather scurrilously in a letter that Isidore Ducasse[10] wrote to his publisher on October 23, 1869, in an attempt to give a plausible account of his work. He places himself in a lineage that includes Mickiewicz, Milton, Southey, Alfred de Musset, and Baudelaire, and says, "Naturally I have assumed a somewhat more robust tone, in order to introduce something new to this literature, which after all only sings of desperation in order to oppress the reader and so that the latter will long all the more strongly for the good, as a remedy. Thus, in the end, one only sings of the good, except that the method is more philosophical and less naïve than that of the old school, of whose members only Victor Hugo and a few others survive." But if Lautréamont's erratic book exists in any context at all, or can be assigned to one, it is that of insurrection. Thus, Soupault's attempt, in 1927, to write a political biography of Isidore Ducasse was quite comprehensible and not without insight. Unfortunately, there are no documents to draw on, and Soupault's sources were based on mistaken identity. Happily, a similar effort was successful in the case of Rimbaud, and we have Marcel Coulon to thank for defending Rimbaud's true image against its Catholic usurpation by Claudel and Berrichon. Rimbaud is a Catholic, indeed, but by his own account he is Catholic in his most wretched part, which he never tires of denouncing and offering up for himself and everyone else to detest and despise—the part of himself that forces him to confess that he doesn't understand revolt. But this is the confession of a Communard who failed to live up to his own expectations, and who by the time he turned his back on poetry had long since, in his earliest writings, bade farewell to religion. "Hatred, to you I have entrusted my treasure," he writes in *A Season in Hell*. A poetics of surrealism could grow up around this statement, too, and would sink its roots even more profoundly into the depths of poetic thought than the theory of *surprise*,[11] of a poetry written in surprise, which stems from Apollinaire.

Since Bakunin, no radical concept of freedom has existed in Europe. The surrealists have one. They are the first to put an end to the liberal, moralistically and humanistically sclerotic ideal of freedom, because they are sure that "freedom, which on this earth is purchased only with a thousand of the most difficult sacrifices, wants to be enjoyed unreservedly, in its fullness and without any pragmatic calculus, as long as it lasts." And for them this proves "that the liberation struggle of humanity in its simplest revolutionary form (which, after all, is precisely liberation in every regard) remains the only thing to which it is worth devoting oneself." But do they succeed in forging unity between this experience of freedom and the other revolutionary experience, which we must acknowledge because after all we have had it: the constructive, dictatorial experience of revolution? In short, to tie the revolt to the revolution? How are we to imagine an existence that is oriented completely to the Boulevard Bonne-Nouvelle, in spaces designed by Le Corbusier and Oud? To win the forces of intoxication for the revolution: this is the center around which all of surrealism's books and projects revolve. Surrealism can claim this as its most unique task. For this task, it is not enough that, as we know, an element of intoxication inheres in every revolutionary act— this is the same as anarchism. But to place all the stress on it would be to de-emphasize the methodical and disciplined preparation for revolution in favor of a practice that vacillates between preparatory training and anticipatory celebration. To this is added a foreshortened, undialectical view of the nature of intoxication. The aesthetic of the *peintre*,[12] of the *poète en état de surprise*,[13] of art as the reaction of the person who has been surprised, is caught up in a number of very pernicious romantic prejudices. Any serious inquiry into occult, surrealist, phantasmagorical gifts and phenomena presupposes a dialectical imbrication that no romantic thinker will ever master. Passionately or fanatically emphasizing the mysterious side of the mysterious gets us nowhere; on the contrary, we penetrate the mystery only to the degree that we rediscover it in the quotidian, on the strength of a dialectical optics that recognizes the ordinary as impenetrable, the impenetrable as ordinary. The most impassioned analysis of telepathic phenomena, for example, will not teach us half as much about reading (which is an eminently telepathic process) as the profane epiphany of reading teaches us about telepathic phenomena. Or the most impassioned analysis of hashish smoking will not teach us half as much about thinking (which is an eminent narcotic) as the profane epiphany of thinking teaches us about smoking hashish. The reader, the thinker, the loiterer, the flaneur are as much figures of epiphany as the opium eater, the dreamer, the drinker. And more profane. Not to mention that most fearful drug— ourselves—which we imbibe in solitude.

"To win the forces of intoxication for the revolution"—in other words, a poetic politics? "We have had a taste of that already. Anything but that!" Well—you will be all the more interested to see how an excursus on poetry can clear things up. For what is the program of the bourgeois parties? A bad poem about springtime. Stuffed to the gills with similes. The socialist sees the "better future for our children and grandchildren" in people acting "as if they were angels," everyone having as much "as if he were wealthy" and living "as if he were free." Of angels, wealth, or freedom, not a trace. All nothing but similes. And the stock images of these Social Democratic Club poets? Their *gradus ad parnassum*? Optimism. A very different air is breathed in the essay by Naville that makes the "organization of pessimism" the order of the day. In the name of his literary friends, he delivers an ultimatum that unfailingly forces this optimism, with its lack of conscience and its dilettantism, to show its true colors. Where do you find the preconditions for the revolution, he asks? In changing hearts and minds, or in changing the external conditions? This is the cardinal question that decides the relation between politics and morality, and it must not be glossed over. Surrealism has come ever closer to the communist response. And this means pessimism from start to finish—positively and absolutely. Mistrust in the fate of literature, mistrust in the fate of freedom, mistrust in the fate of European humanity, but above all, mistrust, mistrust, and mistrust in every kind of rapprochement—between classes, between peoples, between individuals. And unlimited trust only in I. G. Farben and the peaceful perfecting of the air force. But what next, what then?

Here we must give due recognition to the insight that in the *Treatise on Style*, Aragon's last book, asks us to distinguish between simile and image. A fortuitous insight into a question of style that bears extending. For nowhere do these two—simile and image—collide as drastically and irreconcilably as in politics. To organize pessimism means nothing other than to expel all the moralizing metaphors from politics and to discover, in the realm of political action, the one-hundred-percent image-space. But the measure of this image-space can no longer be taken contemplatively. If the twofold task of the revolutionary intelligentsia is to overthrow the intellectual hegemony of the bourgeoisie and to forge a link with the proletarian masses, then it has failed almost completely at the second task, because the latter cannot be accomplished contemplatively. Yet this has prevented hardly any of these intellectuals from continuing to present it, as if it *were* possible, or from sounding the call for proletarian poets, thinkers, and artists. To counter this, Trotsky—in *Literature and Revolution*—was already compelled to point out that such figures will emerge only from a victorious revolution. Actually, it is much less a matter of turning the bourgeois-born artist into a master of "proletarian art" than it is of sending him—even at the price of his artistic activity—to important sites within the image-space. Indeed, might not the interruption of his "artistic career" be an important aspect of this function?

The jokes he tells only improve as a result. And he tells them better. For in jokes, too, in insults, misunderstandings, whenever an action bodies forth as image, is itself the image, seizes and ingests it, where proximity sees with its own eyes, the image-space we seek opens up, the world of all-sided and integral actuality, in which "good breeding" goes missing—the space, in a word, in which political materialism and the physical creative animal share the inner human being, the psyche, the individual, or whatever else we want to toss their way, with dialectical justice, so that no limb is not rent asunder. And yet—precisely after this kind of dialectical destruction—this space will remain an image-space and, more concretely, a space of the body. For there is no help for it, it is time we admitted that the metaphysical materialism of Vogtian and Bukharinian persuasion, and as attested to by the experiences of the surrealists, and before that of Hebel, George Büchner, Nietzsche, and Rimbaud, cannot be converted easily into anthropological materialism. There is a remainder. The collectivity is a body too. And the physical world that is being organized for it technologically can only be created, in its entire political and objective reality, within the image-space to which profane epiphany has initiated us. Only when the body and the image-space have become so deeply interpenetrated that all revolutionary tension becomes bodily collective innervation, and all bodily innervations of the collective become revolutionary discharge, will reality have transcended itself to the extent that the *Communist Manifesto* demands. For the moment, only the surrealists have comprehended its orders of the day. Man for man, they trade the play of their features for the face of an alarm clock that rings sixty seconds a minute.

Surrealism Reconsidered

Theodor W. Adorno

THE COMMONLY ACCEPTED THEORY of surrealism, as laid out in Breton's manifestos, dominates the secondary literature, relates it to dreams, to the unconscious, in some instances even to Jungian archetypes, which, it is claimed, found in the collages and automatic texts a language of images freed from the admixture of the conscious self. Dreams, it is assumed, deal with elements of the real the way surrealism does. But if no art is necessarily expected to understand itself—and one is tempted to think of its self-understanding as nearly irreconcilable with its success— then we are not compelled to go along with this programmatic view, so insistently repeated by its purveyors. In any case, what is deadly in even philosophically responsible art interpretation is that it is compelled to reduce what is alien and strange to a concept, thus expressing it in terms of the familiar, and explaining away the very thing that would be in need of explanation: however much works of art may call for their explanation, each and every explanation, even the most well-intentioned, is an act of betrayal to conformism. If in fact surrealism were nothing more than a collection of literary and graphic illustrations of Jung or even Freud, it would not just be replicating unnecessarily what the theory itself already states, without any metaphorical garb, but would also be so innocuous as to leave no room for the *scandale*[1] that surrealism intends and that is its vital element. To reduce surrealism to the level of psychological dream theory already subordinates it to the ignominy of the official. The well-versed "That is a father figure" is met by the self-satisfied "Yes, we know," and, as Cocteau realized, what is intended to be nothing but a dream leaves reality unharmed, however damaged its image.

But this theory does not do justice to the thing itself. We do not dream that way; no one does. The surrealist constructs are only analogous to dreams in the way they suspend customary logic and the rules of the game of empirical existence, while respecting the individual things that have been forcibly broken apart and indeed bringing all their content, precisely in its human aspect, closer to the form of the object. Things are shattered, reassembled, but not dissolved. Certainly, dreams behave no differently, but in them the object world appears considerably more veiled, less posited as reality than it does in surrealism, where art shakes the foundations of art. The subject, which in surrealism is at work much more openly and uninhibitedly than in dreams, applies its energies to its own self-annihilation, for which in dreams no energy is required; but as a result surrealism renders everything apparently more objective than in dreams, where the subject, absent from the outset, colors and permeates events from behind the scenes. The surrealists themselves have meanwhile discovered that even in the psychoanalytic situation people do not free-associate the way the surrealists make art. As a matter of fact, even the supposedly inadvertent nature of psychoanalytic association is by no means inadvertent. Every analyst knows what exertion and hard work, what an effort of will it takes to get hold of the inadvertent expression that, in the analytic situation, forms as a result of this exertion—how much more so in the artistic situation of the surrealists. In the ruins of the world that are surrealism's, it is not the unconscious per se that comes to light. Measured against the latter, the surrealist symbols would prove much too rationalistic. This kind of decoding would reduce the luxuriant diversity of surrealism to a small number of impoverished categories, like the Oedipus complex, without reaching the power that emanated, if not always from the surrealist artworks, at any rate from their idea; indeed, this is how Freud seems to have reacted to Dalí.

After the European catastrophe, the surrealist shocks lost their force. It is as though they had saved Paris by preparing it for fear: the destruction of the city was their center. If we want to grasp surrealism in these terms conceptually, recourse must be had not to psychology but to surrealism's artistic techniques. Their schema, unquestionably, is montage. It would be easy to demonstrate that even authentic surrealist painting makes use of the motifs of montage, and that the discontinuous juxtaposition of images in surrealist lyric poetry has montage character. As we know, these images derive, sometimes literally, sometimes in spirit, from the late nineteenth-century illustrations with which the generation of Max Ernst's parents was familiar. As early as the 1920s, in a more familiar realm than surrealism, there were collections of visual material, such as *Our Fathers* by Alan Bott,[2] that participated—parasitically—in the surrealist shock and kindly spared the public the trouble of being alienated by montage. Actual surrealist practice, however, introduced unfamiliar elements into their midst. It was these, precisely, that at the instant of alarm lent them their familiar air, their "Where have I seen that before?" The affinity with psychoanalysis, then, will have to be sought not in some symbolism of the unconscious but in the attempt to uncover experiences of childhood by means of explosions. What surrealism adds to the reproductions of the object world is what we have lost of childhood: those illustrated magazines, already outmoded at the time, must have jumped out at us then the way the surrealist images do now. The subjective element in this lies in the way the montage is handled. It wants, perhaps in vain but unmistakably in its intention, to produce perceptions as they must have been then. The giant egg from which at any moment a doomsday monster can hatch is so big because we ourselves were so little when we shuddered at our first sight of an egg.

This effect is assisted by the element of the obsolete. Modernism—always already under the spell of the ever-sameness of mass production—appears paradoxical by virtue of having any history at all. The presence of this paradox is alienating, and in these children's images of the modern era it becomes the expression of a subjectivity that in becoming estranged from the world has become estranged from itself. The tension in surrealism that discharges itself in the shock is the tension between schizophrenia and reification, in other words, precisely not psychologically inspired. The subject that has become absolute—now free to do with itself as it wishes, uncommitted to any consideration of the empirical world—reveals, in the face of total reification, which throws it back completely onto itself and its protest, that it itself is bereft of spirit, virtually dead. The dialectical images of surrealism are those of a dialectic of subjective freedom in the state of objective unfreedom. In them, European weltschmerz freezes, like Niobe who has lost her children; in them, bourgeois society casts off its hope of survival. It is hardly likely that any of the surrealists were familiar with Hegel's *Phenomenology*, but a sentence taken from it, which one must think together with the more general one about history as progress in the consciousness of freedom, defines surrealist content: "The sole work and deed of universal freedom is thus *death*, a death that has no inner significance or fulfillment."[3] The critique this insight contains is one that surrealism has made its own; it explains its political impulses against anarchy, which after all were incommensurable with that content. It has been said of Hegel's pronouncement that in it the Enlightenment destroyed itself with the means of its own realization. It will not be possible to comprehend surrealism at any lesser price, not as a language of immediacy, but as witness to the relapse of abstract freedom into the supremacy of objects and thus into mere nature. Its montages are the real still lives. By rigorously composing out things that are obsolete, they create *nature morte*.

These images are not so much those of something internal, as, rather, fetishes—commodity fetishes—to which at one time something subjective, libido, was attached. Through these fetishes, not by immersion in the self, the images dredge up childhood. Surrealism's models would be the pornographies. What happens in the collages, what comes to a convulsive standstill like the tense mark of lasciviousness at the corner of a mouth, resembles the changes a pornographic representation undergoes at the moment of gratification of the voyeur. Severed breasts, silk-stocking-clad legs of mannequins in the collages—these are the remembered characteristics of objects of the partial drives that once served to awaken the libido. What has been forgotten reveals itself in them, thing-like and dead, as what love actually wanted, what it wants to resemble, what we resemble. As a freezing at the moment of awakening, surrealism is akin to photography. It may be imaginings that it captures, but not the invariant, ahistorical ones of the unconscious subject, which conventional opinion, in neutralizing them, confers. Instead, they are historical imaginings in which the most intimate part of the subject becomes aware of itself as its external aspect, as the imitation of something social and historical. "Come on, Joe, play that old song they always played!"[4]

In this regard, surrealism is the complement of [the New] Objectivity, which emerged at the same time. The horror that the latter felt, in Adolf Loos's sense of ornament as crime, was mobilized by the shock of surrealism. The house has a tumor, its bay window. Surrealism paints it as a fleshy, proliferating growth. The childlike images of modernism are the essence of what the New Objectivity covers with a taboo, because they remind it of its own thing-like nature and the fact that it hasn't come to terms with it, that its rationality remains irrational. Surrealism gathers up what the New Objectivity denies to human beings; its distortions are evidence of the harm that the denial has inflicted on desire. In them, it salvages the obsolete, an album of idiosyncrasies in which the claim to happiness, which people find denied to them in their technologically sophisticated world, goes up in smoke. But if surrealism itself now seems obsolete, it is because people already deny themselves the consciousness of denial that is preserved in surrealism's photographic negative.

Critical Theory and Surreal Practice

Elisabeth Lenk

LADIES AND GENTLEMEN:
Do not expect me to wax enthusiastic for you about the beauty of surrealism when it was still young or about the revolutionary power of the Frankfurt School when it had not yet abandoned the *Zeitschrift für Sozialforschung* (Journal for social research). I don't think much of nostalgia. Instead, I would like to pose the question of their relevance for today.[1] What good are they, these two movements that have been declared dead? Is it possible, with their models, to shed light on the events of today, which come at us so thick and fast? "No one can make himself the subject of any moment but the present," said Max Horkheimer. And surrealism itself can, in my opinion, be viewed as the effort to break up the darkness of the present, admittedly at the cost of sundering not only the world but the eye that observes it as well. If, therefore, there is a strict criterion to which both movements, surrealism and the Frankfurt School, might have adhered, it would be this: cognition of the present. Surrealism and the Frankfurt School can, accordingly, only be explored if one attempts to apply them to the present moment. This is the challenge I face, as well.

My book on André Breton[2] was written under the fresh impressions of the events of May 1968, and while writing it I always envisioned Adorno as the ideal reader. At that time, the two movements seemed to be of great contemporary relevance. Was it not they, ultimately, that unleashed the May events? This is literally true of the Frankfurt School but also, in a metaphorical sense, of surrealism.

In his article on Breton's hundredth birthday, Julien Gracq states correctly that 1968, with its slogan "Empower fantasy," was something like a practical test of surrealism.[3] This is by no means contradicted by the fact that things actually turned out quite differently. Even in 1989, when, without any clue about the events that would take place in November, I wrote my plaidoyer in defense of Adorno,[4] the historical moment seemed favorable for a return of the Frankfurt School under a new, aesthetic constellation. But today?

In seeking to bring this up to date, I discover something unforeseen either by surrealism or by the Frankfurt School: a contented, almost relieved awareness of the failure of all efforts to change the world in a planned way, while its unplanned change advances inexorably. The 68ers were passionate; the 98ers, by contrast, are prosaic. What was at stake were the rights of the quotidian—something the idealistic materialists had failed to consider. At stake was the "desire to bring . . . enjoyment to the majority," which for Max Horkheimer, by the way, was an absolutely legitimate reason for any revolution.[5]

The events of 1989 scrambled all the pigeonholes we Marxists had erected in our heads, in which, until then, everything had been so nicely compartmentalized. We were all expecting the end of the epoch, when the capitalist regimes would be swept away in a chain reaction. "[Critical] theory may be stamped with the approval of every logical criterion," wrote Horkheimer, "but until the era comes to its end it lacks the confirmation that victory confers."[6] The longed-for end was approaching, and the chain reaction came too, but it went in the wrong direction. It was not the capitalist but the socialist systems that were swept away like a bad dream. We Western Marxists were forced to recognize that we had quite obviously had our heads in the theoretical sand, while we were actually deeply mired in capitalism. It was not victorious, this theory. And while some of us asked shyly, "Does this necessarily mean the theory was wrong?" others see the situation with merciless clarity.

"The planet—having abandoned itself to the market and succumbed to the drug Internet—seems to be experiencing the end of history," writes Ignacio Ramonet, and Hans Tietmeyer, the head of the German Bundesbank, repeats a sentence that good old Karl Marx could almost have written: "Politicians, too (at pain of elimination) are forced to submit to the rules of the financial markets."[7]

For the historical blink of an eye, when Helmut Kohl wrapped himself in the magic mantle of history and wanted to force capital to be national, things seemed to be different.

To the best of my knowledge, only one member of the Frankfurt School lived to experience this decisive turn of events and raise his voice in warning: Fritz Neumark, who had borne responsibility for financial research at the *Zeitschrift für Sozialforschung*. In 1990, *Die Zeit* asked Neumark about the monetary union that was about to be created between East and West Germany. Neumark warned against Germany's going it alone and proposed an international conference, since capital, whether people liked it or not, was an international and not a national matter. He argued that the impact of such a step on world markets and their rebound effect on Germany should be carefully calculated, and that international experts should consider this. He predicted that hasty German exceptionalism would result in catastrophe.

That catastrophe has now come to pass. The national enthusiasm has evaporated, and all at once even those Germans who cheered Kohl on are discovering that there is a world market, which gives succor to everyone who dreams of liberalizing tariffs or massively reducing domestic jobs and expanding them elsewhere. In the era of the electronic and commuications revolutions, every big businessman is free to produce practically anywhere on earth and to operate transnationally in a global economy. This means the emancipation of enterprises and consequently of taxes from location. Only the losses remain national.

To become familiar with the stuff of which the current moment is made, one need only follow the stock exchange, which responds with extreme sensitivity. If new jobs are created, as has happened recently in the United States, the international stock exchanges have an allergic reaction, but if hundreds of thousands are fired, they are jubilant. The criterion of this new morality, which has replaced the old, socialistically infected one, is the shareholder principle. It is no longer places or workforces that matter, but the global stockholders. Everyone of importance goes to the stock market, the successful people who generously offer up funds that don't belong to them, the people who, in their almost uncanny lack of bias when it comes to risking the fate of millions, are outdone only by politicians. "It was as if we were trading soap bubbles,"[8] said Nick Leeson, who broke Barings Bank. Confronted with certain magnitudes, controls fail. Stock exchanges represent sheer fascination with cash-free, ever-present global money that is earned or lost in seconds. We normal mortals hear about it only when the swindle goes bust and another enormous financial structure has collapsed into nothing. The "Frankfurters" were quite accurate when it came to predicting the developments we see today, that competition within countries would decline in comparison to bitter struggles at the global level and that it would no longer be independent owners but leadership cliques that would run the world markets.

I was examined by Adorno on the topic "Money and God in Marxist Theory." Today, the slightly updated topic would have to read "On the Godlike Nature of the Lords of Finance in the Paralytic Phase of Capitalism." (Paralysis, let us recall, was once the term for megalomania; today it is a capacity that is required of all top leaders of huge global corporations: the ability to rule freely over increasingly large sums and companies).

No doubt, both the Frankfurt School and the surrealists desired a more humane world in which wealth would be more equitably distributed. But their great strength—and this is something they shared—was their negativity, the pleasure they took in contradiction, in dialectics, in the absurd image. Their strength was critique, which today is more necessary than ever. Admittedly, we would have to include Marxism more radically in the critique of traditional theory than Max Horkheimer did in 1937 in his famous essay "Traditional and Critical Theory." Fundamentally, we must question the traditional relationship between theory and practice. Marxism is obsolete in that it knows only one form of authentic philosophical practice: revolution, whether the revolution is seen as having taken place once and for all, in the past, to be followed only by nonantagonistic contradictions, or looks for revolution, like the Messiah, in some misty future. May 1968 was already no longer a classical revolution; its unorthodox slogan, as concisely formulated by Daniel Cohn-Bendit, was "Reforms, yes, but by revolutionary means."

It is by no means impossible—one does not have to be a Marxist to predict this—that social movements will arise that could sweep capitalism away the same way they put an end to socialism. But such movements cannot be planned. They don't need a party of socialist unity, even the most avant-garde one, to channel them. If one sets aside revolution, that most irrational of events, toward which Marxism was nonetheless oriented, then the Marxist concept of practice simply followed the rules of traditional theory. Like other traditional theories, Marxism, too, presented itself as a closed system of scientific statements. It elaborated a system of concepts and judgments that were supposedly able to grasp the manifold of occurrences under its rules once and for all—except that it included dialectics among the rules. Thus, it was more difficult to contradict Marxism than other traditional theories, because Marxism degraded contradiction—the last critical weapon of the individual against society—into a mechanically clanking method. This lovely old dialectical apparatus no longer functions; it has been consigned to the dustbin of history with other relics of the past. All the great words and great systems of concepts and judgments fail permanently when confronted with the current historical situation. The new thinking that is needed would be a function of the present moment, as unfinalizable as history itself.

What distinguishes Max Horkheimer's definition of critical theory from Marxism is above all its tendency to blur the classical Marxist distinction between theory and practice. Horkheimer calls critical theory, in contrast to traditional theory, a comportment, a philosophical mode of behavior, because it has a whole—society—as its object and, moreover, negates this object. "This activity," Horkheimer adds, "is termed 'critical' in what follows."[9] This different concept of practice necessarily collided head on with those that preceded it.

What Horkheimer is referring to is not the application of theory to industrial practice, however insistently such applications may present themselves as the latest revolutionary development (take, for example, the recent "information revolution"). Nor does he refer to a political practice that, from left to right, can best be grasped theoretically by the phrase "muddling through." The behavior Horkheimer had in mind is paradoxically something that involves more passivity than activity, that is closer to experience than to action. Horkheimer salvaged contradiction from the dialectical machine and tied it to *experience*.

The "Frankfurters" never stated precisely what this behavior is, but again and again, in keeping with the historical moment, they attempted to describe what it is not.

The question I would like to ask today is whether surrealism—whatever its practitioners may have thought—was and is not precisely the practice that is appropriate to critical theory; and whether, on the other hand, critical theory was and is not precisely the theory toward which surreal practice was oriented. Surreal practice, here, is by no means identified solely with art, that is, the production of artworks, much less with the art business. Nor is critical theory identical with a dogmatic Marxism that claimed to have a monopoly on revolution. What the two movements have in common is that they add another dimension to politics, an aesthetic dimension—something that has not been well understood, particularly in Germany.

From an aesthetic point of view, German intellectuals, no matter how theoretically well versed, are unfortunately still underdeveloped. The crudeness of theoretical culture in Germany and the hostility of German political culture to the art of the past have contributed to the fact that neither surrealism nor Adorno's critical theory have received adequate attention. "In Germany, anyone who doesn't swallow the sword right up to the hilt is attacked as an aesthete," said Alfred Kerr.[10] Even the Green Party is unfortunately no exception to the rule of aesthetic obliviousness, despite Joseph Beuys and Heinrich Böll, who would both like to broaden the definition of art. In his "Frankfurt Lectures" of 1964, more or less in parallel with Adorno, Böll attempted to develop an "aesthetics of the humane" and complained bitterly that almost twenty years after the end of Fascism the German public was not capable of understanding metaphors. "When in a radio play or a novel a chimney sweep falls off a roof," writes Böll, "for compositional or dramatic, i.e., for aesthetic reasons *must* fall off a roof, protests start pouring in from the chimney sweeps' union: a chimney sweep does not fall off a roof! The protests, irritations, commotions never actually go much deeper than that, in other words they are not worth the trouble, and it is not the business of the author to give the chimney sweeps' union an overview of the whole of Western aesthetics from Aristotle to Brecht. The minimal preconditions are lacking."[11]

Thirty years later, the situation is hardly any better aesthetically. When Günter Grass, for example, in his novel *Too Far Afield,* describes the chaotic conditions that followed the creation of the German currency union, the Treuhand[12] and its representatives immediately object, and even *Spiegel* editor Rudolf Augstein gets into the act to prove that there is a mistake in Grass's "facts." Please note, my concern here is not to take a position in support of Grass's novel—to do that I would have to discuss the compositional, dramatic, or aesthetic grounds that may have caused him to conceive his novel the way he did, and not some other way. For the moment, rather, I am merely trying to establish that the German public, now as in the past, lacks the minimal preconditions for this kind of debate. The critics, like Lukács, refuse to leave the realm of bare facts and apply aesthetic criteria to aesthetic creations. They attempt to reduce the aesthetic—never the political—to ideology. Their concept of practice is characterized by the fact that destruction, perfect calculability up to and including the perpetration of violence, is allowed, if not actually required, but not its representation in images and words.

Even ancient peoples understood that fictional reality is a different reality than everyday life. "The religious festivals of primitive peoples are not those 'of a complete ecstasy and illusion.' . . . There is no lack of an underlying consciousness of things 'not being authentic,'" it says in the Paralipomena of *Aesthetic Theory*.[13] What was good enough for savages should be acceptable to today's critics. Their pre-aesthetic decision in favor of content and communication is barbaric. The barbarian, loosely following Schiller (who, as is well known, made an unsuccessful attempt at the aesthetic education of Germans), is not the savage whose emotions overmaster his principles, but rather civilized man, whose principles annihilate the emotions. The true barbarian is man without form. "Being responsive only to the crude element, he must first shatter the aesthetic organization of a work before he finds enjoyment in it, and carefully disinter the particular qualities which the master with infinite art has caused to vanish in the harmony of the whole."[14]

The concept of surreal practice itself already implies that we are dealing not with practice in the literal sense but rather with symbolic action, action as gesture and sign. "More and more, our things will have to become this kind of gesture, derived from concepts, and less and less theory in the traditional sense," Adorno wrote to Horkheimer during the Second World War.[15] Here, the two of them harked back to a concept developed by the European avant-garde, born of experience: gesture and sign as a nonviolent alternative to politics.

"Strange incidents," writes the founder of Dada's Cabaret Voltaire, Hugo Ball. "When we had the Cabaret Voltaire in Zurich, at Spiegelgasse 1, there lived at Spiegelgasse 6, opposite us, if I am not mistaken, Mr. Ulyanov-Lenin. He must have heard our music and tirades every evening; I do not know if he enjoyed them or profited from them. And when we were opening the gallery in the Bahnhofstrasse, the Russians went to Petersburg to launch the revolution. Is Dadaism perhaps, *as sign and gesture,* the opposite of Bolshevism? Does it contrast the completely Quixotic, inexpedient, and incomprehensible side of the world with destruction and consummate calculation? It will be interesting to observe what happens here and there."[16]

Like Böll, I will have to leave you without a comprehensive overview of the history of aesthetics from Aristotle to the European avant-gardes. But one thing already seems evident—that a dark, forgotten history remains to be told, one that unfolded underneath the traditional history of philosophy and orthogonal to it. Is it astonishing, after this dadaistic prelude in the spirit of Voltaire, that, for example, the surrealist theoretician Georges Bataille, in all seriousness, called Max Ernst a philosopher? The young Max Ernst, writes Bataille, wanted to become a philosopher, and in a completely paradoxical sense remained true to this vocation.[17] Philosophy, Bataille continues, has two possibilities. The first is the possibility of labor or work, in other words, the philosopher develops, one by one, the questions that pose themselves for him and then tries to deduce them from each other in a way that doesn't leave any gaps. The other possibility is *play*. In the first case, the philosopher behaves as if he had a great deal of time. In the other case, by contrast, he chooses, as the vanishing point of his perspective, the very moment in time when all questions dissolve into nothingness—a moment that laughs at the philosopher. This sounds like a continuation and radicalization of the reflections that Adorno and Horkheimer exchanged in their wartime correspondence. While Adorno, in his letter to Horkheimer—almost as if he were afraid of his own courage—reaffirms Hegel's formula about the work of concepts, Bataille follows the paradigm change through to the end, from the work of concepts to the image: "What is the foundation of the turbulent and violent world of Max Ernst if not the catastrophic substitution of a game, of an end in itself, for laborious work, with a view to a desired result? The serious philosopher conceives philosophy as a laborious activity and in so doing he imitates carpenters and locksmiths. . . . He constructs his philosophical furniture, a well-oiled philosophy responding as a lock does to the key made for it. The person who recognizes the powerlessness of work, on the contrary, is dazzled and fascinated by the play, which serves no purpose."[18]

It is characteristic of the reception of surrealism in Germany that although Max Ernst's paintings are exhibited in museums and celebrated everywhere in the abstract, even today his writings are available only in French or English, and not in German. By the way, not even Adorno, who advised me, when I departed for Paris in 1962, that I should absolutely read Bataille, recognized the cognitive quality of Max Ernst's gestures, otherwise he would not have written so condescendingly about him. Horkheimer is the only one who seems to have sensed something of the philosophical meaning of these images. Surrealist pictures are considered today to be values in which one can invest all the more dependably because they do not need to be understood. If they were, it would be clear that surrealism and critical theory belong together.

Max Ernst was the painter of the nonidentical. "Who knows," writes André Breton in one of the earliest interpretations of Ernst's paintings, "whether, in this way, we are not preparing to someday escape the principle of identity?"[19] To want to escape from naïve definition and thus from identity—surrealism and the Frankfurt School have this in common. Adorno, in his essay "Surrealism Reconsidered," applied Walter Benjamin's analysis of Aragon to Max Ernst.[20] Max Ernst, he said, exploded the energies of outdated things, childhood memories that were attached to a world of past objects. But for this it was not, as Adorno thought, sufficient to reproduce mechanically the world of images of a bygone era. The spark is struck only when there is a countervailing gesture: a few additions, scarcely perceptible lines in a drawing, a horizon traced on a dry catalog of teaching aids for paleontology and mineralogy. If one were to see Ernst's collages as Adorno does, without the flying ghosts—which by the way are imperceptible to the figures in the woodcuts because they are still in the future— the result would be the New Objectivity. Accordingly, Adorno's own texts of the 1930s, which have been described as "surrealistic," are closer to New Objectivity than to the actual writings of surrealism.[21]

Max Ernst's reflections culminate in an entirely new type of passive practice: "It is as a spectator that the author, now indifferent, now passionate, is present at the birth of his work,"[22] he writes, and next to it inserts the image of the Sphinx, which stares blankly ahead while a monster in its lap barks furiously at it. In a way that harks back strongly to Max Horkheimer's project, the surrealists would also like to carry over the passivity of sensual perception, as experience, over into the moral world. Ernst quotes André Breton: "Man will know how to behave at the moment when, like a painter, he is satisfied with simply copying, without any correction, what an inner screen projects for him concerning his future actions."[23]

Max Ernst recognized himself in Georges Bataille's portrait of a tragic player. "Are you a philosopher?" he interrogates himself in the essay "Woman's Nudity Is Wiser Than the Philosopher's Teachings." "Yes I am," he responds, "in the sense of the lines that Georges Bataille has written about me."[24]

Like the Dadaists, with whom he had already allied himself in Cologne, Max Ernst opposed the well-worn myth of the artist as artisan. In his opinion, painters are complicit with poets. Like the latter, they represent not the result (the idea), but the process of thinking. Pursued by the technical reproductions that surrounded them, the visual and performing arts were forced to think back to their poetic core, in other words, to the thing that separated them from their copy. According to Max Ernst, the painted, drawn, or found images participate in the fiction-creating, hallucinatory function of language. Many sentences from his text "Beyond Painting" are written in the style of Rimbaud: "*J'ai vu*—I saw." "I saw myself with the head of a kite," he writes, for example, "and with a knife in my hand, in the attitude of *The Thinker*, of Rodin. But it was actually the liberated attitude of Rimbaud's Seer."[25]

In his manifesto painting *Pietà, or Revolution by Night*, Max Ernst affirmed the surrealist conception of a revolution that takes place not in the daytime but in the dark cave of the unconscious. It consists in the production of images that come from the nocturnal realm, and its goal is to allow these images to revolutionize reality retroactively.

"The dove *closed herself in her wings* and swallowed the key forever"[26]— these are Max Ernst's riddling images, to which *Oedipus Rex* also belongs. Like a smuggler evading capture, Ernst, who knows his Freud, has swallowed the key. For him, surrealism is the making visible of thought that observes itself in the act of thinking. With eyes wide open, he writes, he wants to see into himself; like Rimbaud, he wants to free what sees within him from its shroud. This shroud, which begins as a poetic metaphor, flits ghostlike through Max Ernst's work. It must be rent and cut apart again and again. Max Ernst saw himself as a painter who paints not with a brush, but with the knife of critique. The shroud is everyday perception. Max Ernst cuts it open and thus liberates a mode of thought that calls into question the truth of what we hold to be true. The artist, looking inward with open eyes, awakens beings that have slept for a long time, for too long. He writes picture books for grown-ups.

Horkheimer protested against dividing objects and propositions into the subjects of separate disciplines. Max Ernst rejoins and reconnects these severed things in surprising ways, as a child does. The objective is to rediscover the earliest developmental stage, which Freud calls animist, in which thought is not yet de-eroticized and denuded of images—thought that from the perspective of adults is inward looking. Ernst forces the images to return. His mythical thinking mixes the remains of words and perceptions, like the famous umbrella in Lautréamont that meets up with a sewing machine. In the absence of more suitable furniture, the two make

love on a dissecting table, suggesting that this new mythology was preceded by a process of cutting up and dividing, that is, of image surgery.

The beautiful gardener, since Max Ernst invented her, has become a
mythical figure; before that, it was just the name of a Paris department
store. The painting became a showpiece in National Socialism's chamber
of horrors of "Bolshevik art."

With the help of the new techniques, the reproduction is peeled off like
a skin, leaving subcutaneous reality behind. The origin and meaning of
these remnants of word and image, which the critics typically latch onto,
are of no import. They simply are as they are, ready to have a new meaning inserted. What counts is only the new thing that is produced by the
coming together of these beings who are enamored of their opposite. In
this world there are no longer any humans, only prehuman husks, object-
marionettes. A flower of white lace, its neck pierced by a stone, sits peacefully on a stool. Ernst shows the Hottentot Venus, not Venus de Milo; not
humans, but the sperm, the egg, from which the vanished beings can
always body forth again. He shows bottles that begin to move, ghostlike, as
if of their own volition; parachutes, light pistols, gaslights. The city appears
to be populated by phantoms. A woman, always the same one except that
her head is constantly changing: Wirrwarr, the hundred-headed woman.
There is no planning hand at work here, only the armed, wounded hand
of the artist. The very first image in the *Hundred-headed Woman*[27] defines
the utopia of this world of fragmented objects: a human being falls from
the sky. In the entire cycle, this is the only image that appears more than
once; its caption reads, "Crime or miracle, a complete human being." The
central question in Georges Bataille's "The Sorcerer's Apprentice" has a
similar resonance: "Is a complete human being socially possible?"[28] But all
efforts to bring humans down to earth end in failure, although numerous
graybeards, workers, and scientists have tried to do so, right down to Pas-
teur, who attempts to bring dead people back to life. The experiment fails.
Thus the initial image returns at the end. This time, the caption reads:
"End and sequel."

Suddenly we find ourselves in a cave, in which, as in Plato, light falls from
above. The cave is the most philosophical of all locations, the place of
damnation as well as of refuge. At a critical moment in his life, Adorno
wrote a singspiel whose central stage setting is a cave: *The Treasure of
Indian Joe*, after Mark Twain's *The Adventures of Tom Sawyer*.[29] The bulk

of work on the project was carried out during the early months of the Nazi regime, when the socialist and stigmatized "half-Jew" Adorno had already lost his position as assistant professor at the university but was still hesitating to emigrate. The singspiel's plot is straightforward enough. One night the two boys, Huck and Tom, witness a crime in a cemetery. The half-breed Indian Joe kills the town doctor, Robinson, and then tries to pin the crime on his buddy Muff Potter. The children swear to the murderer that they will not betray him. Indian Joe escapes. The boys feel like accomplices. They have witnessed a murder, and someone else is being accused of having committed it. When they hear old Potter, with whom Adorno felt a deep, lifelong kinship, singing heartrendingly in the tower about his innocence, they decide to break their oath. Potter's song, which Adorno never set to music, echoes Heinrich Heine as it swerves suddenly from a folksong-like idyll to brutality.

Muff Potter (invisible) sings inside the tower:
In the woods, the lovely, green, green woods,
It is so beauteous there,
The sun does shine, the moon does shine,
As if they'd never set.

Then the hunters go off to hunt
Rabbits and deer run away.
They are murdered, each and every one,
The hunters feel their pain.

The play takes place in an imaginary, unlivable America, and at the end of the first act the three friends Huck, Tom, and Ben are already singing the song of homecoming. In his exchanges with Walter Benjamin, who misunderstood the piece as an idyll, Adorno characterized it as a "depiction of fear." It is actually about overcoming a shock. Fear is produced under pressure of social insecurity. The fear can become so powerful that the person regresses—here the term "regression" is used in a way that is completely value neutral, as the ability of time to flow backward. Freud, in a similar situation, before he was forced to leave Austria, regressed thousands of years and created his own Moses in a text that he initially termed a "historical novel." Adorno regressed by abandoning a discourse that was emotionally neutral in order to recover, underneath it, the power of repressed images. At the moment of catastrophe, Adorno bet everything on a single card and played it. He put the thing he feared on stage and retreated into the cave of the unconscious. But this cave is no darker than the cave of Max Ernst, for it is illuminated by the gaze of the person peering into it, however passively, as if paralyzed but with a wakeful consciousness. Inside the cave, the boys find the immaterial treasure that saves their lives. The cave is the social unconscious, a privileged location where outworn images are exchanged for new ones.

Earlier, I wrote that both the "Frankfurters" and the surrealists sought to add a new dimension to the political. This new dimension may be nothing but the philosophical cave in which they were able to immerse themselves under the pressure of contemporary problems and from which they regularly reemerged with the solution—an always surprising solution, which they could not have arrived at by mechanically applying conceptual apparatuses. Among the surrealists, art's resemblance to theory corresponds to theory's resemblance to art.

What links the Frankfurt School and surrealism is the protest against specialization, which, at the same time, is being played out at the highest level of the various specialized fields. They set the arts, disciplinary languages, and professional knowledge from the most diverse realms on a collision course, in order to force them, through the resulting shock, to set free a new way of thinking. The Frankfurt School realized this program in the *Zeitschrift für Sozialforschung* (Journal for social research), which brought together scholars from the most disparate disciplines: experts on finance, economists, psychoanalysts, philosophers, and historians, all of whom, in their diversity, sought to contribute something to an overarching social rationality that transcended the one-sidedness of their field—never mind if it was only the analysis of its absence. For their part, the surrealists, in the early years of their journal *Révolution Surréaliste*, laid claim to a similarly broad social engagement as surreal practice. This they did with a vehemence that anticipated, in a nutshell, all the protest movements of the 1960s: antipsychiatry, prisoners' movement, antimilitarism, critique of fossilized universities; however, the impulse was soon abandoned in favor of surrealism in the service of the Marxist revolution.

The *Zeitschrift für Sozialforschung* did not continue after the war. But Georges Bataille founded the journal *Critique,* whose concept—interdisciplinary social critique at the highest level—is entirely congruent with that of the earlier journal. On one point, freedom of thought, *Critique,* coming as it did after the experience of totalitarianism, is even more radical. The authors of articles, it states, may "freely develop an opinion that is of interest only to themselves, provided they can present this opinion with rational arguments and forego cheap polemics."[30] Bataille, who preserved a portion of Benjamin's legacy through the end of the war, developed his theory in a living, radically anti-Fascist context. As a theoretician of surrealism, he served as an honest broker between surrealism and critical theory.

In the 1980s, former members of the leadership of the German student movement sponsored a conference at which Ulrich K. Preuss, a lawyer who had formerly been active in SDS, addressed the subject of ecological democracy: "We must develop a culture of dissent, of heterogeneity and experiment," he said, "as opposed to a culture of consensus and homogeneity, of forced agreement and thus the exclusion of everything heterogeneous."[31] The categories homogenous/heterogeneous are borrowed from Georges Bataille.[32]

In contrast to actually existing socialism, which had not yet collapsed, the society of which Preuss went on to speak would be based not on an abstract humanity of producers, as posited by socialism, but on humankind's real cultural diversity. It would consist of social beings in specific life circumstances, for whom these life circumstances would be neither privatized, as in bourgeois utopias, nor ultimately spiritualized, but rather would form part of a project of social liberation. Socialism, which condemns the maximization of profit as the sole criterion of the economy, cannot simultaneously endorse the limitless exploitation of human and natural resources. Ecological democracy means deference both to external nature and to the nature of human beings, including all those capabilities that are not immediately useful. "Man is not the master, but the dream of the universe."[33] This implies a new definition of humanity—no longer as producers whose technology allows us to rule over all of nature, as in Marx's vision, but as capable, in our sovereignty, of renouncing this superiority.

Economically and politically, a contemporary perspective that would include the whole of society no longer seems available. Can such a perspective be developed? I have to answer this question as Radio Yerevan once did. Radio Yerevan, the mythical and often scurrilous Armenian station, specialized in dealing with these kinds of questions. Its response was: in principle, yes, such a perspective is possible, though not as Marxism, as an alternative to traditional theory, but as critical theory, understood in a surreal fashion, as an alternative to Marxism.

There are, to say the least, reasons to be skeptical. Capitalism has entered its paralytic phase, and even artists and intellectuals are crippled. One can hardly imagine that once again artists and scientists, experts and philosophers could be energized for a critique of society at the highest disciplinary levels. What is missing, I think, from what today—unfortunately only in a sectarian mode—is offered up as critical theory or as a manifestation of what remains of surrealism, is precisely the requisite tension between specialization and the view of the whole. The critique in critical theory does not consist in bureaucratized thinkers ceasing to think, and what is surreal about surrealist practice cannot consist in artists writing bureaucratic letters asking for support. Impulses toward overcoming the current crisis could only come from a new social movement of the type that has already been gauged as a moderate earthquake in France. Perhaps our sister Wirrwarr, the hundred-headed woman, will help.

Correspondence between Theodor W. Adorno and Elisabeth Lenk, 1962–1969

Introduction to the Correspondence

Elisabeth Lenk

O N THE THIRTIETH ANNIVERSARY of Adorno's death, when I was looking for a quotation from one of his letters, I discovered to my surprise that my letters to him were still extant. The Theodor W. Adorno Archive contains the carbon copies of Adorno's letters and my responses to him. They had been filed away by Frau Olbrich, his personal secretary, in the order in which they were received—with the last to arrive on top. This was the state of affairs when I sat down to read in the Adorno Archive. For me, who was very much alive, Benjamin's characterization of the experience of reading correspondence rang true: "The letters, as one reads them in order, with only the briefest of intervals, undergo an objective change, out of their own life. They live in another rhythm than when their recipients were living, and they change in other ways as well."[1] Letters don't stand for themselves; one could almost say that they belong more to their context than to themselves. There are common themes constituted only over the course of the exchange, and there are preconditions of these commonalities. With them I would like to begin.

The Priority of the Political

Adorno, for me, was that individual who most consistently demanded a reckoning with the past, and—almost alone—actively pursued it. He was viewed as an avenging angel—the poet Paul Celan, with his famous "Death Fugue," evoked a similar response. Adorno was a troublemaker, and this won me entirely over to his side. For me Adorno was not the man who had rescued Western Marxism from the Weimar period for the Federal

Republic of Germany; he was the person who, earlier than many others, understood the significance of Auschwitz for thought, including his own, and drew the practical consequences. "After everything that has occurred, there is no longer anything harmless and neutral," he said in a lecture on philosophy. *Dialectic of Enlightenment,* which appeared in 1947, stands for this. In this book, Horkheimer and Adorno didn't go back to thinking as they had before, without a break. They called that thinking into question. They were not nostalgic. The nonfulfillment of all their Marxist hopes didn't leave them speechless but set off a rethinking, a new thinking, that looks horror in the eye. When I say that Adorno was viewed as an avenging angel, I don't mean that he was filled with a desire for revenge. What drove him to return to Germany was the exact opposite: love for Germany and above all for the German language. "His thought . . . could not be separated from the German language," writes Joachim Perels in his lovely portrait of Adorno, and he goes on to quote Adorno himself: "The substance of my thoughts cannot be separated from the German tradition, even when they turn sharply against it; to do this I would have had to deny my intellectual nature. That I harbored the feeling of doing some good in Germany, of being able to work against the hardening and repetition of the catastrophe, is probably only another aspect of the same thing."[2]

Adorno's authority was due solely to the fact that he took his stand on the side of the victims; his was a moral authority, not an authority of power. He himself was not particularly sanguine about it, even at the beginning. He gambled on a bare minimum of morality. Seen from today, the brief period in which Adorno played his role has something scarcely believable, spectral, and impotent about it. We see him, armed only with the word, crossing swords with a whole society.[3] It is admirable, the way he succeeded in introducing a system of education aimed at civic maturity and against the organization of historical oblivion. Still, there are words that can wound and hit home. The last book that Adorno prepared for publication was *Catchwords,* and in the foreword we read, "The association with polemics that the title conveys is something the author welcomes."[4] In fact, *Catchwords* once again linked the political acuity he had shown, in essays such as "Education after Auschwitz," "What Is German?" and above all in his splendid "Marginalia on Theory and Practice," to more philosophical concerns. But Adorno also knew that the memory of something of which one does not wish to be reminded triggers rage. Society's revenge was that soon after his death he was already forgotten, indeed erased from public consciousness in a kind of fury.

The Aesthetic Dimension

What characterizes this correspondence with Adorno is its paradoxical mix. It is formal and academic, which in Adorno's case is expressed by the fact that he dictates the letters to his secretary, and in my case by the retention, to the end, of the salutation "Dear Professor Adorno" and the formal *Sie* form of address.[5] But it is also spontaneous and lively. It is characteristic of these letters that they constantly disavow their character as letters and refer to the oral exchanges in which they regularly culminate, to which they refer, and toward which they are usually aimed. This may have to do with the teacher–student relationship or the fact that Adorno was always much more direct and understandable for us in oral, improvised expression than in his writing. But the need is articulated just as clearly on Adorno's side. I am thinking of such casual remarks as "I have to tell you about that," "We should discuss this in detail," "We should talk about this at leisure very soon." However much these conversations may have fallen short of the ideal of a calm, leisurely exchange, the letters live from them and not the other way around. And yet written work, texts that have just been completed (especially by Adorno) or are currently being worked on, play the main role. For my part, this priority is simply a result of my position as Adorno's doctoral student. One cannot avoid a certain sense of tragic irony in observing how I constantly put off the completion of my dissertation, which was incessantly conjured up by both of us, as if I were attempting to preserve the floating state that made possible what we shared. Adorno, for his part, occasionally refers to his writings simply by mentioning a piece he has just completed. Some of his letters, especially the later ones, after 1967, are almost lists of works that he has written or, as he says, "put to bed." As monotonous as such a listing may at first be for the reader, if one begins to read the texts they introduce an entirely different dimension into the correspondence, and one suddenly understands why each work held such great importance for him, emotionally as well as intellectually.

From a purely external standpoint, the correspondence had become necessary because after my university examination I left Frankfurt to complete my doctorate in Paris. Adorno represented the entire optic through which I viewed the world; whether he liked it or not, he provided me with a system. I wanted to break out of this system, and the way out was literature, a certain kind of literature, which for me was embodied in the word *Paris*. The funny thing was that Adorno and I converged in our love of this kind of literature, which he called hermetic, and which for him, too, meant an escape from his own thinking, a chance to breathe for an individual who was in danger of suffocating in his self-constructed conceptuality. "The person who comes from philosophy and would like to escape from it," I remember writing at the time, "first grasps the isolated sensual object, until he notices that there is no such thing as an isolated sensual object, that it exists as such only in its difference from the concept. This discovery is so astonishing that the person coming from philosophy breaks into a happy dance. Equidistant from the sensual thing and the concept, he starts to spin around and around." If I was seeking to gain some distance, this was evidently the precondition for an entirely new relationship with Adorno—one that was no longer that of a pupil, but would be dialogical. The myth of Paris existed not only for Benjamin but also for Adorno—and consequently for me as well.

Adorno and I had settled on a strictly sociological theme. I wanted to write on the Durkheim school. But chance, which is not really chance but a walking in traces, caught up with me again: André Breton was there, along with his category of the self-negating objective accident. Breton and "his" surrealism became essential to me, at times more important than Adorno was. I saw Breton every day except Sunday, between 6:00 and 8:00 p.m. in the Café Promenade de Vénus. I had been fascinated by a sentence that I had heard the surrealist José Pierre[6] utter concerning the surrealist group: "Politics, with us, happens on a different level." I had already been prepared for this other conception of politics by Walter Benjamin, who had written, with reference to the great period of prewar surrealism, that this movement was concerned neither with literature in the narrow sense nor with traditional politics, but with winning the forces of intoxication for the revolution.[7] We discussed everything, but at a considerable remove from day-to-day politics and including the arts and whatever we happened to be reading. By no means did the literature we talked about have to be the latest thing; it could come from any century. André Breton was able to conduct a conversation about levitating tables in a novel by Victor Hugo and make it as suspenseful as if he himself had been present the evening before. Since I was the only German in the group, Breton turned to me when it came to things German.

Later, when I was living in Giessen and wanted to return to Paris, he wrote me a recommendation for Nanterre. The questions he put to me about Heidegger provoked me to write an article on Heidegger that was published in his magazine *La Brèche*[8] in 1964. Breton enjoyed the fuss that the text created in France, especially for Heidegger's French interlocutor Jean Beaufret. Like Adorno, Breton was political to the core. As with other political formations, our *groupe* had its struggles among different tendencies, especially between the Trotskyists and the anarchists. But we also partied and improvised in a wonderfully old-fashioned cinema hall that some film people had put at the group's disposal. We played. The playwright Arabal[9] dropped into the café leading a girlfriend on a long leash—which did not prevent the feminist and writer Christiane Rochefort[10] from appearing with girlfriends as well. After all, it was the Café Promenade of Venus! Breton enjoyed himself capitally on days like these. I watched him as he observed the whole colorful bunch, and himself, in the mirror opposite his perch. This moment partly inspired the title of my book on Breton, *Leaping Narcissus*[11]—a leap that derived from the heroic period of surrealism. "The future poet," Breton had stated, "will overcome the tiresome notion of the irreconcilable breach between dream and deed." Surrealism—this was my thesis—was the first attempt by an art that was autonomous, but had become anemic, to reconquer the energies that had been split off from it. It had begun with marvelous élan but, according to Breton, was like a person who repeatedly rehearses in his mind the leap that he does not dare to take in reality. According to Breton, surrealism ultimately remained in the realm of dreams and of art. Like the smile on the face of a statue, the initial spasm of interrupted élan had left its imprint on all of surrealism's living expressions as *convulsive beauty*. Never tiring of gazing at himself, Narcissus prepares to leap. He would like to cross the river of the mirror, to heal the breach between dream and deed, but at this most beautiful, wildest moment, he succumbs to the temptation of looking at himself, and thus the movement freezes in a convulsive gesture.

The group displayed all the unfortunate symptoms of a political clique. After André Breton's death, I was formally expelled for "situationist deviation" in an act modeled on Communist Party ritual. These formalities included not only group interrogation but also breaking off personal ties with me following my expulsion. Few disobeyed this injunction. My misstep had occurred in the spring of 1967 when I responded to a Danish surrealist, who asked what "we" surrealists thought of Situationism, in a way that diverged from the opinion of the new chief of the surrealist group, Jean Schuster.[12] Schuster had dismissed the Situationists, while I lauded them as the new avant-garde of Europe and pointed to their actions in Nanterre—insisting that if a student revolt was to be expected at all, it would come from this quarter. To Schuster's credit, he rehabilitated me after May 1968. Situationism was haunting Nanterre, where I taught, and I found it politically more relevant than surrealism. Its two theoreticians, Guy Debord[13] and Asger Jorn,[14] were close to surrealism in one respect: they included the arts in the revolutionary struggle. At the same time, they paid much more attention to the "new media." *Society of the Spectacle* was the then little-known title of Debord's work, which, like the chapter on the mass media in *Dialectic of Enlightenment,* advanced the thesis that ideology was being replaced by the self-replication of society. The Situationists further radicalized the concept of politics that I had come to know among the surrealists by voting, for example, to run for election to the student council on a program of dissolving themselves if they were elected. Thanks to their brochure *The Poverty of the Students,* which was acutely theoretical but also packed with witty comics, they were elected by the students and, as promised, immediately dissolved themselves.[15] This new political style struck fire with Rudi Dutschke and Bernd Rabehl as well.[16] The German section of the Situationist International, Subversive Action, recruited them as members in 1964 with a poster that was heavily larded with quotes from Adorno and of questionable standing when it came to intellectual property.

As I sat in the Adorno Archive and paged through my old correspondence with my former teacher, all of these contexts floated up to me from the yellowed files as vividly as if I had bitten into the famous magic madeleine.

I recalled that in our correspondence Adorno, like me, betrayed subversive tendencies, although he expressed them quite differently. Adorno was stoically strict with himself; he rigorously sacrificed his inclinations in favor of the self-imposed duty to work against the hardening and repetition of the catastrophe. But after completing *Negative Dialectics,* which was still entirely dedicated to that dutiful program, he adopted a new tone. He allowed himself some side trips to the forbidden country of utopia, the promised land of the concrete. In this late period, there emerges a new style, a high-spirited, more carefree tone, mostly in pieces that Adorno calls "little things," ephemera, for example in "Is Art Light-Hearted?," which held particular importance for him.[17] The essay is more a musical composition than a scholarly text. Not that difficulties are being papered over—Adorno even launches into an entirely new interpretation of his own Auschwitz thesis—but the movement of the language, the tempo, the pleasures of this text are irresistible. One could almost say that he skips lightly over all dialectical intentions. "Is Art Light-Hearted?" is not only brief but breaks down into eight smaller segments—one is tempted to call them capriccios rather than theses, although they are composed of language, not tones.

The Construction of Happiness

The path from the political to the aesthetic and back took place, in our correspondence, under the sign of Charles Fourier. In the days leading up to May 1968, I was ready to interrupt my surrealism dissertation and devote myself again to politics. Adorno never uttered a word of disapproval. He stood for a third thing that united us—quite unequal—correspondents: the utopian belief in happiness. Adorno, from his earliest thinking, always rebelled against the splitting off of happiness from the project of modernity. The central idea of happiness is present in him even in his theory of anti-Semitism, in that he characterizes anti-Semites and racists as enemies of happiness. The potential killer, he thought, is always prepared to attack those who are weaker, especially when he can accuse them of allowing themselves something that he himself is forbidden to enjoy. In this individual, the place of passion and its fulfillment has been usurped by the passion for punishment. Adorno had an exalted, not an idyllic, concept of happiness. The pleasure of thinking, the pleasure of combat were a part of it, hence his enthusiasm for Fourier's category of joy in combat. In my introduction to the Fourier text that Adorno edited, where I said that the error of humankind had not been—as the moralists claimed—to have demanded too much, but rather to have demanded too little, he wrote in the margin: "Yes!"[18]

This resonates with May '68 and its notorious motto "Be realistic; attempt the impossible!" Not only Adorno but also Herbert Marcuse took happiness seriously. In his critique of hedonism, Marcuse writes: "Love, friendship, comradeship are . . . personal relations, to which Western culture has relegated man's highest earthly happiness. But they cannot contain happiness, precisely when they are what they are intended to be."[19] Both agreed with Fourier that happiness is by nature social, and therefore its

establishment presupposes a reorganization of society—a theory that nowadays is meant to be applied in reverse, by reprogramming human beings.

For Adorno, happiness is inseparable from eroticism. He repeatedly
wrote on the theme of antipathy to happiness, for example, in connection with Vera Brühne, who as we now know was unjustly condemned.[20]
Because she was beautiful, and because it was obvious merely from looking at her that sexual frustration was not in her repertoire, a hysterical mob
was prepared to believe that she had committed murder. From Vera Brühne
to Adelheid von Weislingen,[21] whom Adorno called "one of my earliest
lovers from books," Adorno (who once called himself "a martyr for happiness")[22] came to the defense of the marginalized and excluded. In my
Fourier introduction, in a section titled "The Construction of Happiness,"
I emphasized the streaks of happiness that Fourier had come up with in
analogy to streaks of bad luck. In this context, I mentioned the example
of a certain Leander, who is successful with a woman he has wooed (first
pleasure), who secures through her a lucrative position (second pleasure),
and then meets a friend whom he had believed dead (third pleasure). Fourier went so far as to claim that this Leander's streak of good luck exceeded
the pleasures of civilized monarchs. To all this, Adorno wrote in the margin, "The latter would probably have exceeded the happiness of our petit
bourgeois." Adorno, as strict and unbelievably productive as he was, was
always ready to apply his imagination to picturing the happiness of kings.

The "Adorno Line" and Its Supposed Failure

Our correspondence began in 1962, soon after the expulsion of the Socialist German Students' Union (SDS) from the Social Democratic Party of
Germany (SPD), and ended with the 1968 movement and its failure,
shortly before Adorno's death. Dissatisfaction with postwar German society had first led me to Adorno as well as to SDS, which had begun to con-
front the past in earnest in 1962, when it organized a traveling exhibition
on Nazi judges who were still in office.[23] When Adorno first wrote to me,
on November 20, 1962, I had just given the keynote address at the Seventeenth Representative Conference of SDS and been scornfully dismissed
as "Frankfurt's chief lady theorist." My invitation was viewed as part of an
attempt to define the work of SDS in a way that would bring the organization closer to critical theory and to Adorno in particular—in other words,
closer to the "Adorno line." Indeed, I was critical of "blind practice," calling

instead for "theoretical practice as a form of politics." "The capacity of SDS to survive politically following its expulsion from the SPD was probably also enhanced by critical theory, which, in claiming that the workers' movement was socially co-opted, coincided with the new left's objective of distancing itself from the tradition of the old left and its bureaucratic organizations."[24] Adorno maintained a lifelong commitment to his theoretically radical but always nonviolent concept of practice. SDS, however, strayed further and further from it, to the detriment of democracy. A coarsening and vulgarization occurred among some members that alienated many, especially intellectuals and women. New forms of blind actionism emerged among the protesters, which provoked equally blind reactions on the part of the authorities.

"Strike at Lukács" was a slogan popular during the era when I was studying with Adorno. Today, the motto more likely to be heard is "Strike at Adorno." Distancing oneself from him has become a routine exercise. Strangely, it is not SDS, or even the SPD, but the theoreticians of the Frankfurt School, and above all Adorno, who are held responsible for this. It is a vicious circle when, for example, in speeches celebrating the seventy-fifth anniversary of the founding of the Institute for Social Research, it is said that "the historico-philosophical and sociological foundations of the Frankfurt School" can no longer be upheld "today," because this school "failed, as a result of the implementation of its extremely demanding program of critique." Evidently the same people who developed an excessively demanding political program are to be held responsible for the anti-intellectualism of some 68ers and for the desperate actions of the Red Army Fraction.[25]

Correspondence between Theodor W. Adorno and Elisabeth Lenk, 1962–1969

Commentary to the Correspondence by Elisabeth Lenk

1

Frankfurt am Main, November 20, 1962
Kettenhofweg 123

Dear Ms. Lenk,

This is only to tell you that, as you suggested, I had the formal letter of recommendation for you sent to Frau Lorenz, in triplicate, since I do not know the address of the office to which it should go. It has turned out to be formidable, but no more so than corresponds to my honest conviction: trust me in this regard.

And please keep me up-to-date, not only about the scholarship but also about your Parisian impressions overall, about the questions connected with your project, and in general. Please also give me your address and telephone number. It is by no means impossible that I will turn up in Paris in the not-too-distant future, this time without any official duties, in which case I would obviously like to see you and would write to you in advance.

Have you gotten in touch with the people whose names I gave you? I envy your being in Paris a little; actually, I regard every year in which I don't manage to get there as lost. But I am immersed so deeply in my work that I don't have time for envy even if I had more talent for it.

I think the Munster lecture on the dialectic of progress corresponds more or less to what I required of it and of myself; others have confirmed this, which gives me the courage to continue working on the extremely fraught text, whose first draft I have almost finished dictating. The text is admittedly still awfully chaotic, but I take comfort from Nietzsche's dictum on chaos, even if I am careful not to breathe a word of this.

All best wishes from
your warmly devoted
Adorno

Ms. Lenk: In the original German, Adorno addresses his unmarried graduate student with the honorific "Frau" (Mrs.), as a mark of respect. There is no literal equivalent for this practice in English, but since the 1960s "Ms." has come to play a similar role when a female is addressed in a situation that emphasizes her professional role rather than her marital status. Adorno soon begins to address "Frau Lenk" simply as "Elisabeth."—Ed.

Frau Lorenz: Erika Lorenz had been an assistant to Ernst Bloch in Leipzig with her husband Richard Lorenz. She was forced to emigrate from the German Democratic Republic (GDR). At the time she had a temporary position at the Institute for Social Research and was my best friend.

With the people whose names I gave you: Adorno had given me some business cards with his introduction to a number of individuals in Paris. There was also a list of important people, in his handwriting, whom he suggested I seek out, among them Lucien Goldmann, who was teaching sociology of literature at the École Pratique des Hautes Études. As soon as I arrived, I began studying under Goldmann. I met him personally in November 1962 (see note to Letter 2). The list included French sociologist Jean Stoetzel and Raymond Aron, whom I never did get in touch with. Roger Caillois was also on the list. At the time he was the president of UNESCO in Paris. I wrote down "le mythe de Paris," and I remember that Adorno, in explaining who Callois was, spoke of the Collège de Sociologie and mentioned the name of Georges Bataille, whom I had never heard of. (In the "Entretiens" with Jean-Marie Monnoyer, Pierre Klossowski confirms that during the period of the Collège's existence, 1937–1939, he met Adorno as part of the group around Benjamin; see "Le peintre et son démon" (Paris 1985, 187). I got in touch with Callois and Bataille only to the extent that I began to read their works. Georges Bataille had passed away a few months before I arrived in Paris. (See also note to Letter 26.)

The Munster lecture on the dialectic of progress: A lecture at the Munster Philosophers Congress on October 22, 1962, which was first published in

Argumentationen: Festschrift für Josef König, ed. Harald Delius and Günther Patzig (Göttingen, 1964), 1ff. A revised version titled "Fortschritt" (Progress) appeared in *Stichworte.* It was published in English in *Critical Models: Interventions and Catchwords,* trans. Henry W. Pickford (New York: Columbia University Press, 1998), 143–60.

Nietzsche's dictum on chaos: This may possibly refer to: "I tell you: one must still have chaos in one, to give birth to a dancing star." Friedrich Nietzsche, *Thus Spake Zarathustra,* trans. Thomas Common (New York: Modern Library, n.d.), 11.

2

Paris 6e, April 10, 1963
chez Mlle Michot
24, rue Servandoni

Dear Professor Adorno,

Unfortunately I had no time during my brief visit to Frankfurt to come to see you. I nevertheless hope very much that you have not entirely forgotten me and my dissertation plans. Unfortunately, after my enthusiastic launch I must report the first failure: the application to the German Academic Exchange Service (DAAD) for a scholarship was turned down. I must confess that at first I was quite upset, above all about the "how" of the whole affair. First, they kept us supplicants, most of whom came from far away and like me had driven through part of the night, waiting for four or five hours. The gentlemen from the commission were not introduced to us. The rejection gives no concrete reason; it is a mimeographed form letter. The documents, letters of recommendation, etc., remain with them. Now I have a big request to make of you: would it be possible for you to ask the DAAD about the reason why they turned me down, and, in addition, request the return of the letters of recommendation? Naturally, you can judge better than I whether a request of this kind would make sense and be of use.

It seems that in our society it is really an adventurous undertaking to live on one's own and follow one's own inclination. I would appreciate it very much if I could have a conversation with you about my plans and studies. I wonder whether you intend to come to Paris? If not, I would like to send you a rough draft no more than two months from now. In the meanwhile, I have landed at the École Pratique des Hautes Études, have had some discussions with Goldmann and Lefebvre, and in general I already feel myself somewhat established here. The "no" from the inexplicable commission, which makes my further stay here completely uncertain, is a blow that is all the more difficult to accept.

Please do not be annoyed with me if I bother you, who surely have more important things in mind, with my student worries.

Respectfully, I remain
your Elisabeth Lenk

Lucien Goldmann: Goldmann, a sociologist of literature from Bucharest, became a professor in Paris in 1958, at the time of the Hungarian Revolution, thanks to the votes of the Communists. He had written a book on Racine and Jansenism, *The Hidden God*. He took an interest in me, in his somewhat abrupt but friendly way, until his death in 1970. I often met him in the sixth arondissement, where I lived, or in Montparnasse. He almost always had two books under his arm, demonstratively the same ones: *History and Class Struggle,* by Georg Lukács, and *Being and Time,* by Martin Heidegger. The third book that one absolutely had to have, according to him as a sociologist of literature, was Erich Auerbach's *Mimesis*.

3

Frankfurt am Main, April 17, 1963
Kettenhofweg 123

Dear Ms. Lenk,

It is really a shame that you didn't come to see me. No, don't worry, I have not forgotten (first of all) you and (second) your academic concerns. Naturally I will be glad to ask the DAAD about the reason why they turned you down.

At the moment, unfortunately, there can be no thought of Paris; until mid-June I am no human being at all but a work machine and glad if I am still living at that time. What will be in the fall I cannot yet foresee; for certain in August I will once again be in Sils Maria. In any case it would be good if you would like to send me a rough draft as soon as you have it. I promise you that I will react very rapidly.

Very warmly,
always your
T. W. Adorno

4

Paris, 6e, 5.5.1963
24, rue Servandoni, chez Mlle Michot

Dear Professor Adorno,

Many thanks for your friendly letter! If I am bold enough to write to you again—despite all the work that you have—it is because I would like to ask your advice about my dissertation.

I believe I told you in the letter before last that I have fallen in with a surrealist group. I must confess that the atmosphere of the group, but above all the personality of Breton, has made an extraordinary impression. I have started to work on the history of surrealism. Now I have a question: would you be in agreement if I were to write my dissertation on surrealism? In contrast to the official, preliminary theme of French sociology, this subject would be of passionate interest to me. Naturally it will again be a borderline theme that is situated between all the fields; nevertheless, I believe one could responsibly regard it as a sociology project. Technically there would be no problem. Through the contact with Breton and his friends I could get access to the Fond Doucet and other less well-known materials.

This project would fascinate me because it would be empirical not in the usual sociological sense but rather in the sense that I could capture a slice of life and atmosphere.

I would be very grateful if you could write to me what you think of this suggestion. In early July I will come to Germany for a short time. Are you still in Frankfurt then? Perhaps I could stop by with my draft?

With warm regards, I am
your devoted
Elisabeth Lenk

P.S. I asked Frau Dr. Pross to inquire about a formal recommendation from you. I apologize for the fact that I am such an awkward student for you.

that I have fallen in with a surrealist group: I got into this group, as is proper for a surrealistic encounter, by chance. I had been active in the Frankfurt branch of the Socialist German Students' Union (SDS); among other things I had supported deserters from the war in Algeria, together with Monika Mitscherlich-Seifert, the daughter of the well-known public intellectual Alexander Mitscherlich. Often, when I traveled to Paris, I would be carrying some letter or other from these emigrants to family members or people of like persuasion. Thus I was invited to a celebratory dinner party when Pierre Hessel, a prominent deserter, worker, and former Communist, was released from prison; and at this party I was introduced to the surrealists, whose "chief," André Breton, was a co-initiator and naturally a signatory of the "Declaration of the 121 on the Right Not to Serve in the War in Algeria," a manifesto that on September 1, 1960, called for desertion from that war. Soon after this first encounter, Breton encouraged me to come to the regular meetings of the group in the Café Promenade de Vénus, near les Halles, which at that time had not yet been relocated. I owed this privilege not to my love of poetry but to my political engagement, especially since a Trotskyist acquaintance of Breton's had been present as an observer in Frankfurt when I gave the keynote address at the Seventeenth Representative Conference of the Socialist German Students' Union (SDS), the first conference to take place after the SDS was expelled from the Social Democratic Party of Germany (SPD).

Naturally . . . a borderline theme . . . between all the fields: A reference to my thesis on "Neo-Romantic Traits in Georg Simmel's Image of Society," which had already brought me halfway into the study of literature.

Fond Doucet: The Biliothèque littéraire Jacques Doucet is an archive containing essential documents for researchers interested in surrealism.—Ed.

5

Frankfurt am Main
May 31, 1963
Kettenhofweg 123

Dear Ms. Lenk:

Please excuse my unduly long silence. But I have been acutely and very seriously ill; I am now back to normal, but still a bit weak and suffering from it. I really need your indulgence.

In early July I will certainly be in Frankfurt. It would be good if you would let me know beforehand exactly when you will come, so that we can find a quiet time to talk to one another.

A surrealism project would naturally be of burning interest to me, although the irksome question of institutional competence does play a role. If you are looking at literary surrealism, the historians of literature and Romance language will bark; but if you are concerned with surrealist painting, the art historians will make their claims known. Then again, to present the story purely as a "sociology of . . ." would go against my own intentions, since I do not believe that one can write the sociology of an intellectual phenomenon without delving into it oneself. How much the subject would interest me I don't need to tell you—after all, someone in Italy has written a paper, which I could not read, on my relationship to surrealism. So the best thing will be for us to talk about the whole set of issues. Perhaps, after all, one should attempt to separate the purely academic aspect somewhat from that of the actually substantive interest. But even there I am by no means *entêté*.

The matter of the formal recommendation will of course be taken care of.

I look forward very much to seeing you again, and am, with the most cordial greetings

Always your
Adorno

someone in Italy has written a paper . . . on my relationship to surrealism: Roberto Calasso, "Theodor W. Adorno il surrealismo e il 'Mana,'" *Paragone* 138 (June 1961). See also Letters 57 and 58.

6

[Paris 6e, rue Servandoni, chez Mlle Michot]

Dear Professor Adorno,

Although I do not yet know the exact date when I will be in Frankfurt, I would like to thank you for your friendly letter and above all wish you a good recovery. Too bad I don't know Italian, or I would have gladly read the article you mention. I, too, in fact, have noticed some parallels between you and the surrealist intentions.

As soon as I know exactly when I will come I will send a postcard. It is very nice of you to want to take the time.

With the best wishes for your health and warm regards, I am

Your
Elisabeth Lenk

7

Institute for Social Research
An der Senckenberganlage 26
Johann Wolfgang Goethe University
Frankfurt am Main, July 12, 1963

Dear Ms. Lenk:

Today there is good news to report. I have spoken with the new Romance languages professor, the incidentally very pleasant Herr Müller, informed him about your plan to write a dissertation on surrealism, and asked him whether he would take on the codirection. He responded enthusiastically that he is in agreement, without being a real expert, but at least he followed the most important surrealist journals quite closely at the time and has considerable interest in the subject. So far, I should think, we are on firm ground.

Please let me know as soon as possible whether the matter of the scholarship has finally worked out; if not, we must try something else.

With friendliest regards,

Your warmly devoted
Adorno

8

Savournon (Hautes Alpes), July 23, 1963

Dear Professor Adorno,

I only now received your letter, which was forwarded to me where I am on vacation. I thank you most cordially for your friendliness. I am delighted that you, to whom I owe so much intellectually, would go to so much trouble on my behalf, and I will try to write a dissertation that vindicates this trust. What I have learned from you, above all, is this: to take the intellect just as seriously as so-called reality. This means that there is also, especially in intellectual affairs, a strict morality that permits absolutely no sloppiness and dishonesty. Hence I was very impressed by a remark of Lautréamont's to the effect that "all the water in the ocean would not suffice to wash out a single drop of intellectual blood." Not that I imagine I am already moral in the intellectual sense, but you have honed the intellectual conscience of your students, and I believe that is very important, infinitely more important than if someone merely parrots the results of your thinking or even just imitates your style (which is unfortunately also the danger of some "Adorno students").

Excuse these rather fervent words, but your letter awakened these thoughts in me, and the advantage of vacation is that one has time to pick up and analyze impressions that flit by in the heat of everyday life.

Unfortunately I cannot yet enclose the draft that you asked for in Frankfurt. But at the moment I have a translation project to complete for which the deadline has already passed, and in this wonderfully beautiful landscape I must struggle against my tendency to indolence and dreaming, so I haven't completed it yet. As soon as my draft is done I will send it off, even if it should reach you after the holidays.

What will happen with the scholarship I don't yet know, but in view of your "formidable" reference I am quite optimistic. Once again many thanks!

> [Warm regards
> from your
> Elisabeth Lenk]

a translation project: Lucien Goldmann had arranged for me to revise a German translation of Eric Weil.

9

Frankfurt am Main, October 31, 1963
Kettenhofweg 123

Dear Ms. Lenk:

Very best thanks for your letter, which I found waiting for me on my return.

I congratulate you—and us!—cordially on the fact that you have now received a scholarship after all. That the foundation declined to give it to you says something about it and not about you. It does feel good when this kind of thing is rectified in the external world.

It is very unfortunate that you did not phone on my birthday. You would certainly have been most welcome at the reception at the Institute, of which I count you a member. Please do let me know when you might be turning up here again. I would certainly not want to miss you. Many thanks, as well, for your congratulations.

> Most warmly and devotedly,
> always your
> T. W. Adorno

on my birthday: It was his sixtieth, and it attracted considerable public interest in the form of newspaper articles, events, and a television appearance.

10

Frankfurt am Main, July 29, 1964
Kettenhofweg 123

Dear Ms. Lenk:

Forgive a person who is literally hounded to death that it is only today he answers your so lovely letter of May 27 with the report. You can really only with difficulty imagine what I had to contend with, and probably even less the entirely desolate condition in which I found myself. It even prevented me from paying close attention to your dissertation, concerning which I meanwhile have only the worry whether it will be able to be presented as being sufficiently sociological. We must talk about that, although you have no cause to worry on that account.

I am now leaving on vacation to Switzerland and must practice complete intellectual abstinence—that only the most serious motives force me to do this, you will believe. But from the middle of September on I am here, and it would be lovely if you would pay a visit in September or October so that we could talk with each other extensively and seriously.

Only, I would really like to ask you to arrange your coming in good time so that I don't happen to be absent for a couple of days when you are here.

Please forgive me this organizational incivility, which is admittedly very difficult to bring together with the spirit of surrealism.

Otherwise I look forward with special pleasure to seeing you again.

Most warmly, always your
Adorno

11

Frankfurt am Main, September 17, 1964
Kettenhofweg 123

Dear Ms. Lenk,

My very best thanks for your letter.

My proposal would be for you to come here sometime between October 10 and 20. Before that things will be a bit topsy-turvy, and after the 20th I am in Vienna. Within the given dates, however, we will have plenty of time to speak together. Perhaps you will be so good as to let me know an exact time soon.

I look forward with very special pleasure to seeing you again.

Most warmly,
always your
Adorno

12

Frankfurt am Main, November 2, 1964
Kettenhofweg 123

Dear Elisabeth,

I am back from Vienna. You will be in Paris again, and I would like to say how very happy I am about the two afternoons. Please let me know in plenty of time when you are coming here again, so that we can spend more time together and less in the academic shadow, which is not that of young girls. By the way, I am coming to Paris in early March, as is now firmly settled. The definitive acceptance owes more than a little to your presence there.

Today, however, I would like to mention an idea whose realization I cannot guarantee, but that you should know about now. Suhrkamp publishers, whose director, Dr. Unseld, now also controls the Insel publishing company, asked me to make a few proposals for the latter. I came up with the idea of putting together a selection of original source texts on surrealism, perhaps drawing on its prehistory as well, to the extent that it is not already documented in the available editions of Lautréamont, Jarry, and others. How Unseld will react to the plan is something I can't predict. The main question will probably be whether the plan overlaps with projects of other publishers. Obviously, however, I was thinking that you will make the selection and introduce it all. Perhaps you will be so good as to let me know now whether you would be interested. If I were to approach Unseld with something positive, the chances would naturally be greater. My only concern would be that the work doesn't hurt the progress of the dissertation. Since they are so closely related, however, I think that can be avoided.

Today I am leaving for the Rhineland for a few days, but I will be back toward the end of the week and would be *very* glad of a word from you.

In this sense, I am, most warmly,

> your
> Adorno

I am coming to Paris in early March: Adorno flew to Paris, where he had lectures and seminars to give on March 3, 1965.

13

Paris, November 5, 1964
[75, avenue Ledru-Rollin 12e,
chez Danielle Bohler]

Dear Professor Adorno,

For your so charming letter, my warmest thanks! For me the so completely unacademic conversations were very lovely and valuable despite the academic shadow. Some of the personal things you said, things that I felt vaguely but didn't know, have touched me and made me thoughtful: for example, the remark about the clash between art and research. You were right to warn me of the dangers of this kind of dual existence. I believe people who think that doing academic research and writing poetry can be reconciled (poetry here merely as an example for all artistic activity), or who even think they are identical, whether it is the surrealists, Brecht, Benjamin, or the modern structural poets, are in error. When the analytic thinker and the poet get along well, as they claim, it is mere appearance and comes about, like many a "good marriage," because one part has submitted more or less unconditionally to the other—here the artist to the analytic thinker. In some cases the artist, although he may be outwardly adjusted, remains stubborn and therefore intact. But often the artistic is poisoned right at the source, and this leads to tormented and utterly joyless products, as are common in structural lyrics.

But I want to come to the most important thing, your proposal: it has greatly excited and pleased me, and I am very grateful that you are getting so involved on behalf of surrealism (and me). I don't believe that work on a project such as this can hurt my dissertation—on the contrary. But it would be quite a lot of responsibility for me. Everything would depend on not presenting surrealism as a series of classic texts but rather *situating* it in relation to contemporary tendencies. It seems that Max Hölzer, for example—for all his goodwill—has failed at this task. Texts of Breton, for example, are "raw" and indigestible by the German public for two reasons. On the one hand, the fascinating quality of his language, which consists of the tension between the classical French sentence and certain linguistic accidents (or quite intentionally selected individual words), which set this very sentence in motion, is nowhere to be felt in the German translations. And on the other hand, many concepts that Breton can use naïvely in France are freighted with meaning in German. Here they provoke reactions, whole complexes of feelings that have nothing to do with what Breton wants to say. For example, when he speaks of romanticism, the true life, or his hatred of logic, in Germany people too quickly associate irrationalism, hostility to the intellect, Ludwig Klages— and have "done" with the matter.

In order to prevent such misunderstandings, we would need to emphasize the aspects that you mentioned: the mixture of romanticism and modernism, the organic and the mechanical, irrationalism and revolution—all of which seem unusual to the German way of thinking, the fact that they don't reject modern works in the name of a deep romantic soul, but at least make an attempt to digest this world (Dalí's ravenous hunger!). Perhaps such an interpretation could help German intellectuals be less frenetic as they drown their inner romantic, day in and day out!

These are just a few very sidelong associations that came to me on the subject of your so tempting proposal. My letter has unfortunately become awfully long, but that is also an expression of my pleasure at yours.

I look forward very much to seeing you in March in Paris.

Very warm regards from

your
Elisabeth Lenk

modern structural poets: The movement more commonly known as concrete poetry.

Max Hölzer: Max Hölzer had translated *Sacred Eros,* by Georges Bataille, and *Nadja,* by André Breton, into German and edited the short-lived journal *Surrealistische Publikationen* but did not compile an anthology of surrealism. He left a body of poems of his own, which is still largely unpublished.—Ed.

14

Frankfurt am Main, November 9, 1964
Kettenhofweg 123

Dear Elisabeth,

A thousand thanks for the letter, which has truly been a joy to me.

The question about the legacy of theoretical consciousness and artistic production is indeed central to my own intellectual fate, that is to say, still unresolved—I continue to hope, against all reason, that I will yet be able to realize something of what I thought I could accomplish as an artist, and that competent people also thought I could accomplish, so I am not afraid of being caught in the Nero-like *qualis artifix pereo*. This implies, admittedly, that I don't, after all, consider the two to be as incompatible as you suggest; I have had the experience precisely with artists of the highest caliber that lack of reflection and adequate intellectual awareness—often overcompensated for by ad hoc pseudo-theories based on weltanschauung—today, when there is nothing for them to hold onto, has also affected their own production in the most grievous way. The greatest example of this is Schoenberg, who in the lesser texts of his so-called major works truly raged against himself. However, I am of the opinion that the reason for the falseness lies in the relationship between the two spheres, [in the fact] that so many artists are trying to achieve the atrocity of a synthesis of intellectual content and art. In other words, they pump some sort of ideas into the works and mistake that for meaningful content. The relation of the intellect to art can only consist in the intellect, above all the critical intellect, giving directives as to what is possible and what is not possible; it cannot become the immediate object or content of art. Beckett, a person who embodies truly indescribably advanced consciousness and at the same time maintains a strict distance from all interpretation of his works, and from mine as well, seems exemplary to me in this regard. And I myself forget, when I am composing, literally everything that I have ever thought about it, without, I hope, forgetting it after all.

But this is mostly just talking about unhatched chickens, and this, as we all know, is something we are not supposed to do. As for the hatched ones, I hope someday to be able to show you some. You said, by the way, that you would be coming to Germany in December, around Christmas. Could we not meet? March is a long way off.

I am extraordinarily happy about your reaction to the surrealism idea and will speak with Unseld about it over the next few days. What you have to say about the project, in principle, is in complete agreement with my own view, and I will put it forward too.

This evening, at one of the Suhrkamp publisher's evenings, I am reading from the book version of *The Jargon of Authenticity*. It is really too bad you won't be there. Please don't buy it, you will receive one as soon as I get my copies. And please write back as soon as you have a chance; I wait for your letter.

Most warmly,
your
Teddie Adorno

qualis artifex pereo: "What an artist dies with me!" (Nero)—Ed.

15

Frankfurt am Main, November 10, 1964
Kettenhofweg 123

Dear Elisabeth,

Yesterday evening, after my reading at a reception given by Unseld, I had an opportunity to speak with him about our project, and he expressed a lively interest. He asks you to send him, soon, a brief proposal for a timely documentation of surrealism. It would be important to point out clearly the differences from Hölzer's book. If the proposal, as I certainly hope, impresses him, I can only imagine that you will receive an invitation to come here to discuss the details with him. Perhaps then we could also agree on an advance for your work that would appropriately increase your, in my opinion, much too small fellowship. Of my egotistical interest in seeing you as soon as possible, I need say nothing, I hope.

I enclose a little literary piece that I wrote together with a friend before 1933 but that only appeared last June. I should think it would interest you. While it cannot be classified as surrealism, it nevertheless shares some characteristics with it. At the time, I had said in the foreword to the piece that its purpose was to express the feeling one has when climbing a flight of stairs and starting to take another step after already reaching the top. It seems to me that in this piece quite a few much later tendencies are anticipated. Since scarcely any human being knows that I am the author, I would be grateful to you if you would keep the secret. By itself, that would be a pleasure for me.

Most warmly,
your
T. W. A.

from Hölzer's book: See note to Letter 13.

literary piece: These are the "Surrealistische Lesestücke" ("Surrealist Readings"), which were written with Carl Dreyfus and published under the pseudonym Castor Zwieback in *Akzente 10* (1963) and are included in this volume. A selection appeared in 1931 in the *Frankfurter Zeitung*. Adorno's *Collected Works* also contain a selection in volume 20.2, 587–97.

16

Paris, November 13, 1964
(74, avenue Ledru-Rollin 12e,
chez Danielle Bohler)

Dear Professor Adorno,

Warmest thanks for your two letters, which arrived here with some delay
on account of the Fête de la Victoire. (I believe French nationalism is
ineradicable if only because every victory, even the most remote, results
in a day off, year after year.) You make me very happy by placing so much
trust in me. I was always convinced that you are fundamentally an artist,
and for this reason I was sometimes annoyed (I can say this openly?)
that you allowed yourself to be put on the defensive by the positivist
academics. That sometimes gave them a triumphal feeling of superiority.
They accuse you of subjectivism and believe they are closer to the truth
(objectivity) because they go about their work without passion and
imagination.

  I would indeed have been interested in your reading from *The Jargon
of Authenticity*. I already greatly enjoyed reading the essay that I
discovered in the *Neue Rundschau*. It seems to me that you have really
identified the most sensitive spot in the Federal Republic, one of the
reasons why the intellectual atmosphere is so stale there. Who goes so
far as to dare to make a joke about the church? Even the Left respects
the taboo and is silent. I am afraid that against this inflation of blabber
only very radical measures can help (for example, doing away with the
church tax).

  That Unseld is interested makes me very happy. I will start to draft a
proposal right away. Do you really think it would be possible to arrange
an advance with the publisher? That would open up a whole new
perspective for me. I had been thinking of possibly going to Giessen, not
least because I thought my economic base would soon be getting shaky,
but also for other reasons. (Naturally only with your assent.) But if a
solution like the one you mention were possible, I see it as the only
chance to maintain my free and surely more productive existence in
regard to surrealism for a little while. But perhaps it would be better if
I could speak with you in person about all that. If you had time for me
around Christmas, I would find that very lovely.

Warmest thanks for sending *Akzente*. The pseudonym is already nice and—I find—anticipates the spirit of the *Readings* a little bit: that banal events are given a tiny little nudge and as a result become noteworthy. I especially liked "Meeting," "Regent," and "Memory." Encouraged by the "secret," I enclose a poem.

Many warm regards
from your
Elisabeth Lenk

essay that I discovered in the Neue Rundschau: This was an excerpt from the still unfinished book *The Jargon of Authenticity*, which had appeared in the *Neue Rundschau* 3 (1963). In my article "L'Être caché" (Hidden being) in the journal *La Brèche: Action Surréaliste* 6 (June 1964), published by André Breton, I called Adorno as a witness against Heidegger and quoted from this text. See also the note to Letter 18.

to Giessen: Professor Helge Pross had offered me an assistantship there.

The pseudonym: What I didn't notice at the time was the twin emphasis of the twin authorship: Castor refers to Pollux (his twin), who is inseparable from him, and Zwieback to the twice-baked character of the text. If one takes into account the motto under which the texts were first published, the reference to surrealism and its tendency to collective writing becomes even clearer. The motto was "Knock on the door, cry 'Enter!' and don't enter." It is the penultimate sentence of the book *L'Immaculée Conception* (1930), which was cowritten by André Breton and Paul Éluard, and which obviously inspired Adorno and Dreyfus to their joint production. This inclination of Adorno's to overcome the sterile monological principle by means of "symphilosophy" or "sympoetry," as the early German romantics called it, can also be seen in the joint authorship of *Dialectic of Enlightenment*.

I enclose a poem:

With my horror I bedeck you as with a ribbon
And my grief enfolds you
Thus am I in time
Moonbeam
Not yet drowned in wonders

Saba I call you but you are far off
On a mirror-pond you make graceful circles

And around you the poplars nod in the wind
To move the stars thrills you
And you smile at the night birds' wailing

They will find you Saba watch out
Pick up the thistle hidden on the shore
Don't you hear the rattle behind the wall
And the evil whisper of trees
You're a bother here you are not welcome

Leave your dance alone Saba flee
Now you see yourself in the ice mirror
For a ray slips past you
Moonbeam I
Don't be frightened you are no longer you
Moss has grown around your neck
At your temples curls the ribbon of horror
And the strong red of grief enfolds you

A confused pleasure grips you
You would like to throw your arms away
And when they come back you feel glad
How you nod in the wind Saba
You don't know it is I who caress you

Now they come don't you see them a darkling army
The bushes surround you
Already you need to take back the arms that stood far from you

They constrict you
With their branches of iron they scratch themselves into you
Down fall horror and grief
You are still moving Saba
Your dream the dream dance you will end now
They do not allow it
You're a bother here you are not welcome

Alas their mouth no longer shuts
It stands stiffly surrounded by rattling bushes
At daybreak I am full of foreboding when the sky bleeds violet
I flee a moonbeam not yet drowned in wonders

17

Frankfurt am Main, November 24, 1964
Kettenhofweg 123

Dear Elisabeth,

Forgive me for only today answering your letter, which gave me much joy—in the meanwhile the news of the death of my friend Eduard Steuermann reached me, the heaviest blow that has struck me since Benjamin's death, and I was as if under a spell all these days, from which I have only extricated myself with difficulty, with an obituary for my friend, which I have written. I ask you most cordially for your understanding. Otherwise believe me that I am quite immune to attacks aimed at me under the rubric of subjectivism. Thus, what I may have written in this connection is hardly in the nature of an apology—in general I don't think much of defenses—but is more aggressive-polemical. And yet there seems to be quite a bit happening; the most interesting [is] probably in connection with the Popper controversy, on which Habermas wrote an essay in *Zeugnisse,* to which Hans Albert has now replied in the *Kölner Zeitschrift,* admittedly somewhat mean-spiritedly but at least with some kind of quality. You have probably already seen all that, quite apart from whatever happens with Giessen.

In any case, send your memorandum to Unseld as quickly as possible so that I can speak with him about the matter. In the meanwhile, I have initiated something else on your behalf but don't know how it will go. Anyway, I will attend intensively to the external matters.

To say something about the poem itself is not possible for me—this is not meant negatively in the slightest, but says only that precisely with things of this kind one needs a larger context, a structure, if one wants to say something not too awfully meaningless. I have endless longing, and longing is certainly not such a small word, to talk with you about the question of philosophy and art at length and in all seriousness. By the way, my text on music and painting, which you will certainly get to see soon, will contribute something to it at least formally—namely, that the two realms converge precisely through their extremes and not by becoming outwardly more similar to each other. But surely you know that as well as I.

As to temporal dispositions, on December 17 there is another lecture and seminar, then vacation. I think I will be able to escape from my so-called office hours on Friday the 18th. Nothing would be as important to me as to meet with you soon. Perhaps you will now already say a word about this so that we agree when and where in good time. Don't think that I am overly organized on that account, just a person who, if he doesn't do a minimum of planning, fails to get to the most important things. You can naturally also place a collect call to me at the Institute any morning except Saturday if you prefer that to writing. In any case, please let me hear from you as soon as humanly possible. I can't think of anything that would be more important to me.

Most warmly,

your

Teddie Adorno

news of the death of my friend Eduard Steuermann: Eduard Steuermann was the leading pianist of the Schoenberg circle and Adorno's piano teacher and friend since 1925 (see also Letter 19).

an obituary for my friend, which I have written: The obituary, "Nachruf auf einen Pianisten: Zum Tode von Eduard Steuermann" (Obituary on a pianist: On the death of Eduard Steuermann), appeared in the *Süddeutsche Zeitung* on November 28–29, 1964, and is published under the title "Nach Steuermanns Tod" (After Steuermann's death) in *Gesammelte Schriften*, 17:311–17.—Ed.

Habermas wrote an essay in Zeugnisse: Jürgen Habermas, "Analytische Wissenschaftstheorie und Dialektik: Ein Nachtrag zur Kontroverse zwischen Popper und Adorno" (Analytical theory of science and dialectics: An addendum to the controversy between Popper and Adorno), in *Zeugnisse: Theodor W. Adorno zum sechsigsten Geburtstag* (Testimonies: For Theodor W. Adorno on his sixtieth birthday), ed. Max Horkheimer (Frankfurt: Europäische Verlagsanstalt, 1963), 473–501.

in the Kölner Zeitschrift: Hans Albert, "Der Mythos der totalen Vernunft: Dialektische Ansprüche im Lichte undialektischer Kritik" (The myth of total reason: Dialectical claims in the light of undialectical critique), in *Kölner Zeitschrift für Soziologie* 16, no. 2 (1964): 225–55. Habermas responded in issue 4 the same year with "Gegen einen positivistisch halbierten Rationalismus" (Against a positivistically bisected rationalism),

635–59. See Theodor W. Adorno, *The Positivist Dispute in German Sociology*, trans. Glyn Adey and David Frisby (Ann Arbor: University of Michigan Press, 2009).—Ed.

I have initiated something else: I assume he was attempting to secure a position for me as an assistant at the Institute (see also Letter 23).

my text on music and painting: "Über einige Relationen zwische Musik und Malerei" ("On Some Relationships between Music and Painting"), first published in *Pour Daniel-Henry Kahnweiler* (Stuttgart, 1965) and included in *Gesammelte Werke*, 16:628–42. English trans. Susan H. Gillespie, in *Musical Quarterly* 79, no. 1 (Spring 1995): 66–79.

18

Paris 17e, November 24, 1964
new address
58, rue des Batignolles
tel.: MAR 3319

Dear Professor Adorno,

I would like to express many, many thanks for the book. Only now have I found time to read this dense, thoroughly through-composed book. I was busy moving; I have had the good fortune, really unheard of in Paris, to find an affordable apartment.

In reading, it became clear to me how much German ideology has changed since Marx's time. "Make a joke" in my last letter was the wrong phrase. It seems almost diabolical, this theology without God, which condemns human beings to an immanence without hope, worse, to an *amor fati*. I think it would be important to translate this book into French. It would provoke some second thoughts in the people who have picked Heidegger as the godfather of their humanism—as well as those who want to shield him from any sort of understanding.

Once again warm thanks, for the dedication as well, which fills me with childlike pride.

Many regards from your
Elisabeth Lenk

P.S. By the way, I recently learned that the *Diskus* has dug up and published an essay of mine that I had sent them a long time ago. It is the expression of my anger at the high-handed way Enzensberger dismissed surrealism (and the avant-garde altogether). But when I try to read it with your eyes, I almost think you would write in the margin "too simplistic!"

the book: *The Jargon of Authenticity,* subtitled "On German Ideology."
German ideology: Marx's *The German Ideology* was published in 1845.—Ed.
the people who have picked Heidegger as the godfather of their humanism: This refers to Sartre in particular.
those who want to shield him from any kind of understanding: I was thinking primarily of Beaufret, to whom Heidegger had addressed his "Letter on 'Humanism.'" Beaufret, by the way, was extremely critical of my article in a letter to André Breton, published in *La Brèche,* no. 8 (November 1965).
that the Diskus has dug up and published an essay of mine: Elisabeth Lenk, "Die Aporien des Herrn Heidegger" (The aporias of Herr Heidegger), *Diskus,* no. 7 (1964). It was my answer to Enzensberger's "Aporien der Avantgarde" (Aporias of the avant-garde), a text that had appeared in 1962 in *Einzelheiten* (Details). The *Diskus* was the Frankfurt student newspaper.

19

Frankfurt am Main
November 30, 1964
Kettenhofweg 123

Dear Elisabeth,

Our letters crossed. My last one went to the old address. I hope it has reached you.

Today I would just like to congratulate you on the new apartment and simultaneously attach the little essay in which I have attempted to express at least a little bit of what the death of my friend Eduard Steuermann has meant for me.

A strange coincidence was that, a few hours after I received your last letter, I introduced Enzensberger as the current visiting lecturer for poetics in front of a huge crowd of students. You probably do not know that years ago I had a radio discussion with him about the very point that your essay in *Diskus* addresses, the question of avant-gardism, in which I, like you, defended this concept. I am planning an essay on it, "Defense of Isms." On the other hand, the danger that the avant-garde will become rigid cannot be overlooked either—I became extremely conscious of it two years ago at the surrealist exhibition in Vienna. Everything depends on holding fast to the intent and not allowing it be marketed, yet not becoming immured within it but instead really moving it forward. As for Enzensberger himself, I am friendly with him and like him very much. I am almost sure that if you were to meet him in person you would like him and would get along well; he is, God knows, free of arrogance and moreover theoretically to a large extent shaped by my writings. In other words it is a kind of fight between brothers, which I would like to put to rest.

Please write as quickly as possible when you are coming. December 17 is my last lecture before Christmas, and then you have, as they say so nicely in America, *first priority*. As indeed it would be.

> All imaginable love from
> your
> Teddie Adorno

the little essay: Theodor W. Adorno, "Nachruf auf einen Pianisten: Zum Tode von Eduard Steuermann" (Obituary for a pianist: On the death of Eduard Steuermann), in *Süddeutsche Zeitung,* November 28–29, 1964 (see also the note to Letter 17).

Your essay in Diskus: See note to Letter 18.

years ago I had a radio discussion with him: The conversation with Enzensberger on the avant-garde was taped for the *Süddeutscher Rundfunk* (Stuttgart), probably on March 6, 1961. It was scheduled to be broadcast on April 7 and 10, 1961, on several channels.

I am planning an essay on it, "Defense of Isms": Handwritten note in the margin. This became a brief passage in *Aesthetic Theory.*—Ed.

20

Frankfurt, December 7, 1964
Kettenhofweg 123

My dear Elisabeth,

A thousand thanks for the letter.

I am immensely happy and await your call. The 19th is a Saturday; the best time to reach me will be in the morning, at home, 77 18 24.

Until very soon then—and if you are kind you will write a few words beforehand,

your
Teddie Adorno

In frightful haste, due to tests, hence so short. I am embarrassed—

21

Paris 17e, December 13, 1964
58, rue des Batignoles

Dear Professor Adorno,

I enclose the carbon copy of my letter to Herr Unseld. I had the idea—unfortunately a day too late—that it would be better to put the poetry, which properly takes up the most space, at the beginning. This would not only correspond better to the spirit of surrealism, but also to the facts, for almost all of the surrealists mentioned were poets even before they became (militant) surrealists.

In addition I thank you very much for your little letter. It will remain the 19th, then.*

Very warm regards

from your
Elisabeth Lenk

*Unless the strike that is planned for next week wreaks havoc with our plans. But it is unlikely that it would also paralyze the "grandes lignes."

wreaks havoc with our plans: The meeting must have taken place. There is a trace of it in the book *Jakob von Gunten*, by Robert Walser, which Adorno gave me and which bears the dedication: "To Elisabeth the surréaliste, who wants to go to Giessen, Christmas 1964 from the papan's grandson." We looked at Max Ernst's collage-novel *Le Lion de Belfort*, which he owned, and on this occasion Adorno told me about his *papan*, his maternal grandfather from Corsica with the picturesque name Giovanni Francesco Calvelli-Adorno. He was a fencing master and settled in the Bockenheim section of Frankfurt, where in 1862 he married Elisabeth Henning, the daughter of a master tailor. Elisabeth did not follow in her father's footsteps. Like her daughter Maria, Adorno's mother, she was a singer and gave concerts. When the Franco-German War broke out on July 19, 1870, for which the monumental statue of the Lion of Belfort is a well-known patriotic symbol, his grandfather had the following statement entered into his passport by the English consul in Frankfurt, who was responsible for the affairs of French citizens in the city: "Pour se rendre directement en France" (to return directly to France). On October 29, 1870, he received an entry in his passport from the Légation de France in Brussels that stated "Pour la France" (for France). Whether he actually took part in the war on the side of France the family does not know. (I am indebted to Frau Elisabeth Reinhuber-Adorno for these facts.)

22

[Frankfurt am /Main, March 1, 1965
Kettenhofweg 123]

Dear Elisabeth,

On Wednesday, as planned, I am coming to France—but have discarded your telephone number. Is it immodest if I ask you to call me, preferably in the course of the late afternoon on Wednesday? I am staying in the Hotel Port Royal (telephone 43–50).

> Most warmly,
> your
> [Adorno]

23

Paris 17e, March 21, 1965
58, rue des Batignolles

Dear Professor Adorno,

I have hesitated so long with this letter because I would have liked to send along the promised picture as well. But the photographer who was supposed to develop it has fallen ill, and I want to send the *Brèche,* at any rate, and a brief greeting. The time you were in Paris was very rich and lovely for me, and I wish very much that such hours of intensive time together may be possible in Germany as well.

I hope that in spite of all the work you have found time to recover from the—after all—very strenuous days.

At the moment I am playing with the reality chapter that I spoke with you about; I am attempting to define the concept of myth, which is central to the surrealist universe. But it is not turning out to be all that much, because I am always looking out of the corner of my eye at "life," which in Giessen I am afraid will only be snatched at odd moments.

Still, I am looking forward a little bit to Germany above all because Giessen is not all that far away from Frankfurt . . . *

Very warm regards from your

Elisabeth Lenk

* After I turned down the position in Frankfurt that sounds paradoxical, but it is true and not just a polite formula.

want to send the Brèche, *at any rate*: See notes to Letters 16 and 18. With the letter Lenk enclosed a copy of Beaufret's response to her anti-Heidegger article, both of which appeared in *La Brèche*.—Ed.

The time you were in Paris: Adorno stayed at the Hotel Port Royal (see Letter 22) and received guests in the lobby. There I met Samuel Beckett and René Leibowitz. Although it is true, as Adorno writes in Letter 14, that Beckett did not think highly of interpretations of his work, even Adorno's, the two seemed to understand each other splendidly. At any rate Beckett, who refused almost all requests to meet him, came to see Adorno every time the latter was in Paris; the two also met in Berlin (see Letter 78). For his part, Adorno forgot everything else when Beckett entered the room. "Did you see," he whispered to me at the Port Royal, "he took off his glasses to please me?" In "Ist die Kunst heiter?" ("Is Art Lighthearted?") Beckett is mentioned as the individual whose plays induce infectious laughter at the ridiculousness of laughing. Leibowitz didn't like Beckett. He claimed Beckett was to blame for the illness of Joyce's daughter; on Leibowitz, see also the note to Letter 54.

"Is Art Lighthearted" appears in *Notes to Literature II,* trans. Shierry Weber Nicholson (New York: Columbia University Press, 1992, 247–53).—Ed.

the—after all—very strenuous days: Among other things he gave a talk at the Deutsches Haus in the Cité Internationale, "Schwierigkeiten" (Difficulties). On March 8, Adorno read "Sittlichkeit und Kriminalität" ("Morals and Criminality"), his text on Karl Kraus, to an audience at the Amphithéâtre Descartes.

The essay "Schwierigkeiten" appeared in English under the title "On Some Difficulties of Composing Today," trans. Susan H. Gillespie, in *Essays on Music: Theodor W. Adorno,* ed. Richard Leppert (Berkeley and Los Angeles: University of California Press, 2002), 644–79. The essay "Morals and Criminality," trans. Shierry Weber Nicholsen, appears in *Notes to Literature II,* 40–57).—Ed.

reality chapter: In the book it would appear as the third chapter, "Vanishing Point Reality." See Elisabeth Lenk, *Der springende Narziss: André Bretons poetischer Materialismus* (Leaping Narcissus: André Breton's poetic materialism) (Munich: Rogner and Bernhard, 1971), 103 ff.

in Giessen: Since Unseld remained silent on the subject of the anthology of surrealism project, I had meanwhile accepted the position offered by Frau Pross, starting in April 1965. My departure was rapidly approaching.

turned down the position in Frankfurt: I felt verbally committed to Frau Pross, particularly since she had been the first to offer me a position and had also supported me in all manner of difficult situations in a way that was not usual for university professors.

24

Dutenhofen, April 26, 1965
County Wetzlar
Auf dem Kronberg

Dear Professor Adorno,

I would finally like to report in from the diaspora. Until recently I was rather dejected and quasi-paralyzed. Here one can only protest, in the spirit of Heidegger: the intellect sits high and dry and doesn't know how to get back into the water. But now at least I am back in touch with the surrealist project. I would be very, very glad to discuss it once more with you. Our conversations in Paris were so lovely and gave me wings. But I don't want to be immodest. You are surely very busy once again.

I hope that you were able to recover a bit in Baden Baden.
Very warm regards, to your wife as well,

your
Elisabeth Lenk

the intellect sits high and dry: Heidegger wrote: "One judges thinking by
a standard that is unsuitable for it. This judgment resembles the procedure
of judging a fish's nature and capabilities by the extent to which it is able to
live on dry land. For a long time, for too long, thinking has been sitting
high and dry. Can one, now, call the effort to bring thought back to its element 'irrationalism'?" Heidegger, "Über den 'Humanismus.'" I was living
in the countryside not far from Giessen, which, as I noted in my journal at
the time, means "to make something flow out by tipping it."

Heidegger's famous "Letter on Humanism" was addressed to French
philosopher Jean Beaufret in 1946 as a response to questions that Beaufret
had posed. It was Heidegger's first public statement following the end of
the National Socialist regime and unleashed an international controversy.
A revised version was published a year later in Germany, *Brief über den
Humanismus* (Frankfurt: Vittorio Klostermann, 1949). The "Letter" appears
in volume eight of the *Heidegger Gesamtausgabe* (Heidegger collected
works) (Frankfurt: Klostermann, 1975).—Ed.

25

Frankfurt am Main, April 27, 1965
Kettenhofweg 123

Dear Elisabeth,

All my thanks for your letter.

Must I tell you that my need to see you is as great as yours? Please do
telephone, so that we can make some plan—you probably don't have a
telephone yet?

And as to the time—for you I can always arrange it, you know that.
All warm regards,

as always your
Teddie Adorno

26

Dutenhofen, May 9, 1965
Kreis Wetzlar
Auf dem Kronberg

Dear Professor Adorno,

Unfortunately, on Friday placing a call from my damned hamlet didn't work (I must get a telephone myself as soon as possible).

Meanwhile I have had a look at the Salomon text. Should I try to reconstruct the sense that Salomon wanted to give the entire piece as closely as possible, or would a few corrections, including some substantive ones, be possible? Namely, it bothers me that Fourier appears too much as an eccentric petit bourgeois who is only interested in comfort and pleasure. This may be accurate *à peu près* for his person, but surely not for his theory. In the latter, in my opinion, he is closer to Sade (whom Salomon treats as abnormal), in the sense that in Fourier, as in Sade, the liberation of the drives becomes so central that it explodes the eighteenth-century idea of happiness. I also find questionable the claim that for Fourier happiness and pleasure are purely individual. What is really new about his theory is actually precisely the fact that he doesn't oppose corrupt society with the isolated, self-absorbed individual (nor even the couple) as authentic, but instead sees sociability, based on sympathy, as the natural condition of humanity, the precondition for liberation and the intensification of individual drives.

Other than that, I would naturally stick closely to Salomon's original and only make the text more accurate in those places where it is necessary.

Unfortunately, I have discovered that the seminar of Prof. Pross, in which I am supposed to participate, takes place here on Tuesdays precisely from 5:00 to 7:00 p.m. Before that, I could come to the Philosophical Seminar in Frankfurt. I wonder whether this is possible and makes sense?

Very warm regards,

from your
Elisabeth Lenk

[*Enclosure*]:

Thoughts on the Relationship between Sade and Fourier

Both undertake a complete rehabilitation of the passions. If it were possible to free the latter from subjugation to morality, as it has existed up to now, a new morality could be derived from them. What is good, accordingly, is no longer moderation but precisely the exaltation of the passions, say Fourier and Sade: "Everything is good when it is excessive." Evil and falsehood only sneak in the moment the passions give way to some internal or external pressure, get mired down halfway. This halfwayness and inner agony, brought about by (Christian) morality as it has existed up to now, is the source of all unhappiness. True happiness, unknown until now, consists in giving in to the inner, passionate impulses, raising them to principles of action. Sade: "Happiness depends on the energy of principles, there would be no way a person who is endlessly floating could have any."

Sade and Fourier also share the idea that in the passions the fate of every human being is already foreshadowed hieroglypically. "The attractions are proportional to the destinies" is the motto at the core of Fourier's thought. Jean Gaulmier, interpreting this sentence, comments, "Since God, or rather nature, has endowed man with passions, it would be absurd to leave them unused: the number of passions with which a being is equipped at its inception announces the destiny that it is promised." Sade, for his part, assures us, "It is in our mother's breast that the organs are produced that will render us susceptible to this or that fantasy. The first objects that are presented to us, the first words that are heard determine the tensions; education can do what it will, it no longer changes anything." Both of them, Sade and Fourier, ultimately strive to enable man's individual destiny, his purpose, by liberating the energies that slumber within him—this against the pull of all societal and ethical tendencies, which can never drive out the passions but only paralyze and distort them.

Admittedly—and here they part company—Sade sees this liberation of the previously truncated passions only in its negative aspect, as radical destruction. The Sadist places himself outside the law, negates God, and thus also humankind, which has already negated itself in the idea of God; finally, as Maurice Blanchot has shown, he negates even nature herself, in whose name he had risen up against God and the law. The monstrous freedom of the Sadist is that of the domination of all other human beings and ultimately their annihilation.

For Fourier, by contrast, the very total isolation of the individual from which Sade derives the passions, as powers that don't shrink from any crime or perversion, is itself merely the product of specific epochs that truncate the passions. The true human passions may be incompatible with the societal state of contemporary civilization, but this does not make them anarchic or destructive in principle. Fourier believes he has found the philosopher's stone in the law of *attraction passionelle,* and that if one only pushes the passions far enough, this will redeem them from their violently destructive social condition and open them up to harmony.

Sade and Fourier are both committed to the ideas of the eighteenth century to the extent that they first appeal to nature to justify the truth of their theses. But the conclusion they derive from their starting point exceeds the eighteenth century's idea of nature. If, at first, nature's role was to defend the passions against all moral and religious views, the view that prevailed at that time, in the end the newfound sovereignty of the passions ultimately turned nature against itself. In Sade, the initial faith in nature turns into actual hatred: "Yes, my friend, I abhor nature" and "This is the expression of a primordial and elementary feeling: to outrage nature, this is man's most profound necessity; this need in him is a thousand times stronger than the need to offend God." But even Fourier, who never tires of preaching the future harmony of man and nature, can't help criticizing the state of nature as it currently exists: the ugliness of bedbugs and toads, the wildness of many animals and their aggression toward humankind, and the pallor of moonlight as the only nocturnal illumination are all things that should be ameliorated as soon as possible.

Thus, although initially nature is called on to justify the liberation of human passions, the latter—once they have become sovereign—prove to be lacking in respect, not only for the existing state of society with all its conventions but ultimately for the state of creation itself. In Sade, this takes the form of an irreconcilable hatred that in the individual is directed in equal measure against society, God, and nature; in Fourier, it comes through indirectly in the innumerable reforms that are wrung from society *and* nature by the law of passionate attraction.

Meanwhile I have had a look at the Salomon text: This refers to the draft of the introduction to Charles Fourier's *Theory of the Four Movements,* which Gottfried Salomon-Delatour had had translated into German. After Salomon's sudden demise, Adorno approached me with the task of completing the introduction. Gottfried Salomon was extremely well informed about the early socialists and the history of social movements in Germany and France. In 1923, he had already published P. J. Proudhon's *Confessions of a Revolutionary* in a new translation by A. Ruge.

closer to Sade: From the surrealists, in particular André Breton's "Ode to Charles Fourier," I had acquired a completely different view of Fourier. In December 1965, the Eleventh International Exhibition of Surrealism would take place in Paris under Fourier's motto "L'Écart Absolue" (Absolute deviation). However, my comparison of Sade and Fourier owes its genesis more to the circle around Bataille. Walter Benjamin had already pointed the group in this direction during the era of the Collège de Sociologie: "He anticipated the advent of total liberation through universalized play, in the sense of Fourier, for whom he had boundless admiration," wrote Pierre Klossowski in his "Letter on Walter Benjamin." See Pierre Klossowski, *Tableaux vivants: Essais critiques 1936–1983* (Living pictures: Critical essays 1936–1983) (Paris: Gallimard, 2001), 87. Both Sade and Fourier counted on an economy of fully living out, and not suppressing, the passions, which may have stimulated Georges Bataille to his "economy of waste."

Jean Gaulmier: French orientalist, 1905–1997.—Ed.

As Maurice Blanchot has shown: The reference is to Blanchot's *Lautréamont et Sade,* originally published in 1949. An English edition, trans. Michelle Kendall and Stuart Kendall, was published by Stanford University Press in 2004.—Ed.

27

Institute for Social Research, Frankfurt am Main, May 20, 1965
Senckenberg-Anlage 26

Dear Elisabeth,

Today I spoke to Helge Pross on the telephone—she had called me about something else—and inquired on your behalf and also about the question of editing the Salomon text. She told me that you have already written to me about this, and only after a long search did I find the letter in a frightful flood of paper. I am utterly inconsolable that I overlooked it and made you wait such a long time; that there is no reason for this other than the disappearance of the letter I don't have to tell you. I am all the more pleased that you want to take this on. I consider it not only legitimate but necessary to make the substantive corrections you propose. This can then either be indicated in the text, or I can clarify the situation in the foreword, which I want to write in any case. That it is necessary to intervene deeply in the Salomon text not only for substantive reasons, but in many cases out of the simplest logic, is evident, and you have my fullest agreement.

Helge also told me that you must give a seminar there exactly when I hold my own. That really is awfully unfortunate.

Tomorrow I leave for Berlin, where, *horribile dictu,* I have to give three lectures; I will return on Monday. Then we will want to make a date as soon as possible in order to come to a final agreement, a contract, or whatever you want to call it. The best would probably be if you were to call me on Tuesday morning, since all of Monday is filled with institutional stuff.

À bientôt and most warmly,

> your
> T. W. A.

28

Dutenhofen, July 13, 1965
Auf dem Kronberg

Dear Professor Adorno,

I would have liked to write to you long ago, but put it off because I wasn't coming along so well with the foreword. I was so taken with Fourier that I first read his collected writings. The difficulty now is to extricate myself from the thing again; and if Salomon has spoken about it only very superficially, I have—I fear—fallen into the opposite error, out of sheer enthusiasm, of identifying myself with him too closely.

I would like *very* much to come to you in Frankfurt again, in order also, perhaps, to discuss the draft. It would be very nice if you could let me know very briefly whether this is still possible before the holidays, and when. I will also be here all of August, only I think you already have travel plans?

> Very warm regards, to your
> wife as well, from
> your
> Elisabeth Lenk

29

Institute for Social Research, Frankfurt am Main 1, July 19, 1965
Senckenberg-Anlage 26

Dear Elisabeth,

I was really disappointed that you didn't get in touch for all these weeks.
Now it is a little bit difficult to agree on something, not because I am
pouting, but simply because the next few days until the end of the
semester are filled so full with faculty and committee meetings and
examinations that I don't know whether I am coming or going.

Nevertheless it should and must be possible somehow.

My suggestion would be Wednesday, July 28, at 3:00 at the Institute.
Please confirm whether this is all right with you.

Warmly, as always,

your
Teddie Adorno

30

Dutenhofen, July 21, 1965

Dear Professor Adorno,

Thank you most warmly for your letter. Many thanks, as well, for wanting
to make it possible to see me despite your many obligations.

Spontaneously, I often feel like calling or writing to you, but I am held
back by a kind of intellectual shame. I always believe I should only make
claims on your time when I have gotten further along in my work.

I would feel very sad, if—merely out of fear of disappointing you—
I should now have disappointed you. I shall therefore be there on
Wednesday at 3:00, and will appear at the Institute with the draft in my
head (even better, in my pocket).

Very warmly,
your
Elisabeth Lenk

31

Hotel Waldhaus Sils Maria Engadin
September 4, 1965

Ma très chère,

You will—at least I am bold enough, in the depths of the not at all so unconscious, to hope, as a question—be a bit disappointed that I did not write until today; the reason, the only one, is a writer's block the likes of which I have not experienced in this form, a complete incapacity for decision that could be called paralyzing if it were not a reaction to utter intellectual overexertion. I even lost my fountain pen in order to not be able to write at all—in its place this dreadful ballpoint pen, which I entreat you to pardon; and as to the psychopathic state I *passionément* take your understanding for granted.

Now, five weeks later, I feel myself not only restored but also active again; as a test I have drafted a couple of pages on the play of a Viennese acquaintance, and see here, after total abstinence, I still have the power to write.

The abstinence was interrupted by reading the Fourier pages you sent me, and I am keenly enthusiastic. I have never, really never, met a woman whom I consider to be as endowed with genius as you are, in the areas that are closest to me; and please, don't ascribe that to my feeling of being in love, to which it merely contributes even more. If there is something that is lovely for me, then that you care for me—that this time really *everything* comes together. What impressed me most is the independence, the real freedom of your fragment—that you really don't say anything just to be part of the conversation, that every sentence expresses a productive resistance against all claptrap. And if I could teach you something further, in a sense that exceeds the academic, then that would be splendid for me.

Here there has been all manner of contact with surrealism, with an old friend, a young painter named Roman (a student, not an *élève*, but a disciple of Balthus), also with Peter Szondi. All this I hope to tell you about as rapidly as possible.

Next week we return to Frankfurt. Please call me Wednesday morning at the Institute, so we can quickly arrange something. Words fail me to

tell you how much I look forward to going away with you; we want to
think it through together.

Entirely your Teddie

This letter, written on stationery of the Hotel Waldkopf, is handwritten
and not, like other letters to Lenk, dictated to Adorno's secretary.

Ma très chère: The salutation is an allusion to Baudelaire's "Hymne" in
Les Épaves (Scraps).

*You will—at least I am bold enough, in the depths of the not at all so
unconscious, to hope*: For the first time, Adorno addresses Lenk using the
familiar form of address, as "Du." It occurs only twice in the correspondence, in this letter and the following one.—Ed.

a couple of pages on the play of a Viennese acquaintance: The essay refers
to the comedy *Der Himbeerpflücker* (The raspberry picker), by Fritz Hoch-
wälder. See Adorno's "Reflection on the *Volksstück*," trans. Shierry Weber
Nicholsen, in *Notes to Literature II*, 334–35.

Balthus: Balthazar Klossowski de Rola, known as Balthus (1909–2001),
surrealist painter, son of Baladine Klossowska, Rilke's "Merline," and
brother of Pierre Klossowski.

Peter Szondi: See note to Letter 41.

we want to think it through together: This dream journey never took place.

32

Frankfurt am Main, September 13, 1965

Ma très chère,

I don't know whether you received my letter. And today I send back your
pages, which inspired my keen enthusiasm, really only as an excuse to
write to you.

Please be so good as to call me soon at the Institute, in any case, so we
can arrange something.

All warm regards,
Your Teddie

I don't know whether you received my letter: Again, Adorno uses the
intimate "Du."—Ed.

Your Teddie: "Your" is in the familiar form.—Ed.

33

Frankfurt am Main
September 23, 1965
Kettenhofweg 123

Dear Elisabeth,

This now in great haste—I must travel to Southern Germany to give a couple of lectures.

A thousand thanks for the manuscript. I have only had a peek; Gretel has read it and is enthusiastic. I will be able to study and annotate it only in the next few days—then we must get together as rapidly as possible. Perhaps you will be so good as to call me next Wednesday at the Institute—a pity that you have no telephone, otherwise I would naturally call you.

As far as being angry is concerned—hopefully you are not somehow angry that I could not keep our appointment. But it really was a case of *force majeure*; a very urgent consultation with friends, a theater director who had to talk to me about engagements, had been arranged without my secretary's knowledge, and this is how the chaos came about. I earnestly entreat you to pardon it. Everything else orally.

Most warmly,
your
Teddie Adorno

the manuscript: Adorno refers to the first draft of my introduction to the *Four Movements* of Charles Fourier.

annotate: Adorno inserted a wealth of handwritten marginal notes into my text; see notes to Letters 35 and 36.

As far as being angry is concerned: I must have written something of the kind, perhaps in a letter accompanying the typescript. Unfortunately such a letter could not be found either in the Theodor W. Adorno Archive or in my collection.

34

Frankfurt, October 19, 1965

HOPITAL ST GEORGES MONS
WARMEST WISHES FOR RAPID RECOVERY, AM ENTHUSIASTIC
ABOUT FOURIER INTRODUCTION MOST WARMLY ADORN

Hopital St. Georges Mons: On October 15, I had had an automobile accident halfway between Paris and Giessen and been admitted to the local
hospital.
Adorn: The "O" is lacking in the original telegram.—Ed.

35

Hôpital St. Georges
Mons Belgique [undated]

Dear Professor Adorno,

I felt very, very happy about your truly charming and so unexpected
telegram. If it is only now that an answer comes, then not because I am
incapable of writing (I am already feeling quite fine) but because it is
difficult to find someone to post the letter.

I would already be quite capable even of weathering your critique of
the Fourier introduction. In any case I am in suspense about your notes
and would like very much to do a bit of fiddling with it, naturally if it is
not too inconvenient for you to send the manuscript.

As soon as I am back in Germany and more or less presentable (my
face took the worst beating), I will get in touch with you.

I must say once again how much your telegram cheered me and how
happy I felt.

> Very warm regards, to your
> wife as well,
> Your
> Elisabeth Lenk

Your notes: See note to Letter 33.

36

Dutenhofen, November 1, 1965
Auf dem Kronberg

Dear Professor Adorno,

I must remark that an accident also has its rather pleasant aspects: one receives sympathy and is spoiled. What pleased me most of all was your so spontaneous and warm reaction. A thousand thanks for the manuscript, which arrived just in time, and also for the lovely catalogue. I am surprised how many surrealists I do not yet know (only a single member of the *groupe* is there, the Cuban Camacho).

I succeeded in deciphering your notes like a philologist, with alternate readings, conjectures, etc. Even where I was unable to make out some of the words, I believe I understood your critique, for it referred mostly to passages about which I myself had an uncomfortable feeling. I will now proceed with the revision.

One more thing: it was not until I returned that I found the telegram from your wife, for which I thank her warmly. In Paris I had already spoken with Breton about it, and he is prepared to give the publishing house a photograph of the picture of Fourier. I will be glad to take care of it, only I would have to know exactly—because I am inexperienced at this kind of thing—what needs to be done (stipulations, etc.)—I think I will soon be able to show myself in Frankfurt.

With very warm regards to
you and your wife, I am

your
Elisabeth Lenk

the lovely catalogue: Catalogue of the exhibition "Surrealism Today," which opened in the municipal museum Schloss Morsbroich, in Leverkusen, on October 22, 1965.

of the **groupe**: The group that had formed around Breton, to which I belonged and which met regularly in the Café Promenade de Vénus. See note to Letter 4.

your notes: They were all handwritten, and Adorno's tiny Sütterlin handwriting (in a style that was in common use before 1941) was difficult to decipher. Ever since Adorno had graced my first report with his "notes," I had sought help from his secretary, Frau Olbrich, who could read everything, or almost everything, from "ça ne vas pas" to "find more precise concept," or "this sentence is not quite thought through," to open contradiction: "Precisely this is what idealism does not say." Most of these notes, of which there were about ninety, were written in the tone of a coach who has run out of patience. At the end, then, Adorno's completely positive conclusion was almost astonishing to me.

37

Frankfurt, November 23, 1965
after the 28th, again Dutenhofen

Dear Professor Adorno,

Whenever I have not written for some time and also have heard nothing from you (even if it is only a couple of weeks), I am seized with restlessness, as if the cordial understanding between you and me, which makes me very happy, were at the same time very vulnerable.

I actually only wanted to write that I am once again *disponible* and could come to Frankfurt. But the bad luck, which seems to follow Fourier-like laws, won't let me go. I have to go back into the clinic (this time an "aesthetic" clinic, for plastic surgery) for a few days. But I am trying to be optimistic, and so I have the idea that I will certainly be healthy and cheerful again by the time of your lecture in Giessen.

I have done some honing of the Fourier, the chapter on the passions, which suddenly seemed to me to be the weakest of all—have even rewritten it completely.

I look forward very much to seeing you again soon and am,

with warm affection,
your
Elisabeth Lenk

P.S. Many, many thanks for *Deutsche Menschen* (German men and women). Today I am a bit tongue-tied and sad, so that the ideas about Benjamin/ surrealism that came to mind as I was reading your postscript are not occurring to me; but will certainly come again!

the bad luck, which seems to follow Fourier-like laws: A streak of bad luck, according to Fourier, is a sevenfold multiplication of bad luck, just as a streak of good luck, which he constructs in parallel, is a sevenfold multiplication of good luck. See in this volume the introduction to the German edition of *Theory of the Four Movements,* by Charles Fourier, especially the section on "The Construction of Happiness."

an "aesthetic" clinic, for plastic surgery: The doctor, a professor at the University of Giessen, had determined that I could no longer close my left eye, which he said was dangerous to the eye. Since he had a clinic in Giessen, he offered to operate on the eyelid, a stroke of luck by today's standards.

your lecture in Giessen: See note to Letter 38.

many thanks for Deutsche Menschen: Adorno had published a new edition of the collection of letters that bore this title, which Walter Benjamin, under the pseudonym Detlef Holz, had published in Switzerland in 1936 while he was in exile in Paris. Adorno sent me a copy of the new edition, to which he had written a postscript (see "On Benjamin's *Deutsche Menschen, a Book of Letters,*" in *Notes to Literature II,* 328–33). What seemed important to me at the time about Adorno's postscript was his comparison of Heidegger's early concept of facticity to the concrete in Benjamin. The vision of a naked concreteness, forsaken by God and even by meaning, was completely at odds with Lukács and had a powerful influence on my theory of surrealism. As I noted in "Sense and Sensibility," my afterword to *Paris Peasant,* "Lukács very accurately recognized Walter Benjamin as his theoretical adversary on this question. For Benjamin, the modernity of Baroque allegory lay in the way it freed the details from their duty to mean something and reproduced them as naked, deserted by God and meaning." Lenk, *Kritische Phantasie* (Critical imagination) (Munich: Matthes & Seitz, 1986), 61–77. See also the note to Letter 97.

"Sense and Sensibility" is included in this volume.—Ed.

38

Frankfurt am Main, November 25, 1965
Kettenhofweg 123

My dear Elisabeth,

Your letter moved me greatly. As to what you so tenderly and beautifully call our understanding, at least where I am concerned, it is not vulnerable, and the fact that you know this may perhaps contribute a wee bit to its being that way for you too. There is nothing that I wish more.

Hopefully the surgery achieved all that was desired.

I am writing to you in Dutenhofen, where you will find my letter when you return, and am already looking forward to Friday a week from now, on your account—to our seeing each other. Not that you would miss much as far as the lecture is concerned; especially since you will like the main text, which I admit is important to me, better in print than when I read it.

How nice it is, or perhaps not nice at all but a good sign of your *daimon,* that you have started working on Fourier again, and on the chapter on the passions, no less. I am looking forward to it with great anticipation. As soon as you have put this behind you, we should find an occasion to talk very extensively, with plenty of time, about the questions surrounding surrealism, among many other things. By the way, in December I have been invited to Paris for a few days, to Royaumont, by Goldmann, from the 10th to the 13th. But as lovely as the idea would be of us being together in Paris, this would probably be as far as possible from a peaceful situation such as I wish for us and as we finally need to have.

> *En attendant,* all warm
> regards and love,
> your Teddie Adorno

the lecture: Adorno had agreed with Helge Pross to give a lecture on the concept of society. For the text of the lecture, see "Society," in *The Legacy of the German Refugee Intellectuals*, ed. Robert Boyers, trans. Fredric Jameson (New York: Schocken, 1972), 144–53.

Royaumont is a former convent near Paris, where Lucien Goldmann, among others, held sociological-philosophical conferences during the 1960s. —Ed.

39

Dutenhofen, December 11, 1965
Auf dem Kronberg

Dear Frau Adorno,

Very many thanks for your friendly letter. From Herr Adorno I have learned—when he was here—that you are to be operated on Monday.

I would like to send you my wish that it will be not too unpleasant and painful, and that you will recover soon. This sort of thing is awful, even when the doctors tell us it is not serious.

That the book should appear without an image is really too bad. Well, perhaps the demand for Fourier will soon be so great that it can be made good the second time around?!

I will try to have the manuscript ready, in duplicate, by December 20. But could I have a postponement until January for the bibliography? I must make inquiries in Paris about a few things in order for it to be more or less complete and good. If it is very pressing, I will have to try my best without such inquiries. In any case, I will telephone the Institute before the 20th to ask what you think about the deadlines and when I can come by to discuss all these things with you.

Once again all good wishes for your health

And warm regards from
your Elisabeth Lenk

the book ... without an image: This refers to the Fourier book (see Letter 36).

the demand for Fourier: The comment is ironic. Salomon's seminar on the early socialists typically had only four or five people.

40

Elfriede Olbrich to Lenk
Secretary to
Prof. Dr. Theodor W. Adorno

Frau Elisabeth Lenk
6331 Dutenhofen, by way of Wetzlar
Auf dem Kronberg

Frankfurt, December 15, 1965

Dear Ms. Lenk:

Professor Adorno, who must administer examinations all day today, asks me to write to you and thank you for your letter.

Since on Monday afternoon there will be a meeting here with the staff, he asks you to come to him at the Institute on Tuesday, December 21, in the afternoon around 4:00. In Paris you can ask about anything that is still unclear, but that has time until the beginning of January.

Professor Adorno sends you his warm regards.

your
[E. Olbrich]

41

Dutenhofen, January 4, 1966

Dear Professor Adorno,

Here come the final chapters and notes, a bit late. Actually there are only tiny changes, but you have perhaps also had the experience that a word, a fortuitous expression, just when one is most in need of it, slinks away in protest and only shows itself again when it is sure that you no longer want anything from it.

One small comment on my dissertation: I am a bit worried because Szondi has canceled for January 4 and has postponed our get-together indefinitely. I wonder whether I can stop by to see you soon about this? I would bring the Fourier translation along too, about which I have one more—as it seems to me—important comment—or is it already in press?

Very cordial greetings, to your wife as well, and wishes for a productive New Year with *many* streaks of good luck!

Your
Elisabeth Lenk

Szondi: Later, from 1970 to 1975, I would become an assistant in Peter Szondi's Seminar for General and Comparative Literature, in Berlin.
streaks of good luck: See note to Letter 37.

42

Giessen, January 28, 1966

Dear Professor Adorno,

If I write to you again so soon, in reference to that business about the lectureship that I mentioned on the telephone, I have a rather guilty conscience. But the situation, unfortunately, is that my application would have to be submitted very quickly. Would it be possible for you, perhaps already in the coming week, to write me a letter of recommendation? I enclose a page with a few keywords, so that hopefully it won't take too much of your time.

The latest from Giessen is a global-total lecture by René König (held at the invitation of the new Faculty, not ours). Sensational result: the extended family has always existed, but the nuclear family too! In light of such international perfection, one is irresistibly reminded of Peeperkorn.

I wonder whether the Fourier text is acceptable in this version?

Very warm greetings, to your wife as well,

Your
Elisabeth Lenk

P.S. Yesterday, by the way, I gave a seminar on your "Essay as Form," and in the process tried to shake up the academic ideal of our students a bit!

that business about the lectureship . . . a letter of recommendation: I had decided to return to France and had applied for a position as lecturer at the University of Nanterre. André Breton had already written a letter of recommendation in which he sang my praises as a potential lecturer in German culture.

René König: From the perspective of today, this characterization of König is unjust. At that time he was already drawing on anthropological research for his sociology, at least for what he referred to as his research on archaic high cultures, and for the latter the thesis of the coexistence of the two forms of family is accurate.

Peeperkorn: Reference to the eponymous figure in Thomas Mann's *Magic Mountain*, who always exclaims, "Perfect, perfect!"

43

Institute for Social Research
An der Senckemberg-Anlage 2
Johann Wolfgang Goethe University
Frankfurt am Main, February 3, 1966

Dear Elisabeth,

Please forgive the delay. The last few days were like a madhouse and I simply did not have the few minutes of self-reflection to write something about you that would be satisfactory to me. Here I enclose my letter of recommendation—as ridiculous as it may be for me to write such a thing about you—so you have it. If you think it is better for me to send it myself, let me know that right away, obviously with the address. If you would like changes for some strategic reason or other, let me know that too, so I can still make them. I hope the delay does not disadvantage you.

Until very soon. And let me know how you are. By the way, I will be in Brussels for a few days in the beginning of March and give lectures there. Perhaps you will be so good, in any case, to give me a call at home on Saturday morning between 10 and 11 (77 18 24).

Very warmly,
your TWA

44

Frankfurt am Main, February 11, 1966
Kettenhofweg 123

Dear Elisabeth,

Today I spoke with the dean, Franz Walter Müller, about the issue of your dissertation and about how research that is philosophically oriented and applied to topics from literature should be treated, in principle. He responded with uncommon understanding and has given me positive affirmation that your dissertation will proceed with me, that he will be the second reviewer, and in addition (at my suggestion) Habermas. More than this we cannot ask for, and I think the matter will now go smoothly as soon as your text is complete. The topic was expressly agreed to be "Sociological Aspects of the Work of Breton."

Concerning my two conversations with Hellmut Becker, Gretel has brought you up to date. He advises most urgently that you should immediately get in touch with Herr Hans Gert Schulte (Paris, 15, rue de Verneuil), whom he has informed in detail, as soon as you get there. He will do everything he can, although he says the outcome is not certain on account of the great number of applicants—you already knew that. He considers your intervention in Paris to be especially important so that you avoid the Godesberg committee, about which he seems to have an opinion much like yours. On the other hand, it is good that your request to Godesberg has already gone in. You should in any case bring a copy of your curriculum vitae along to Herr Schulte.

Let me know how long you are still here, so we can still arrange something.

Most warmly,
your
TWA

dean, Franz Walter Müller: Professor of Romance languages (see Letter 7).

conversations with Hellmut Becker: Hellmut Becker had been director of the Institute for Cultural Research of the Max Planck Society since 1963.

Godesberg committee: This committee had previously turned down my application for a scholarship (see Letter 2).

45

Dutenhofen, February 13, 1966
Auf dem Kronberg

Dear Professor Adorno,

I am so glad that Professor Müller, who always seemed so threatening to me, has agreed to this, and can only ascribe it to your *pouvoir de séduction*. Should I now go to see him (with *exposé*), or is he too busy for that, now that he has become dean?

A thousand thanks to both of you for the tips and information about Herr Schulte. It would be really too bad if it didn't work out now, after all the effort and roundabout bureaucracy. Well, never mind! I am, without daring to compare myself to the lilies of the field, very optimistic. Yesterday I had an idea about our (very temporary) parting, but soon had to abandon it: to invite the two of you, possibly together with Frau Pross, to visit me. With a car (mine) this would have been possible, but it seems like an imposition to tempt you to this trackless backwoods. Can't we have a rain check sometime soon in Paris?

I had planned to leave for Paris on February 28. If it should be possible for you, somehow, I would very much like to stop by the Institute. Shall I give you a call about this next week or the week after?

With very warm affection,

your Elisabeth Lenk

P.S. I will call next week in any case, so that you don't need to write again especially.

46

Frankfurt am Main, March 14, 1966
Kettenhofweg 123

Dear Elisabeth,

From Jutta I hear that you seem to have gotten the lectureship. Please be so good as to let me know immediately whether this is the case, above all whether it is *final* or is still dependent on anything. It is not unimportant for me to know this because I have gotten into a certain complication with Hellmut Becker about the publication of a piece of mine; but I would like to inform him about it only when I know that your appointment has worked out so that he doesn't possibly fail to intervene on your behalf in the way I would like, out of annoyance over the fact that he might not, in the end, get the piece from me. You know how I have formulated the categorical imperative of academic life: if you beat my Jew, I'll beat your Jew.

Fourier is being set in type, and very soon now I will write my foreword as well. Perhaps after all I will find the chapter motto for your text in my notebooks.

I am making better progress with my book than I would have dared to hope. According to the schedule, a large part of it will be set in type on May 1, and the remainder certainly no later than July. But it is an insane effort, and I have the need, for once really a whole month long *rien faire comme une bête*. Since in all likelihood I will be in Italy in October (the lectures with which I am financing it already exist and don't count as work), the prognoses, including Sils Maria, are not bad.

Admittedly, I must still finish up a little volume for Suhrkamp's Edition series, which bears the title *Ohne Leitbild* and will contain aesthetic parerga, among others the Werkbund lecture. Most of it already exists; still, there are a couple of less onerous things that have yet to be written.

When might we see each other again? I am still here until the end of next week, from the 25th in Baden Baden, Brenner's Park Hotel.

As warmly as ever,
your TWA

Jutta: Jutta Burger-Thomae, Adorno's friend and lover—he dedicated *Notes to Literature* to her—and his colleague at the Institute for Social Research.

publication of a piece of mine: "Education after Auschwitz," which Adorno had promised to Hellmut Becker for the *Neue Sammlung* but gave to the minister of culture, Ernst Schütte. On May 3, 1966, he wrote to Becker, "I am now unable to keep my promise and ask for your understanding. I had to give the lightly revised lecture to a publication in which Schütte is most intensely interested. After he has done us the greatest favors in a series of matters—above all in the cases of Friedeburg and Mitscherlich—it would have been impossible for me to deny his request; for him and his friends, my collaboration in this matter was evidently of greater importance than I can objectively ascribe to it. I ask you most warmly for your understanding." "Education after Auschwitz" appeared in *Zum Bildungsbegriff der Gegenwart* (On the contemporary concept of education), ed. Heinz-Joachim Heydorn et al. (Frankfurt am Main: Diesterweg, 1967), 111–23. It is included in volume 10.2 of the *Collected Works*.

The essay appears in English in *Catchwords: Critical Models*, 2:191–204.—Ed.

Perhaps, after all, I will find the chapter motto for your text in my notebooks: Next to the chapter "Unrequited Love of Praxis," Adorno had noted, "On this very concept there is an unpublished aphorism by me (look for it)." He did not find it, however, and thus the chapter remained motto-less.

with my book: *Negative Dialectics*.

Ohne Leitbild: *Ohne Leitbild: Parva aesthetica* (Without a model: Parva aesthetica), which contains various smaller written works, is included in volume 10.1 of Adorno's *Gesammelte Schriften*.—Ed.

Werkbund lecture: The lecture took place on October 23, 1965, at a meeting of the Deutscher Werkbund. It was published under the title "Functionalismus Heute" (Functionalism today). The Werkbund was an association of artists and craftsmen founded in Munich in 1907. Disbanded in 1933, it was re-created after World War II. At its height it also included architects such as Mies van der Rohe and le Corbusier.—Ed.

47

Paris, March 20, 1966

Dear Professor Adorno,

Just now your letter arrived, which made me very glad and simultaneously a little bit moved. It bespeaks a generosity and friendliness that I have not deserved at all.

The lectureship is not yet final; I must still await the decision of the German commission. If it accepts me, it is probably pretty definite that I will come to Professor Sagave in Nanterre. And I don't believe any intervention is required.

In Italy you will certainly be very well received; at least, a lecturer in Italian in Giessen recently told me what a great resonance your books have there. In general, intellectual life must be very lively there, which given the descriptions I have heard I would very much like to experience at some point—*novarum rerum cupida*. But for the time being I am entirely occupied with getting settled back here again. Breton has resurfaced in the *groupe* after a longish illness and talked about a book in which Melmoth and the main character from the *Histoire d'O* meet. Thus I am once again in living contact with surrealism, even though it has been declared dead, and hope that this also benefits my work! I will come to Germany in mid-April; will you be in Baden Baden then?

With the warmest regards,

your Elisabeth Lenk

P.S. My address for the time being: 31, rue Dauphine c/o Euphorion 6e; your letter evidently made a long detour.

Professor Sagave: Germanist in Nanterre.
a lecturer in Italian in Giessen: Nico Pasero.
novarum rerum cupida: Desiring novelty and change.—Ed.
Melmoth and the main character from the "Histoire d'O": The novel *Melmoth the Wanderer*, written by Charles Robert Maturin and published in 1820, gained fame as an example of Gothic writing. *Histoire d'O* is an erotic novel published in France in 1954 on the subject of love, dominance, and submission. The author was Anne Desclos.—Ed.

48

Brenners Park-Hotel, April 8, 1966

That was charming of you, dear Elisabeth, to send me the biography of the original Charlus, and the surroundings here—the part of the Hotel Stefanie that has been salvaged—are remarkably well suited to it. By now you are surely in Germany—I wonder whether my thanks will reach you? And whether your situation has been settled in the meanwhile? We will stay here until the 15th (Friday), then a week in Frankfurt, then a week in Czechoslovakia. It would be nice if we could see each other—please give me a call. The final revision of my galleys is coming along better than I could have hoped.

Warmest regards, your
Teddie Adorno

Most warmly, G.A. Have you received the galleys for the Foreword?

The letter is written on a postcard showing a photograph of Brenner's Park Hotel.

biography of the original Charlus: Philippe Jullien, *Robert de Montesquiou, un Prince 1900* (Paris: Librairie académique Perrin, 1987). The book on the

Count of Montesquiou is preserved in Adorno's library. This eccentric dandy was a friend of Mallarmé and the godfather not only of Marcel Proust's Baron Charlus, but also of the main character Des Esseintes in Joris-Karl Huysman's *À Rebours*.

my galleys: *Negative Dialectics.*

Most warmly, G.A. . . . galleys for the Foreword: Added by Gretel Adorno; she was referring to the galleys of my foreword, not Adorno's.

49

Frankfurt am Main, May 3, 1966
Kettenhofweg 123

Dear Elisabeth,

It is an eternity since I have heard anything from you; the last thing was the book on Montesquiou. I don't even know whether you were in Germany and whether you are now in Paris.

We vacationed for three weeks in Baden Baden; we have a week now in Czechoslovakia, as bleak in the concrete as one imagines it in the abstract. At the end of next week I will go to Vienna, Hotel Erzherzog Rainer.

Please let me know whether your business has finally worked out or not, and above all whether I should and must intervene with Hellmut Becker.

Next week, by the way, I will finally dictate the foreword to Fourier. Only this much for today—I hope very much for a quick word.

Most warmly,
your T. W. A.

the book on Montesquiou: See note to Letter 48.

50

May 8, 1966
[Paris 6e, rue Dauphine
Librarie Euphorion]

Dear Professor Adorno,

I had written to you long ago, in immediate response to your postcard, but I was not happy with it. It was a bit sad and, besides, had no new information about the lectureship.

I was asked to come to Germany after you were already in Czechoslovakia, and so I didn't come to Frankfurt at all.

The examination went well, according to the gentlemen examiners, although such significant events as the founding of the German Reich simply didn't want to occur to me. Now, therefore, I am the only surviving candidate, admittedly for a position that still does not even exist. Whether it is really created must be decided this month.

At the moment I am seriously working only a few hours a day, the rest of the time *for money*. I tramp around Paris, interview, take notes, and write up comments for a series of programs for Radio Cologne—the first one is on anarchism. There are still some odd characters around: the old combatant Lecoin, who in the meanwhile, quite in contravention of the anarchist *régelment,* aspires to win the Nobel Prize; Monsieur Guérin, *homme de lettres,* who by the way gave me a very polite reception after I told him that I am your student; he has made anarchism acceptable again in intellectual circles (to my disappointment he doesn't think much of Fourier). And then the numerous, really numerous *militants,* who now welcome the beatniks into their ranks, since the latter—lounging around peacefully—have also been harassed by the police here.

Does Prague really have nothing Vienna-like, European about it any longer? Too bad! I am also dreaming of vacation, perhaps to the Vallée de la Loue, since I saw Courbet yesterday—even the inevitable stag fails to disturb me. For the moment, I console myself by moving into a hotel from time to time, a hotel that I recently discovered, whose rooms—right on the rue Jacob—all front on an absolutely beautiful *jardin intérieur.* This is what is still exciting about Paris: all centuries, all types of people and landscapes coexist (but already slightly museum-like).

So, now the letter should finally be on its way. And please do not be angry with me about the long silence. To you, in particular, I would not like to write *à n'importe quel moment.*

Very warm regards, to your wife as well, from

> your
> Elisabeth Lenk

P.S. I look forward eagerly to your foreword, but above all to *Negative Dialectics.* It occurred to me that here one might perhaps translate "negative dialectics" with "black dialectics" (*dialectique noire*).

series of programs for Radio Cologne: It was called "Seen in France, with Amazement, by Elisabeth Lenk," and had three parts: 1. Anarchism, 2. Unions, and 3. The Intellectuals. I recall only that for the third theme I interviewed Clara Malraux, who was of German origin.

Courbet . . . the inevitable stag: The realist painter Courbet had produced a famous image of rutting stags. An exhibition of his works opened on May 5, 1966, at the Paris museum that bers his name.—Ed.

moving into a hotel from time to time: To live in a hotel was quite common at that time, even for locals; if you stayed for a month there was a price reduction.

51

Frankfurt am Main, May 12, 1966
Kettenhofweg 123

Dear Elisabeth,

Many thanks for your letter—it is really a shame that we missed each other.

The foreword is done; you receive it herewith.

Otherwise, I would like to report today, under extreme stress, that at Radio Bremen, where I spent a couple of days, I beat the drum for you. This station is probably the most friendly to us. I should think you could land whatever you want there, even if it is not as well paid as the Westdeutscher Rundfunk or the Norddeutscher Rundfunk. Perhaps you will write, mentioning me, to Herr Dr. Helmut Lamprecht (Editorial Department, Studio Bremen, 28 Bremen, Heinrich Hertzstrasse 13), who is fully in the picture.

Negative Dialectics is coming along very nicely; four sections are already being typeset. *Dialectique noire* would not be a bad name, but God only knows if and when it will appear in French.

As warmly as ever,
your TWA

The foreword is done: The foreword to Charles Fourier, *Theorie der Vier Bewegungen und der allgemeinen Bestimmungen* (Theory of the four movements and of the general destinies), which appeared in the same year with the Europäische Verlagsanstalt. An English translation, *The Theory of the Four Movements,* trans. Ian Patterson, appeared with Cambridge University Press in 1996.—Ed.

Helmut Lamprecht: Helmut Lamprecht, whom I did not meet until long after Adorno's death, remained loyal to Adorno (see, for example, Helmut Lamprecht, "Die Katastrophe der Vernunft: Anthropologische Aspekte der Kritischen Theorie" (The catastrophe of reason: Anthropological aspects of critical theory), in *Jahrbuch der Wittheit zu Bremen,* vol. 27, 1983.

Westdeutscher Rundfunk . . . Norddeutscher Rundfunk: West German Radio and North German Radio.—Ed.

God only knows if and when it will appear in French: It appeared in Paris in 1978 under the title *Dialectique negative,* translated by the translation group of the Collège de Philosophie (Paris: Payot).

52

Moncourt, May 22, 1966
From the 25th once again
Paris, 31, rue Dauphine

Dear Professor Adorno,

I have just spent a couple of days with friends in Île de France and would like to send you many greetings from here and thank you for your letter and the foreword. I was delighted with it, and Saloman's people ought to be satisfied too (for this I will gladly show the "piety" that is otherwise not at all my cup of tea).

In the meanwhile I have been named lecturer and will serve three masters at once: the philosopher (Jasperian) Ricoeur, the sociologist Henri Lefebvre, and the Germanist Sagave. My work will consist, above all, in reading and interpreting philosophical, sociological, and literary texts with the students. I am spared the boredom of pure language teaching. I am very happy about this resolution, which I frankly had not expected. I believe that your and Herr Becker's advocacy played the decisive role! I will teach five hours a week; the remaining time can be devoted entirely to the dissertation.

I hope to be able to tell you of new progress on my dissertation before the beginning of the vacation.

> With warm affection,
> your
> Elisabeth Lenk

will gladly show the "piety": Reference to Adorno's comment in the foreword: "The task was resolved by Elisabeth Lenk . . . with . . . delicacy and piety."

53

Frankfurt am Main, May 26, 1966
Kettenhofweg 123

Dear Elisabeth,

With all my heart I congratulate you that the arrangement has worked out; we didn't do badly with that! In a certain sense the position is ideal, because the work suits you and leaves you so much freedom. May this freedom also benefit the dissertation—also in the sense of the freedom of the dissertation itself. Perhaps you will be so good as to write a few lines to Hellmut Becker, as well, who really functioned well this time. The address: Professor Hellmut Becker, 1 Berlin 33, Thielallee 58.

Gretel and I were in Czechoslovakia, where it is, as they say, very interesting, but, as they say less among progressive people, indescribably depressing. Then I was in Vienna for a week, flooded with impressions, although also so busy that I hardly had time to think. The meeting with Frau Berg, now eighty-one years old, was especially lovely. I have gotten myself fairly deeply entangled in Viennese opera politics, and not without success; I must tell you about it sometime.

Meanwhile, my book is making better progress than I would have dared hope. If nothing unforeseen occurs, it will actually be completed by the time I go on vacation, that is, mid-July. It is a little bit of what Benjamin said when he read the last chapter of the *Metacritique,* which was completed while he was still alive: the icy wastes of abstraction that one has to traverse to arrive in the promised land of the concrete. But that is a *captatio benevolentiae.*

I am glad that you accept my foreword to Fourier. Official piety—and piety always has something official about it—is truly not my cup of tea either, but this time yours was needed in order to satisfy the widow, as dumb as she is unlikable, sufficiently for her to hold her tongue; she is a bundle of enthusiasm.

For the next six weeks I remain here, with the exception of a few days in Berlin around June 23, then back to Sils Maria. Please keep me up to date about where and when you are.

All love from
your
Teddie Adorno

Hellmut Becker: See note to Letter 44.
Frau Berg: Alban Berg's widow.
deeply entangled in Viennese opera politics: Adorno had taken part in a podium discussion "Stagione- or Ensemble-Opera," at the Palais Palffy; it was conceived as an anti-Karajan event. Also see Letter 96.
my book: *Negative Dialectics*.
captatio benevolentiae: A rhetorical device to gain the good will of the reader.—Ed.

54

Frankfurt am Main, June 6, 1966
Kettenhofweg 123

Dear Elisabeth,

I just got the news that Kolisch, with whom, as you know, I am the closest of friends, is in Paris and will play the Schoenberg concerto there on the radio; Leibowitz is directing. Kolisch is staying with the latter. I have written him about you and would be really glad if you would get to know each other; *ça vaut la peine*. So please, call him there as soon as possible. You probably have Leibowitz's number; in any case here it is again: Littré 96–90.

Most warmly,
your
T. W. A.

Rudolf Kolisch: The leading violinist of the Schoenberg circle.

Leibowitz is directing: René Leibowitz, conductor and composer, introduced Schoenberg in France. Boulez was his student. He was also a writer and had contacts with the Bataille circle through his friendship with Georges Limbour. Three important books by René Leibowitz are *Le Compositeur et son double* (The composer and his double) (Paris, 1971); *Les Fantômes de l'opéra* (The phantoms of the opera) (Paris, 1972); and *Schoenberg et son école: L'étape contemporaine du langage musical* (Paris: J. B. Janin: 1949), in English as *Schoenberg and His School: The Contemporary Stage in the Language of Music,* trans. Dika Newlin (New York: Philosophocal Library, 1949). See note to Letter 23.

55

Paris 6e, June 14, 1966
31, rue Dauphine

Dear Professor Adorno,

I want to let you know right away that I have met Herr Kolisch; at first my utter ignorance of the new music rather depressed me, but when the conversation turned to Karl Kraus the ice was broken.

A thousand thanks for your detailed and so cheerful letter with the lovely characterization of your new book. For the moment I am stuck fast here, still on account of the stupid radio shows. Ach, I would so much like to simply read and write again without any goal in mind. Even if nothing final should ever come of it, at least that kind of freedom has value in itself. Just one example of my current situation: out of a feeling of journalistic dutifulness I am reading the newspaper *every day*. One must truly be Karl Kraus to bear up under this onslaught of spiritual wasteland and even give it a positive twist. I don't manage it.

I am looking forward impatiently to vacation, when I will finally take up the *thèse* again. I still do not know exactly when I am leaving or where to; but I will stay in touch.

With warmest affection,

your Elisabeth Lenk

56

Paris, July 31, 1966

Dear Professor Adorno,

Today I met someone who claimed to have seen you sitting at Deux Magots. Since on the one hand I was very pleased at the idea that I might be able to meet you here, but on the other hand I can't quite believe it, I want to reassure myself of your nearby or faraway existence by writing.

I would have a few things to tell you, for example, about an academic-surrealist conference in Cérisy, about some little plans. Will you be in Frankfurt at the end of September? I have a great desire and—in case it suits you—the firm intention of coming.

By the way, Herr Behncke has written to me. He wants to do a broadcast with my Fourier text and in addition he proposes to pull together some pieces from the *Quatre Mouvements* (or other works by Fourier) for a program. For this last undertaking, however, I wanted to get your agreement, and that of your wife and the translator, first!

Until mid-August I am still in Paris, then for a while in Spain.

With many kind regards, to your wife as well, I am

With warm affection,
your
Elisabeth Lenk

at Deux Magots: Deux Magots, which along with the Café Flor was situated on the Boulevard Saint-Germain, was *the* intellectual café at the time. Lucien Goldmann was in the habit of riding by on his ancient bicycle. The only alternative was the Select in Montparnasse.

an academic-surrealist conference in Cérisy: "Entretiens sur le Surréalisme du 10 au 18 Juillet 1966" (Conversations on surrealism, July 10–18, 1966). This conference was initially planned as a "purely" academic conference. But then, in May 1966, Ferdinand Alquié, the author of *Philosophie du Surréalisme* (Philosophy of surrealism), decided to include artists and turned to André Breton. "In May 1966," he reported, "I had the great joy of obtaining the participation of the surrealists themselves." On very short notice, in June, Breton asked me whether I would also like to take part in the "Entretiens." I was then invited, with José Pierre, Jean Schuster, and

Gérard Legrand, to attend as a delegate of the *groupe surréaliste*. In my talk, I discussed the difficulties attending the reception of surrealism in Germany, and thus returned to the theme of my letter to Adorno (Letter 13). The essay appeared as "Warum wird in Deutschland der Surrealismus so wenig beachtet?" (Why is surrealism so ignored in Germany?), in *Kritische Phantasie: Gesammelte Essays* (Critical imagination: Collected essays). See also the note to Letter 37.

Herr Behncke: Claus Behncke left Suhrkamp publishers in 1963 to become culture editor of West German Radio in Cologne.

57

Frankfurt am Main, October 27, 1966
Kettenhofweg 123

Dear Elisabeth,

Around the time we were last talking to one another here, Breton must have died in Paris. The news moved me greatly, and I thought of you very much.

Today, now, two things: My friend Nicolas Nabokov, the director of the Berlin Festival Weeks, will be in Paris from the beginning of next week. He is an altogether remarkable man, whose knowledge, both of things and of people, is without peer when it comes to everything that went on artistically in the 1920s. I have spoken to him about you, and he will be very glad to receive your phone call; only you will have to call him in his studio during the first four days of the week because he can no longer be reached on the weekend. The telephone number in Paris is: [. . .]

Then: In Rome I had in-depth conversations about you with my friend Iris von Kaschnitz (the daughter of Marie-Luise). She is a member of the editorial department of the journal *Duemila,* which publishes German writing in Italian and is attempting to give the journal a very specific point of view, in our sense. Among the proposals that I made to her, your introduction to Fourier is first in line. The newspaper pays very decently, and Iris, without question, will make sure that an outstanding translation is made—perhaps by Roberto Calasso, who is equally unusually well-versed in surrealism and in my own things (he wrote an essay on my relationship to surrealism, which I unfortunately cannot read, since it exists only in Italian). I would advise you simply to get in touch with Frl. von Kaschnitz (Via Vittorio 10, Rome), mentioning me. By the way, I believe that in Italy, in general, great publishing opportunities exist for you. The impact of my own things there, without my being able to explain it myself in the slightest, is indescribable.

How are you coming along with your dissertation? When will you turn up here again? And how are things going altogether?

Negative Dialectics comes out on November 24. *En attendant,* I am finishing up the little Suhrkamp volume *Ohne Leitbild* and am already deep in preparation for the next, big book, which I would have preferred to put off a little bit, but which has now assumed such urgency that I cannot extricate myself from the affair.

Jutta and I met in Salerno, were together in Paestum, Ravello, Naples, and saw each other again in Rome. In Sicily this time I was in Segesta and Seliunt—my words are not adequate to give an impression. The question of what a contemporary relation of consciousness to traditional art can actually look like is of extreme interest to me; this will be not be the least of the new book's subjects. I found Ingeborg Bachmann in Rome again, really extraordinarily smart, full of imagination, and productive—you should get to know her.

All warm wishes,
as always your
T. W. A.

weekend: English in original.

Around the time . . . Breton must have died: On September 18, 1966.

The telephone number in Paris: The number is missing in both the original and the copy.

Ohne Leitbild: See note to Letter 46.

Roberto Calasso: See the following letter and the note to Letter 5.

deep in preparation for the next, big book: *Aesthetic Theory*.

Jutta: See note to Letter 46.

a contemporary relation of consciousness to traditional art: These reflections found spontaneous expression in the theses "Über Tradition" (On tradition), in *Gesammelte Schriften*, vol. 10.1, 310–19. Collaborative translation in *Telos* December 21, 1992): 75–82.

58

Paris, November 11, 1966

Dear Professor Adorno,

Once again I have succumbed to the temptation of leading a scattered (for your sake I don't say "inauthentic") life. With astonishment I find that it is already a week since I received your letter. You must think that I am a completely unfeeling person; actually I was so overjoyed at the letter!

That you know Ingeborg Bachmann well interests me very much. Some of her poems are among my favorites, and she impressed me greatly when she gave her lecture courses and seminars on poetry. An Italian friend recently drew my attention to Roberto Calasso's work, by the way. He wants to send it to me, and I think I will be able to find my way through it, more or less. I look forward to it.

Meanwhile I have survived the excitement of the first classes. The students' German is much better than I had thought, so it is possible to read really demanding texts and even to play with German words a little, for the sake of the pleasure principle.

You ask in such a friendly way how things are going "altogether." Actually not very well at all. Perhaps it is a bit on account of Breton's death. The feeling of emptiness that has emerged in the *groupe* has spread to me, as well. I have never before felt so clearly as now that it is exclusively Breton's intellectual originality that attracts me and not the abstraction of surrealism, which had already taken on a life of its own while he was alive. However, this does not do any harm to the project, as I now conceive it; on the contrary.

I envy your productivity a little bit, and the ease with which you— barely emerged from a very extensive project—are already taking on something new and on top of that manage to do a lot of other things. For me, things are getting so complicated at the moment that the details are escaping and walking off in different directions. Perhaps it would be different if I could speak with you more frequently.

Very warm regards, to your wife as well, and many good wishes!

your
Elisabeth Lenk

P.S. Unfortunately I was not able to reach Mr. Nabokov, but I will try again at the beginning of next week.

Roberto Calasso: See Letter 5.
to play with German words: See Letter 52.

59

[Paris 13e, Bd de la Gare]

Dear Professor Adorno,

I would just like to let you know that I have finally gotten my own apartment and thus have a new address: 138, Bd de la Gare (near Place de l'Italie).

I am not entirely moved in yet, which explains the rather scribbled letter! Along with it I enclose the most recent issue of the journal *Critique*, in which—as you will see—your *Jargon of Authenticity* is mentioned. This critique, which is in itself quite blunt, would merit no interest . . . if I didn't have the impression that this is a *règlement de comptes* in which the Master himself is calling the shots!

A few days ago the *Studienstiftung* invited me to the conference "Enlightenment and Myth." The topic appeals to me, but I would mainly be very happy to see you on that occasion; hopefully they will let me off here for the couple of days!

Are you familiar with the *Internationale Situationniste*? I am sending you an issue, enclosed, simply because it has affected me in a way that nothing else has for a long time, because in it I find all my dislikes and prejudices (I had no idea until now that such a lively, fresh, undogmatic protest movement exists).

Warmest regards

from your
Elisabeth Lenk

most recent issue of the journal **Critique**: *Critique* 234 (November 1966): 883–904. The article from the journal can be found in the Theodor W. Adorno Archive. It is by François Fédier, "Trois attaques contre Heidegger" (Three attacks on Heidegger), and is a review of three books: Guido Schneeberger, *Nachlese zu Heidegger* (Gleanings after Heidegger) (Bern: Suhr, 1962); Theodor W. Adorno, *Jargon der Eigentlichkeit* (The jargon of authenticity) (Frankfurt am Main: Suhrkamp, 1964); and Paul Hünerfeld, *In Sachen Heidegger: Versuch über ein Deutsches Genie* (As regards Heidegger: Essay on a German genius) (Hamburg: Hoffmann & Campe, 1959).

the Master: Heidegger. See notes to Letters 16 and 18.

Studienstiftung: German National Merit Foundation, a German national foundation offering scholarships and fellowships.—Ed.

Internationale Situationniste: Situationism was already raising its head in Nanterre; its subversive cartoons and theses were not dissimilar to ideas that could be found in *Dialectic of Enlightenment*, especially in the chapter on media. Is it so very strange that the German section borrowed from that book without—naturally—giving it credit? "May 1964: In Munich, Stuttgart, Tübingen, and West Berlin members of Subversive Action carry out a postering action near their local university under the heading 'Position Wanted.' The poster consists of a collage of quotes from Adorno's work: 'With this world there is no coming to terms; we belong to it only to the extent that we rebel against it.' 'Everyone is unfree, under the appearance of being free.' The German intellectual and artist has known this for a long time. But nothing changes. 'They want to do nothing, and they are done to.' We believe that knowledge is not the imposition of power. If you too find the disproportion between analysis and action unbearable, write, under the code word 'Antithesis,' to Munich 23, *poste restante*. Responsible: Th. W. Adorno, 6 Frankfurt am Main, Kettenhofweg 123." In response to this illegal and intentional claim to Adorno's authorship, Adorno filed a complaint against 'unknown' for unauthorized use of his name. The originators of the postering action, who were subsequently identified as Frank Böckelmann and Dieter Kunzelmann, were found guilty and sentenced to a fine of DM 100 each. But at the same time they accomplished their aim of recruiting members. In West Berlin, the sociology students Rudi Dutschke and Bernd Rabehl, who had come from the German Democratic Republic and were not satisfied with the other opposition groups, joined the micro-cell West Berlin." (Wolfgang Kraushaar, ed., *Frankfurter Schule und Studentenbewegung: Von der Flaschenpost bis zum Molotowcocktail* (The Frankfurt School and the student movement: From letters in a bottle to Molotov cocktails), 3 vols. (Hamburg: Rogner & Bernhard, 1998), 1:208. Returning to *Internationale Situationniste*—the journal's masthead proclaimed generously: "All the texts published in *Internationale Situationniste* may be freely reproduced, translated, or adapted." At the same time, Guy Debord, the founder of *Internationale Situationniste*, was less than enthusiastic when Henri Lefebvre, the teacher of Dany Cohn-Bendit and my "boss" at the time, in his new book simply appropriated Debord's thesis that the Commune had been a festival, and in exchange, in the book's foreword, merely expressed his thanks to a mysterious Guy Debud [*sic*]. See "L'historien Lefèbvre," *Internationale Situationniste*, no. 10 (March 1966).

because it has affected me in a way that nothing else has for a long time: Only a few months after this enthusiastic comment on Situationism, I was expelled from what remained of the surrealist group on the grounds of Situationist deviation.

60

Frankfurt am Main, December 14, 1966
Kettenhofweg 123

Dear Elisabeth,

Very quickly: your letter crossed with the mailing of my book to you. It was going to your old address; I was able to catch it and have your new address inserted.

Is there actually a possibility that you will come here over the Christmas holiday? Please do let me know soon.

Very warmly,
always your TWA

61

December 18
[Paris 13e, 138, Bd de la Gare]

Dear Professor Adorno,

With the book you have given me a very great pleasure, and since today is a long Sunday I will start on it right away. Over the Christmas holiday I am not necessarily coming. But if you happened to have a little time for me, that would be reason enough to come. Would the first days of January be convenient? If not, it could be sooner, as well. My vacation lasts until January 4.

Many warm regards, to your wife as well,

from your
Elisabeth Lenk

With the book: *Negative Dialectics*.

62

Frankfurt am Main, December 21, 1966
Kettenhofweg 123

Dear Elisabeth,

Many thanks for the letter. Of course we can see each other in early January. Please be so nice and call me ahead of time, at home, 77 18 24, preferably around 11:00 in the morning. I will be at the Institute again beginning on January 2.

Most warmly,
always your
TWA

When you read my book, you must forcibly put yourself in the place of a boy who "devours it through night and ice."

When you read my book . . . "through night and ice": Compare Letter 53.

63

Paris, 13e, January 15, 1967
138, Bd de la Gare

Dear Frau Adorno,

I was very glad to have spent time with you both and found the afternoon very lovely; once again many thanks! On Monday I attempted to reach Professor Müller, without success. He had had the flu for some days already. But I will write to him in the next few days!

Today I have another request, which I unfortunately forgot to mention: could it be that in the Institute there is a file on me, containing the very preliminary "chapters" of my surrealism paper? Evidently during one of my numerous moves I have lost two texts that I currently miss very much. They are a text on black humor and one on the dandy (the general title is "Harbingers of Surreality").

It would be frightfully nice if you could have a look to see whether these texts are at the Institute. If yes, would it be possible for you to send them?

With many thanks in advance, and very warm regards to you both,

your
Elisabeth Lenk

64

Frankfurt am Main, March 10, 1967
Kettenhofweg 123

Dear Elisabeth,

This is merely to remind you that you should by all means rapidly get in touch with Peter Szondi in Paris. The simplest thing may be for you to pass by the Collège de France (you probably know where it is, directly across from the Sorbonne), find out the times of his lectures, attend a lecture, and just introduce yourself, with greetings from me. Then you can make an appointment at your leisure. Perhaps this method is better than via Minder, who was very ill and of whom I therefore am not certain whether he will immediately react in the way that I would like someone to react when you speak with him. Naturally, if you call him, you would also have to say that you are calling at my suggestion.

One more thing. It is possible that there are still letters from Benjamin in Breton's possession. Would you be able to do me the favor of speaking with Madame Breton about this and possibly sending them to me? I would then have them photocopied and immediately mail the originals back to Madame Breton. A thousand thanks in advance. That meanwhile in the *Merkur* there was an essay by Heissenbüttel on Benjamin that contained quite foolish things about him and me and above all about my relationship to surrealism, you are probably aware.

Once again I would like to tell you how much I liked your lecture and how altogether lovely it was to see you again.

Most warmly,
always your
Teddie Adorno

Peter Szondi: Scholar of comparative literature and friend of Adorno's. See also the note to Letter 41.

Minder: Robert Minder, a French scholar of German language and literature, taught at the Collège de France and had invited Szondi for a visit there.

letters from Benjamin: Heissenbüttel had speculated that letters from Benjamin to Breton existed and might be found, but this turned out not to be. Benjamin did mention André Breton's *Nadja* in his essay on surrealism, but he was in touch personally only with Georges Bataille, with whom he deposited a portion of his manuscripts for safekeeping. A lecture by Benjamin had been announced in the Collège de Sociologie. See notes to Letters 1 and 26.

an essay by Heissenbüttel on Benjamin: Helmut Heissenbüttel, "Vom Zeugnis des Fortlebens in Briefen" (On the evidence of living on in letters), *Merkur* 21, no. 228 (1967): 232–44. In this essay, Heissenbüttel accused Adorno and his student Tiedemann of treating the entire work of Benjamin as a single complex and measuring it against the criteria of traditional philosophizing; he accused Adorno and Tiedemann of "erasing" the materialist component of the late work, represented by Brecht on one side and surrealism on the other.

your lecture: "Mythos und Aufklärung im Surrealismus" (Myth and Enlightenment in surrealism), given at the conference of the Studienstiftung (see Letter 59). The basic idea of my presentation was that surrealism does not signify a future reality but rather an ever-present possibility—a step beyond the concept of utopia.

65

L'archibras
*le surréalisme**

Le 21 mars [1967]

Dear Professor Adorno,

I was very glad to get your letter, especially given that I was a little bit sad that I was not able to say good-bye to you at all properly. Now I have missed the Szondi lecture after all. As I was just getting interested again in the latest events in Paris, it was already past. Herr Picht, whom I saw over the weekend, told me about it; he liked it very much.

I am now very curious about the essay in *Merkur* that you wrote about. Until now I have been unable to locate it, because Germany, being very parsimonious, has put a stop to journals. By the way, I myself barely escaped the knife of the Grand Coalition, which is cutting out everything superfluously cultural. Everywhere they are simply closing down assistant positions. Sometimes I suspect that it is not so much the economic base but rather a base of hysteria that determines people's political actions.

I found the time we spent together lovely, and I am so relieved that you liked my text; your opinion, for me—you must know this—is the most important!

Many warm regards

from your
Elisabeth Lenk

*here the new, authentically Fourierian stamp I told you about.

here the new, authentically Fourierian stamp: The letter is written on green paper with a letterhead and drawing from an exhibition on Fourier, to which Lenk added the words "L'archibras / le surréalisme." The surrealists had not only provided the 11th International Exhibition of Surrealism with its motto from Fourier (see note to Letter 26) but had also founded a new journal called *L'Archibras*. "L'Archibras" is the third arm that, according to Fourier, humans will develop once "harmony" has been achieved.

Herr Picht: The teacher and philosopher of religion Georg Picht, author of the book *Die deutsche Bildungskatastrophe: Analyse und Dokumentation* (The catastrophe of German education: Analysis and documentation) (Olten: Walter-Verlag, 1964).

essay in Merkur: See note to Letter 64.

my text: See note to Letter 64.

66

April 16, 1967
[Paris 13e, 138, Bd de la Gare]

Dear Professor Adorno,

I must finally tell you what a pleasure it was to me to read the *parva aesthetica*. I had taken them along with me on a vacation trip, from which

I have just returned. I particularly liked "Amorbach" and "Scribbled in the Jeu de Paume," but also the "Theses on Tradition" and the final, foundational essay. If I prefer pieces like these to *Negative Dialectics,* then surely above all because I guess I am not philosophical by temperament. I take them as a model for what I myself would like to write, precisely because they can't be imitated (and because one doesn't notice the effort of thought you have put into them). The second book that accompanied me on vacation was Mallarmé's *Divagations.* You see, I was in good company!

Yes, instead of writing myself, I have only been reading again; but I think such passivity is justified by the pleasure one has in doing it.

I would be glad to know how you are. You are giving lectures again this semester, I believe? At the beginning of the summer holidays, in early June, I will come to Germany, and then I would like to sit in on your lectures again, like the old days. I am already looking forward to it.

Very warm regards, to your wife as well,

from your
Elisabeth Lenk

parva aesthetica: Subtitle to *Ohne Leitbild,* which Adorno had sent me at Easter with the dedication "Hopefully, dear Elisabeth, it is wild enough for you and not too tame." On *Ohne Leitbild,* see note to Letter 46.

the final, foundational essay: "Die Kunst und die Künste" ("Art and the Arts"). In English, trans. Rodney Livingstone, in *Can One Live after Auschwitz? A Philosophical Reader,* ed. Ralph Tiedemann (Stanford, Calif.: Stanford University Press, 1993), 368–88.—Ed.

67

Frankfurt am Main
Kettenhofweg 123

Dear Elisabeth,

This now, somewhat delayed, to thank you for your letter of April 16. It reached me immediately on my return from Vienna, where I lived the obligatory existence *au coté des Guermantes,* which did me, profoundly depressed as I was, quite a lot of good.

I am delighted that the *parva aesthetica* have pleased you. A piece like "Amorbach" is very risky, because it apparently risks so little, is so close to the idyllic, but I felt tempted to enter this sphere without allowing myself to be infected by it. To judge by your reaction I would seem to have been successful, and that naturally makes me very happy.

Meanwhile, I am continuing to work assiduously on my big book, and have managed to put some smaller things to bed, for example, a series of theses on the question "Is Art Lighthearted?" with which I introduced an internal discussion of the PEN Club.

Please now be so good, to the extent that your anarchic character allows, as to let me know in good time approximately when you will be here, so that I can make appropriate arrangements. Around the 7th of July I will be in Berlin. If there would be a possibility to meet there, it would also be something not to turn one's nose up at. In early June I will surely be here, other than on the 3rd, when I have TV circus in Cologne.

Be in touch again soon.

> Most warmly,
> always your
> TWA

my big book: *Aesthetic Theory.*

68

May 10, 1967
[Paris 13e, 138, Bd de la Gare]

Dear Professor Adorno,

Only now do I know how my plans for the next weeks will look, and so that I shall never again be suspected of anarchism I will start right off with that: I could come to Germany between May 22 and June 6. Is that convenient for you at some point? I would be very, very glad.

In the last little while I have, *nolens volens*, been occupied extensively with Kant (because I happen to have it as a topic in the seminar) and even delved into philosophical mathematics. It's just good that no responsible authority has ever accompanied my bold forays into the realm of logic!

With the Breton piece things are also gradually moving forward. For the first time I have the feeling that an end is in sight.

May I call you in the next few days? It seems to me that that would be the best way to agree on a time to meet.

Many warm regards to you both,

your
Elisabeth Lenk

69

Frankfurt am Main, May 18, 1967
Kettenhofweg 123

Dear Elisabeth,

Many thanks for the letter. Of course a time can be found in the period that you mention. Were you planning to come to Frankfurt, or were you thinking we should meet at a third location? That would also be quite possible—I would only like to ask you to get in touch with me in good time regarding the dates. I am, other than on weekends, actually at the Institute every morning, telephone 77 21 47 or 77 21 95.

I am naturally very eager for your logical forays; I look forward to them because there is, after all, something schematic and abstract about the separation of the logical and the material. Not for nothing have I tried so hard, my whole life long, to make logic speak, as I once described it. It would be very lovely if we were to understand each other in this regard too. Along with my big project, which is coming along quite nicely, all kinds of little things have been put to bed, for example, a text on social conflict today (together with Fräulein Jaerisch) and a thesis-like response to the question "Is Art Lighthearted?" as the introduction to a discussion in the PEN Club. At the moment, I am working, for recreation, on writing a little Viennese memorial, without, I admit, quite managing to come to terms with it until now—perhaps what I imagine expressing is too vague. Along with that I would like to respond to the attack by Hochuth, which is in the *Festschrift for Lukács*. That I have done something small on Stefan George for the radio I assume you know. It has an aspect that may amuse you, strange links to surrealism. After what you have told me about the background of Breton this will not astonish you

very much. Hopefully we will have an opportunity to talk about it rather
extensively very soon.

Most warmly,

your

Teddie Adorno

working, for recreation, on writing a little Viennese memorial: The Viennese memorial that is mentioned here is the text "Wien, nach Ostern 1967"
(Vienna, after Easter 1967), not the "Wiener Memorial" (Viennese memorial), which is included in the final volume of the collected works under
the "Miscellanea" and has been dated ca. 1930. It does, however, seem as if
Adorno, "for recreation," was picking up the thread of a fragment that lay
many years back, as so many artists do who have seen their productive
activity interrupted more or less involuntarily over a long period. The idea
of composing texts that seem aimed more at expression than at any grasp-
able meaning continues until it breaks off abruptly with the afterthought
"perhaps what I imagine expressing is too vague."

I would like to respond to the attack by Hochhuth: Here Adorno refers
to Rolf Hochhuth's essay "Die Rettung des Menschen" (The salvation of
mankind), in his *Festschrift zum achtzigsten Geburtstag von Georg Lukács*
(Festschrift on the eightieth birthday of Georg Lukács), ed. Frank Benseler
(Neuwied/Berlin: Luchterhand, 1965), 484ff. His response was "An Open
Letter to Rolf Hochhuth," which appeared in June 1967 in the *Frankfurter
Allgemeine Zeitung*. It is included in *Notes to Literature II*, 240–46.

George: Compare "Stefan George," in *Notes to Literature II*, 178–92.
With "George," a thread originates that I would like to identify as hermetic
poetry. Adorno's affinity with hermetic lyrics is not new, otherwise how
could he have set no less than fourteen poems by Stefan George to music
in his youth? The essay on George, which with its brief title seems to stand
quite alone, deserves attention for another reason as well, for it explicitly
states that the anti-Hitler rebel Stauffenberg was one of George's acolytes.
The poem "Der Täter" (The perpetrator), which depicts an assassin just
prior to the deed, can thus be read in its reflexes toward the future. Equally
astonishing is the surrealist side of George that Adorno reveals by including the poet's prose and dream protocols.

After what you have told me about the background of Breton: I had
described André Breton's *Jugendstil*-oriented origins to Adorno, a strange
world of images that is organized around an entirely unreal, ornamental

woman. To this extent, what Adorno says about the early George is true of early Breton as well: "The most passionate love poems of the misogynist are always directed at images of women."

70

Frankfurt am Main, June 30, 1967
Kettenhofweg 123

Dear Elisabeth,

Herbert Marcuse is meant to be in Paris during these days, and you should by no means fail to get to know him, in case this has not already happened. Please call him and tell him you are calling at my suggestion. He is staying at the Hotel Nice, 4 bis, rue des Beaux Arts (VI).

I ask you urgently to forgive my silence. The last weeks were horrible, not only on account of everything that was weighing me down in the work category, which also includes many things that evoke happy feelings, but on account of the academic *faux frais,* of which one cannot divest oneself after all. The business with the students could easily be made into a full-time job, and it even requires a certain amount of brutality to defend oneself against the claims of moral suasion. After having paid my debt of solidarity, I do not find it too difficult to develop this brutality.

Quand-même—hopefully we can see each other quite soon and finally once in the long-wished-for way.

> your
> Teddie Adorno

full-time job: In English in the original.—Ed.

71

Frankfurt am Main, July 11, 1967
Kettenhofweg 123

Dear Elisabeth,

Back from Berlin, I would like to inform you of something that has, perhaps, considerable significance for you. The Germanists there, and also my friend Szondi, whose title is professor of comparative literature, are seeking a senior assistant in the sociology of literature. Naturally I had suggested you first to Peter Szondi and can hardly doubt that you will receive the position if you so desire. Peter expressed himself unambiguously on this point. So long as you have not yet received the doctorate, you would receive the position provisionally, as it were, but with the same salary. This would begin with the summer semester of next year. After you receive the doctorate, it would become a regular position. If you would like to go to Berlin earlier, i.e., in the coming winter semester, you could only be employed as a research assistant, since the thing is not yet budgeted, and Peter Szondi is a bit embarrassed on this account; but I would like at least to mention the possibility, in case, in regard to the problematic aspect of continuing your work in Paris, you were interested in a solution of this kind. Since the matter is quite urgent, I would be grateful if you would answer me as quickly as possible, and perhaps also Szondi, whose address is 1 Berlin 33, Taubertsr, 16; you should probably write "please forward" on it, since he is in the clinic on account of a sinus operation.

Please forgive the barbaric brevity. I hardly know where my thoughts are. That in Berlin I had a little scandal with the SDS, because I refused to write a recommendation for Herr Teufel under pressure, is probably known to you. Now I am completely in over my head with examinations, and I am somewhat confused. All that is too bad, because I was in the midst of the most productive work. This also includes an improvised report on hermetic poetry that I presented in Szondi's seminar in Berlin.

From the 19th on we are in Switzerland. The address: Crans sur Sierre, Hôtel l'Étrier. In case my letter does not reach you in good time, for example, because you yourself are on vacation, I would be very grateful if you would write to me there.

En attendant, most warmly, as always,

your
Teddie Adorno

Peter Szondi: See note to Letter 64.

a little scandal with the SDS: SDS, the Sozialistischer Deutscher Studentenbund, or Socialist German Students' Union. "Completely unsuspecting, Theodor W. Adorno had accepted the invitation of the Berlin

Germanist Peter Szondi, who was one of his admirers, to give a lecture on July 7 on Goethe's *Iphigenia*. In May, he would probably have garnered general applause for it. But the student body was agitated by the June events (the fatal shooting of the student Benno Ohnesorg by a policeman during a demonstration), and quite a few of them saw this kind of topic as a provocation, not least because Adorno had not responded to the request to support the student Commune I, which had been charged with a crime based on a flyer that supposedly called for arson. Szondi was able, with some effort, to induce the audience to listen to Adorno, but the evening ended in general bad feeling. A private discussion with SDS students did not alter the situation. . . . Rumor has it that on the afternoon of July 9, as Adorno flew back from Tegel airport to Frankfurt, Herbert Marcuse was landing at Tegel." From Günter C. Behrmann's comments in the chapter "Das Audi-max der FU als Intellektuellen-Schaubühne der Bewegung" (The auditorium maximum of the Free University as intellectual theater of the movement), in Clemens Albrecht et al., *Die intellektuelle Gründung der Bundesrepublik* (The intellectual foundation of the Bundesrepublik) (Frankfurt: Campus Verlag, 1999), 326. The authors have a tendency to misunderstand Adorno as a tactician and major standard-bearer of the intellectual scene in the postwar period. For Adorno's own perspective, see Theodor W. Adorno and Peter Szondi, "Von den Unruhen der Studenten. Ein Rundfunkgespräch" (On the disturbances of the students: A radio conversation), in *Frankfurter Adorno Blätter VI* (Munich: edition text + kritik, 2000), 142 ff. The volume contains additional position papers and documents on the events of the year 1967.

I was in the midst of the most productive work: See the note to Letter 78.

an improvised report on hermetic poetry: As Letter 78 indicates, in preparing for his report Adorno had been spending time reviewing the volume *Sprachgitter* (Speech grille), by Paul Celan. The path to a reconciliation with Celan was thus already clear, thanks to Szondi's mediation. In fact, hermetic poetry belongs to the new line of inquiry that Adorno begins to develop after completing *Negative Dialectics*. However, he never produced a written version of the report he gave in Szondi's seminar. The "little scandal with the SDS," which tore him away from his productive work, may have been one of the reasons for this.

72

Paris, July 20, 1967
[138, Bd de la Gare]

Dear Professor Adorno,

When I returned to burning hot Paris (I had fled for a few days), I found your letter. It put me in a state of literal excitation. A possibility like this—out of superstition I won't call it anything else—has something incredibly appealing to me. I will write to Dr. Szondi immediately and ask him whether I can meet him sometime in the next few months, and where. For without this kind of personal contact, he is not likely to be able to make a decision, correct?

I have heard nothing at all about the "little scandal" that you mention. But it seems odd to me that they would ask you for a letter of recommendation for someone you don't even know.

I met Marcuse. We had a very lively discussion, on Vietnam, for example, and were not of one mind. On this point he is as radical as the Berlin students; by contrast I felt almost a little bit reactionary.

As soon as I hear something from Szondi I will let you know. In my life you are really playing the role of the *invisible hand*. I feel like a lucky duck, for I have not deserved so much confidence.

I hope very much that you will soon recover from the stress of the examination maelstrom and that you will once again have peace and quiet for your own work!

Many warm regards to you both,

your
Elisabeth Lenk

I have heard nothing at all about the "little scandal": I was much less aware, in faraway Paris, than Adorno believed. I was preoccupied with the trial of the Situationists in Strassburg, with whom we—some teachers at the university in Nanterre—had declared solidarity. I had certainly heard about the explosive events in Germany, but only from a distance, which may have had its consoling aspect in this more and more turbulent period. Following the founding of the SDS in Paris this changed; the threads of the two movements ran together, for me personally as well. See the note to Letter 83.

Marcuse: I see from notes that I made during that period that we also disagreed about Fourier and surrealism. "By the way," I wrote, "he is quite charming for his age." He had just returned from his first great appearance on the stage of the Free University, in Berlin; he must have made a stop in Paris both before and after. See note to Letter 71.

73

Crans-sue-Sierre (Valais)
Hôtel de l'Étrier
July 22, 1967

Dearest Elisabeth,

Many, many thanks for the letter. As far as Peter Szondi is concerned, the matter should be a *cause jugée*; but naturally it is *you* who must have that impression. Do not be nervous if he does not respond right away; he has just been through a very painful sinus operation, is headed to vacation, and is privately very depressed because Lexi Kluge has left him—in other words, patience, please. We are starting to feel restored; besides that I am working on the Durkheim introduction and the Borchardt selection. I think of you *often*—until very soon, I hope.

Most warmly,
your
TWA

The letter is written on a postcard showing the Matterhorn.

Lexi Kluge: Sister of Alexander Kluge; she was unforgettable as the main character in his film *Abschied von Gestern (Yesterday Girl)*.

Durkheim introduction: Adorno provided the introduction to the German translation of Emile Durkheim, *Soziologie und Philosophie* (Sociology and philosophy) (Frankfurt am Main: Suhrkamp, 1967). The introduction was dedicated to Jürgen Habermas.

Borchardt selection: Adorno was preparing a volume of selected poems by Rudolf Borchardt for Suhrkamp. As the selection itself and the introduction reveal, this intensive interest in Borchardt by the late Adorno belongs to his involvement with hermetic poetry. In the essay "George," Adorno "invents" an analogous situation: "assuming I had the task of preparing a selection of works by George." In both cases he is concerned with breaking through the official canonization and *salvaging* two already almost forgotten outsiders who were hopelessly enmeshed in the German language.

74

Frankfurt am Main, August 23, 1967
Kettenhofweg 123

Dear Elisabeth,

Back from vacation and well restored, I would like to ask whether you have made contact with Peter Szondi, how the matter stands overall, where you are keeping yourself, and how the chances are of seeing each other soon. By the way, I will be in Geneva on September 8 and will give the lecture on art and the arts, in French, with which you are probably familiar from *Ohne Leitbild*. In any case we should see each other soon, as arranged. Please do write a word very soon.

> Most warmly, always your
> Teddie Adorno

Just received letter from Szondi: please let me know as *quickly* as possible how the matter looks from your perspective.

Ohne Leitbild: See note to Letter 46.
Just received letter from Szondi: Handwritten. Szondi's letter of August 18, 1967, says: "In Paris I met Ms. Lenk. We understood each other very well. Unfortunately, nothing came of it after all, since she responded to my sketch of the responsibilities that await her by freely admitting that sociology interests her less and less, and furthermore her dissertation will be more like a philosophical theory of surrealism than a work of literary sociology. Now, you know me well enough, and I am also too much your student not to say to you that I am of your and her opinion and consider the social in the work, and not the work in society, to be the subject of the sociology of literature. But the difficulty is that, given the ever stronger and exclusively literary-sociological interest of the students and the fact that works from the 17th and 18th century often come up for discussion, even the immersion in the work itself, from the vantage point of literary sociology, cannot do without a knowledge of the social and economic facts of

the epoch. . . . This sense of social and economic history is something that the assistant I am seeking would have to awaken, without letting go of the immanent analysis of the work. Ms. Lenk told me with likable openness that she had a horror of this kind of historical description. Since she has a rather good position in Paris as a language teacher with the philosophers of the second university (in Nanterre), I did not have the feeling that she needs my help at the moment." Only following the completion of my doctorate in 1970 did I become Szondi's assistant. My position was not related to social history.

75

Villa Ausseil
Côte rouge
Argelès sur Mer
Pyrénées Orientales
August 30, 1967

Dear Professor Adorno,

Yesterday, in the heat, I read Goethe's *Iphigenia* and tried to guess what you might have said about it. Before I came here, I saw Szondi in Paris. I hope he didn't receive me in such a friendly fashion only on *your* account; I believe that we could understand each other very well. He is, as it seems, immune to the hysteria in Berlin. However, it probably won't work out with the position, for he would like to have an assistant who deals with things that do not interest me (or him, for that matter) very much: instead of the works themselves, the inevitable historical and social conditions. We were in agreement that the sociology of literature presupposes precisely this kind of exact studies of social history; only, I am not the person qualified to give the students a background of this sort. Basically I care neither about this kind of facts—and stupidly this is why I forget them so quickly—nor about locating the place of a work in its epoch. Szondi, as if he had foreseen this, had another suggestion: Professor Taubes is seeking a researcher for the department of hermeneutics.

Until now I have not—as we agreed—written to him about this matter. Far from the Protestant north, I am completely incapable of goal-oriented rational action. I would also appreciate knowing what you think about it.

For about three weeks I will probably remain here, in a landscape of cork oaks, wild cactuses, fig trees, and sea. Where I should look for you I have no idea. But I hope this letter will reach you somehow.

Many dear greetings from
your
Elisabeth Lenk

I saw Szondi in Paris: We met at the home of Jean Bollack, where Szondi was staying.
Professor Taubes: See Letter 77.

76

Frankfurt am Main, September 7, 1967
Kettenhofweg 123

Dear Elisabeth,

Very best thanks for your letter.

I am glad that your meeting with Szondi, according to both of your accounts, went so well; similarly, I must submit to your mutual decision that you will not assume the position that was under consideration—what you say about it is perfectly comprehensible.

It is much more difficult to give you the right advice about the position with Taubes. That you are perfectly well qualified for it in substance, that the issue of your particular talent is to be taken into account, and that he should be happy if you accept it, is beyond question. I have also noticed that Taubes has a lot of élan and good will—he has never done anything incorrect or even unfriendly toward me and exhibits a solidarity of intent toward people who come from me. On the other side—and now I really ask you to treat this with discretion—there is a problematic aspect to him. Scholem, whose student he was and who has the most exact knowledge of him, is completely at odds with him and judges him extremely negatively. While I cannot presume to have a complete picture, and while Taubes ascribes everything to Scholem's authoritarian personality, I consider the latter to be a person of much too pure a nature to speak of another, younger person the way he does merely out of ill will. To this is to be added that Taubes promised my student Rolf Tiedemann everything imaginable when he brought him to Berlin—among other things complete freedom from lesser, routine work so as to facilitate the writing of his second dissertation—and that he evidently did not keep these promises. I myself can recall that when I first met him in Sils Maria he spoke very critically of Martin Buber as soon as he got wind of my own negative position vis-à-vis the Talmudists, while I then heard from Scholem that he had kowtowed to and flattered Buber in the most crude way. I would think that Taubes is a person with a good noumenal and a bad empirical character: one internal authority really wants to do the right thing and respond to the exceptional, but then some kind of emotions that are difficult to control get in the way. However, as I said, all this refers only to the experiences of others, not my own. Certainly Taubes is an individual who is simultaneously highly gifted and deeply disturbed in his productivity, and this constellation leaves considerable characterological scars. *Rebus sic stantibus,* the best thing would probably be for you to have a conversation with him at some point in Berlin and form your own impression, whereby it is true that the immediate personal impression of a man who is extraordinarily quick to respond and sensitive is sometimes better than his actual character. Still, I think it is not out of the question that you could get along with him in spite of everything; particularly after the Tiedemann affair he would likely have an interest in not disappointing me again. Rather, he is feeling disappointed himself, by me, because he had hopes for the professorship in Jewish studies here, which, after Scholem's vote, I absolutely could not give him. You must also know that he is involved with Margherita von Brentano; if you come into contact with the latter you must therefore be very careful with every word that refers to Taubes. Politically, by the way, he is absolutely decent and courageous.

Tomorrow I go to Geneva for two days, where I am speaking at the Rencontres Internationals. Then I am here again, on the 23rd and 24th in Berlin. If you should happen to come there during that time, it would naturally be great fun.

The work is coming along, despite considerable stress, thanks to my hardheadedness.

I would be happy indeed to see you again soon.

> All warm regards from
> your
> Teddie Adorno

Martin Buber: In the 1930s, Adorno is already said to have had this critical perspective and to have called Buber a "professional Jew" *(Berufsjude)*.

See Peter von Haselberg, "Wiesengrund-Adorno," in "Theodor W. Adorno,"
ed. Heinz Ludwig Arnold, special issue, 2nd exp. ed. (Munich: edition text
+ kritik, 1983), 7–21, 12.

Rebus sic stantibus: This being the case.—Ed.

on the 23rd and 24th in Berlin: For a podium discussion and radio program. See the note to Letter 78.

77

Paris, September 21, 1967
[138, Bd de la Gare, 13e]

Dear Professor Adorno,

The thought of meeting you in Berlin was tempting; but I shrank from
the long trip and—if I am honest—was also afraid that we would not
have been able to see each other in peace. Many thanks for your lovely
"Curiosity Shop," which makes me want to read Dickens again.

I enclose one of the Breton poems that I translated over the vacation. I
am very eager to have your judgment of this example of Bretonian poetry.
I am not sure the thing has quite succeeded formally, but my work on it
was full of surprises. There are poems that truly give something away
because they lay bare Breton's inner history (and pessimism!), which are
left out of the prose pieces.

A thousand thanks for your letter concerning Taubes. I will write to
him first thing today, because after all that is what we had agreed. But
after all that I am not so enthusiastic. It is more important to me to see
you soon. In Frankfurt?

> Very warmly!
> your
> Elisabeth Lenk

"Curiosity Shop": Theodor W. Adorno, "Rede über den Raritätenladen"
("On Dickens' 'The Old Curiosity Shop'"). Adorno had sent me an offprint
from *Federlese: Ein Almanach des deutschen PEN-Zentrums der Bundesrepublik* (Munich: Kurt Desch, 1967). The essay is included in *Notes to Literature
II*, 171–77.

one of the Breton poems that I translated:

    Curtain Curtain
Vagabonding seasonal theaters perform my life
To the very end
The front of the stage was my dungeon from there
    I whistled
With hands on the bars I saw against a ground of
    black green
Naked to the belt the heroine
Commit suicide at the beginning of the first act
The play continued inexplicably in the chandelier
While the stage gradually sank into mists
And at times I cried out
I broke the pitcher that someone had given me
Butterflies flitted out of it
And flew up confusedly to the chandelier
On pretext of a ballet interlude
    they were determined to give with my thoughts
Then I tried to slit my wrists with hunks
    of brown earth
But they were lands I had gotten lost in
Impossible to rediscover the trace of these travels
By the bread of the sun I was separated from all
An actor ran around in the hall and he alone
    kept the action going
He had fashioned himself a mask from my features
Disgusting how he sided with the ingenue and the
    traitor
It was announced that the order was set as May June
    July August
Suddenly the cave grew deeper
In the endless corridors at hand level
    bouquets wandered
Too much freedom was given me
Freedom to flee from my bed on a sleigh
Freedom to call back to life the beings I missed

Chairs of aluminum drew closer
      around a mirrored kiosk
Above which rose a dew curtain fringed
      in green blood
Freedom to drive the semblances of reality ahead of myself
The half-basement was wonderful on a white wall appeared
      in a dotted line of fire my outline
      the bullet in the heart.

78

Frankfurt am Main, October 5, 1967
Kettenhofweg 123

Dear Elisabeth,

Taubes sent me the carbon copy of his letter to you—evidently he is
quite serious, after all, about winning you. He has also come to see me
about it again, and I need not say that I have written to him as glowingly
as I can, and that gladly, as I really cannot do for anyone except you. In
my opinion you should at least go to Berlin to speak with him. The
chances that exist there for you are probably too big and far-reaching for
you to cast them to the winds. And, as I said, Taubes also has his merits,
as has been demonstrated in particular by his extremely decent stance in
the matter of the Berlin student conflicts. You would have to come to
your own decision.

    Your translation of the Breton poem seems to me to be faultless. You
will not be angry with me if I am nevertheless unable to strike any real fire
either from the translation or from the original? This kind of poetry rests
entirely on the risk that the irrational sits and fits with perfection; it can
succeed only when it can fail, and in this case that translation did not
happen for me. But that can be my fault as well as the fault of the thing
itself, and perhaps it will change with repeated readings. Perhaps I was
also too preoccupied with my own affairs to be wholly open to something
else; I have managed, in spite of everything, to get the lecture on Rudolf
Borchardt put to bed; its basic idea is to establish the convergence of this
kind of poetry—which is retrospective to an absurd degree—with the
absurd in our sense. I will repeat this little saying on October 20 in
Bremen. How would it be, then, if you were to be present?

The weekend before last I was in Berlin to take part in a conversation on Schoenberg and Stravinsky. Before the event, I spent a long time together with Sam Beckett, and the conversation we had belongs to the most unforgettable things I have experienced in many years. I would like to tell you about that, too; I even, quite against my wont, made notes on it.

Did I tell you that I have decided to write something about Celan after all, and quite soon? Before I gave the seminar with Szondi I had been very much occupied with *Sprachgitter* (Speech grille), made notes on it, and drafted the plan. When I was visiting Böschenstein in Geneva, afterward, Celan phoned at just that moment, by chance, and expressed, on his part as well, the state of peace that has involuntarily broken out between us. I am very glad about this development. If you should see him, which after all is quite possible due to the parallelism of your positions, greet him very warmly from me. He seems to be in a much better state now, and it would be very worthwhile if you would reestablish contact.

Otherwise, in the past few weeks I have made good progress on the main business at hand and am now looking ahead with some horror to the semester, which I almost see only as a handicap, although this time I can get through it entirely with the help of existing materials. In any case, the rough draft of my book is far enough along that with some luck it should be put to bed by the beginning of the summer semester, and the situation that I will then be in with regard to the draft is incomparably more favorable than it is now as long as I continue to press ahead with writing in the face of all obstacles.

This has now become a letter full of literature, and I can only hope that you won't file me away under the literature mongers. But I think we must only be together once properly, above all without any time limits, and then this danger will pass. You see, I am in a slightly manic phase, and this, in turn, may have something to do with the fact that I am writing to you.

> In this sense, most warmly,
> your
> Teddie Adorno

Taubes . . . letter: Taubes sent me a four-page letter, dated October 3, 1967, in which he invited me to come to Berlin on November 16–20 to get acquainted. The occasion was a colloquium with Hans Blumenberg and the Lindauer circle. I was never his assistant, but from that time on enjoyed a lifelong friendship with him and Margherita von Brentano. Here is the lively beginning of this letter: "Very honored Ms. Lenk! I thank you very cordially for your lines. After the conversation with Szondi I was not sure whether I was supposed to write to you, or you to me. As soon as I read your introduction to the *Quatre Mouvements* of Fourier, I tried to locate you. Lukács once said to me, in 1947 in Zurich: Fourier is something for the future. Since then, I have returned to Fourier from time to time but could not make friends with his massive anti-Semitism. You, however, have brought the dialectical moment to light. I would be grateful to you if you would send me what you, with *understatement,* characterize as 'a few little things.'"

his extremely decent stance in the matter of the Berlin student conflicts: Taubes sympathized with SDS insofar as he could interpret it as subversive, anarchistic, and even surrealistic. It was he who had addressed the crowd in the Auditorium Maximum on July 9, 1967, together with Marcuse. "The first panel, moderated by Taubes, consisted of Marcuse, the Free University social scientist Richard Löwenthal, Alexander Schwan, Dieter Claessens, and Peter Furth, along with Rudi Dutschke and Wolfgang Lefèvre from the Berlin SDS" (Albrecht et al., 326 [see note to Letter 71], among other sources). Taubes appreciated Rudi Dutschke and Wolfgang Lefèvre, but later he played a trick or two on left-leaning faculty members in his department. For example, he was so fulsome in his praise of a Polish Scheler specialist that his fellow faculty members offered the scholar a visiting professorship. Only after the papal election did they learn that their candidate had been Karol Wojtyla, the future Pope John Paul II.

if I am nevertheless unable to strike any real fire either from the translation or from the original: It was comments like this that moved me to write in the afterword to my book on Breton, when it finally appeared in 1971 (in other words, two years after Adorno's death): "Adorno, to whom the work was directed as the ideal, but certainly not always well-disposed, reader."

the lecture on Rudolf Borchardt: This lecture was based on Adorno's introduction, "Charmed Language: On the Poetry of Rudolf Borchardt," to Rudolf Borchardt's *Ausgewählte Gedichte* (Selected poems) (Frankfurt: Suhrkamp, 1968). It appeared in English in *Notes to Literature II*, 93–210.

The weekend before last I was in Berlin: On this occasion he met Samuel Beckett at the Hotel Savoy, in the Fasanenstrasse. Beckett was in Berlin for the Berlin Festwochen, where he was producing *Endgame* in the workshop of the Schiller Theater. On this, and on the content of the notes Adorno made on the conversation, "quite against [his] wont," see also Rolf

Tiedemann, "Gegen den Trug der Frage nach dem Sinn: Eine Dokumentation zu Adornos Beckett Lektüre" (Against the deceptive question of meaning: A documentation on Adorno's reading of Beckett)," in *Frankfurter
Adorno-Blätter III* (Munich: edition text + kritik, 1994). The article documents not only Adorno's comments on texts by Beckett but also notes on
conversations and letters, for example, Beckett's inimitable reaction to
Adorno's last letter (February 1969): "I have not yet been *conspiré*, so far as I
know—and that is not far—by the *Marcusejugend*. As you said to me once
at the Iles Marquises, all is misunderstood. Was ever such correctness joined
to such foolishness?" The Iles Marquises was a restaurant in the rue de la
Gaité (fourteenth arrondissement) where the two met on several occasions.

to write something about Celan after all, and quite soon: Here Adorno
mentions a plan that he had conceived earlier, during his preparation for
the seminar with Peter Szondi. However, nothing was ever written down.
Perhaps this was also due to a resistance to surrealist methods, along the
lines revealed by Adorno's comments on Breton's poetry.

the seminar with Szondi: See note to Letter 71.

visiting Böschenstein in Geneva: Bernhard Böschenstein, the Swiss
scholar of literature, was a friend of Peter Szondi and the author of a number
of studies on Celan, for example, on *Die Niemandsrose* (The no-one's rose).

the state of peace that has involuntarily broken out between us: With his
statement that to write poetry after Auschwitz was barbaric, Adorno had
alarmed or at least raised concerns in the minds of many artists. Thus it is
certainly no accident when Celan writes spontaneously to Adorno after the
latter distances himself from the statements he had made in January 1962 in
the *Merkur* (Adorno, *Gesammelte Schriften*, vol. 10.2, 499ff.), and again, even
more radically, in March 1962 on Radio Bremen and in the *Neue Rundschau*
(*Gesammelte Schriften*, 11:409ff.). See *Die Goll-Affäre: Dokumente zu einer
Infamie* (The Goll affair: Documents of infamy), ed. Barbara Wiedemann
(Frankfurt: Suhrkamp, 2000), document 193, 547ff. Subsequently, the
"Goll affair" cast a temporary shadow over the friendship between Adorno
and Celan. The new "state of peace" between them was established by
Peter Szondi, Celan's most loyal defender, who in 1960 had already penned
a courageous response to a certain cabal that was lurking behind the
pseudonym K. Abel—a graduate student with a history of right-wing
sympathies who had written an accusatory article on Celan in *Die Welt*
(November 11, 1960). Szondi also sent corrections to *Christ und Welt* and
the *Neue Deutsche Hefte*.

the parallelism of your positions: Paul Celan was a lecturer in German language and literature at the Sorbonne. My contact with him, however, had come through his wife, Gisèle Lestrange, who was the secretary for the German department at the "Grand Palais"—the building had been subdivided into offices, which the department occupied temporarily. I spent two weeks at Gisèle Lestrange's country home in Moisville, together with Bernhild Boie.

He seems to be in a much better state again now: Celan had to undergo psychiatric treatment from time to time, the first time toward the end of 1962. The Goll affair, which consisted not only in the infamous attacks on the Büchner Prize–winner by Goll's widow but also in the scurrilous and uncritical repetition of these accusations by a considerable part of the German literary world of the era, played no small part in this.

the main business at hand: Aesthetic Theory.

79

Paris, October 23, 1967
[138, Boulevard de la Gare, 13e]

Dear Professor Adorno,

Your ears must have been ringing, for I have been having long tête-à-têtes with the figure of Adorno, which is haunting me. I am meant to write an article on you for Goldmann's *Lexikon der Literatursoziologie*—and that can only turn into a defense of works of art against their methodological compilers. But how is one to do justice to this in five pages? As soon as I have come up with something readable, I will send it to you.

I have written to Taubes that his offer was very tempting to me (if only because I could start right off with my favorite subject) but that I can on no account leave here before the end of June. In fact, they have given me additional hours, and this time my teaching is considered important enough to be examinable.

I have been working very intensively over the last few weeks. (It's a shame you didn't like Breton's poem. However, like all his poetry and poetic prose, it is more hermetic than irrational—and that *malgré lui*.) I believe there is a very specific view of reality at the bottom of Breton's work. There are something like magnetic poles around which his images circle. If it were possible to give them a precise definition—and I have made a fair amount of progress in this regard—the very texts that give me, and not only me, the greatest headaches become transparent. I call Breton's particular view of reality poetic materialism—a materialism that has nothing to do with philosophical or historical materialisms, but has its exact location only in poetry. Materialism is the idea that the body of the word creates the very first sense, the way an inadvertent movement of the human body can bring forth (or come up with) a thought, a rhythm. Material is word material, and Breton has the alchemical notion that it can be purged of its sensual dross. The material in which pure qualities appear is glass—the element of modernity that surpasses water. All this, because I am only giving a vague idea of it, may perhaps sound obscure. However, it is neither a preconceived idea nor a mere working hypothesis but something that is embedded in the texts themselves; I simply hadn't seen it before.

Is it true that you are going to talk about Stefan George, together with Claude David? Or is that only "groundless chatter," as our great philosopher says? (Apropos: I must confess that from time to time I cannot resist the temptation to read *Him,* simply on account of his lovely puns, "until the lack of being rooted in the soil intensifies into complete rootlessness." Then one must intone the lovely old children's ditty "Don't turn around, the humbug's in town," etc.)

Recently I read the article in the *Times Literary Supplement* about you. I would be eager to hear what you think of it. I found it to be very objective and good. The only thing that bothers me is that he simply picks up the banalities about your style that are common coin. Meanwhile, one must perhaps give the author (do you know him?) credit for the fact that as an Englishman he cannot have any feeling for the extent to which the usual "academic German," which he probably takes to be a basic norm, cripples the German language.

Over Christmas I will come to Germany. If, however, this should suit you badly or not at all, I could come for a lightning visit either before or after—somehow between Thursday and Sunday, for I teach on Mondays.

Many warm regards from your

Elisabeth Lenk

an article . . . for Goldmann's Lexikon der Literatursoziologie: Lexicon of the sociology of literature, unpublished.

poetic materialism: The phrase became the subtitle and central theme of my book on Breton, *Der springende Narciss: André Bretons Poetischer Materialismus* (Leaping Narcissus: André Breton's poetic materialism) (Munich: Rogner & Bernhard, 1971).

David: Claude David, a professor of German at the Sorbonne, who wrote on Stefan George.

Him: Martin Heidegger.

article in the Times Literary Supplement: Anon., "Theodor W. Adorno" appeared in the *Times Literary Supplement,* September 28, 1967, 892–94. It was probably authored by George Steiner.

80

Frankfurt am Main, October 31, 1967
Kettenhofweg 123

My dear Elisabeth,

A thousand thanks for your letter.

Naturally I am most eager to see your essay for *Goldmann's Lexikon.* If I had not neglected to write the urgently necessary section on interpretation for the second part of *Negative Dialectics,* the task you face would most likely have been easier. On the main question—the method of the anti-methodical, so to speak—the most usable material is probably to be found in the piece on "The Essay as Form."

I am following with suspense the development of the Taubes matter; I could, in any event, imagine you having fun and productive possibilities there, above all since it is not only Taubes who is there but also people like Szondi and Tiedemann. In the meanwhile you will also receive another offer, with which I am not unconnected. An unusually clever and pleasant Austrian, Harald Kaufmann, has founded an Instutut für Wertungsforschung in Graz, whose concept, despite the rather unappealing name, is based on the consideration of questions of aesthetic criteria that can be linked, simply put, to my writings. Kaufmann is looking desperately for colleagues of like mind, and I have given him your name and that of Nike Wagner (the very charming daughter of Wieland). Graz is a delightful city, which probably resembles the utopia that at one time persuaded you to go to Giessen more than it does the atmosphere in

Oberhessen. There are Nazis there, but where are there none, and Kaufmann's circle resists them energetically; a strong intellectual opposition is coming together there. And Vienna, with its delightful Semmeringbahn, is easy to reach (I had better not mention cars). I would not like to mislead you into an adventure, but only say to you that there is much that speaks in its favor. A small conference on music criticism that he held there three weeks ago was extremely productive; the list of invitees essentially corresponded to my suggestions.

Let us not, on account of the Breton poem, misunderstand each other. I do not reproach the poem its irrationality—how could I. The problem, it seems to me, is much more to be sought elsewhere, namely, in the fact that in many surrealistic productions the individual associations, in their necessity, are not conveyed starting from the articulated image. And this, precisely, is what would count. This is where the risk and the opportunity of such poetry lies, and it is still not evident to me that Breton quite succeeds here. If one does attempt poetry without the crutches of meaning, it requires uttermost strength to lift what is wholly free above the level of chance. Fundamentally, the lay of the land is not altogether different here than when it comes to theory.

That I will speak about George in Paris in January is true, not that it has anything to do with the good Professor David; at least Raczinsky has said nothing to me about it. I think my George text will be of interest to you on account of several very surprising cross-connections to radical art. By the way, I spoke last week in Bremen on Borchardt's poetry. I think it has turned out well. The George story is part of the same layer of reflections.

My main business is coming along well, the end of the rough dictation is probably to be anticipated by spring, and then I am in a much more favorable position in terms of how I envision things.

Here the semester has now broken out, and for the next couple of weeks it will be difficult to make myself as free as I would like. Christmas would probably be the best time. But let us continue to correspond, perhaps an opportunity will turn up earlier, perhaps even in a third location.

Most warmly,
as ever your
Teddie Adorno

the urgently necessary section on interpretation: Since this section was not available to me, I followed "The Essay as Form" and wrote: "The Frankfurt School's thinking about art is internally contradictory. Thus, it did not produce a unified, precisely definable methodology for the sociology of art. The form in which contradictory aspects can coexist without immediately pressing for a decision is the essay. Benjamin, Adorno, and also Bloch, by the way, never wrote about aesthetic subjects in any other form than that of the essay. In this they follow the early Lukács and his teacher Georg Simmel. Benjamin, in the preface to his book on the German tragic drama, calls the esoteric essay 'the alternative of philosophical form.' In Simmel, who could philosophize with playful seriousness about a pot handle or a chair, the essay appears almost as a challenge to traditional philosophy. Adorno picks up this motif in 'The Essay as Form.' The essay, he says, 'frees itself from the dictates of the attributes that since the definition in the *Symposium* have been ascribed to ideas.' 'The essay shies away from the violence of dogma, from the notion that the result of abstraction, the temporally invariable concept, is more deserving of ontological dignity than the individual phenomenon that it grasps.' The essay is meant to defend the individual phenomenon, without considering whether it contains the totality within itself or is somehow typical or meaningful for the whole, but instead for its own sake. It is tempting to conclude that this type of intention contradicts Adorno's theoretical premises. A second passage in 'The Essay as Form' hints at this, when it states that the essay comports itself 'cautiously' in its attitude toward theory, that it consumes even theories that are close to it. To this extent, the form of the essay would not be an expression or final consequence of critical theory but rather its corrective. It is not yet clear whether this entirely inconsequential form, which is capable, as it proceeds, of forgetting its initial hypotheses, is more likely to elicit truths about its fractious subject than a sociology of literature that would apply replicable methods." See "The Essay as Form," trans. Bob Hullot-Kentor, *New German Critique* 32 (Spring–Summer, 1984): 170, 158. Translation modified.

I had better not mention cars: A reference to my automobile accident (see Letter 34).

Instutut für Wertungsforschung in Graz: Institute for Research on Value in Graz. The institute was founded in 1967 as part of the Academy of Music and Performing Arts. It later became an institute for music aesthetics.—Ed.

A small conference on music criticism: The "Symposium on Music Criticism" took place in Eggenberg Castle, near Graz, as a part of the Steirian Academy of 1967. At Adorno's suggestion, Heinz-Klaus Metzger, Andreas Graf Razumovsky, and Luigi Rognoni had been invited to participate.

the good Professor David: See note to Letter 79. In any case, David was good in a positive sense, that is, brave. He not only brought Celan to his institute but also looked after him when he was in difficulty, lending him his apartment from time to time.

Raczynski: Since September 1965, Count Joseph Raczinsky had been the director of the Goethe Institute in Paris (Centre Culturel Allemand). At Raczinsky's invitation, Adorno gave a talk there on January 15, 1968, "Reflections on George." (See "Stefan George," in *Notes to Literature II*, 178–92.) The occasion was George's hundredth birthday and the centenary celebration of Baudelaire's death.

George text: "Die beschworene Sprache" (Charmed language). See the notes to Letters 69 and 73.

on Borchardt's poetry: See notes to Letters 73 and 78.

81

Elfriede Olbrich to Lenk
Secretary to
Prof. Dr. Theodor W. Adorno

Frankfurt am Main, November 3, 1967
Kettenhofweg 123

Dear Ms. Lenk,

With this, Professor Adorno sends you an authentic dream protocol of his, which he thinks could be of interest to you.

With the most friendly regards,

your
Elfriede Olbrich

an authentic dream protocol: Typescript with the title "Dream Protocol, Los Angeles, February 18, 1948." "I dreamed I had a voluminous illustrated work on surrealism, and the dream was nothing but the exact representation of one of the illustrations. It portrayed a large hall. The wall on the left, in the back—far from the observer—was covered by a misshapen wall painting that I immediately recognized as *German Hunting Piece*. Green, as in Trübner, was the dominant color. The subject was an enormous aurochs that, standing on its hind legs, seemed to be dancing. The length of the hall was occupied by a series of precisely oriented objects. Nearest to the painting was a stuffed aurochs, approximately the same size as the one in the painting and also on its hind legs. Then a living, also very large but somewhat smaller, aurochs, in the same pose. The same posture was also assumed by the following animals, the first two not entirely distinct, brown, most likely bears; then two smaller, living aurochs; and finally two ordinary deer. The whole thing seemed to be following the orders of a child, a very graceful girl in a very short green silken dress and long green silk stockings. She led the parade like a musical conductor. But the signature of the painting read Claude Debussy. (While I was writing the big afterword on Stravinsky for *Philosophy of New Music*.)" Adorno, like Benjamin, kept a dream diary. For each of them, as for Freud, a dream protocol could be considered authentic only if it was written down immediately upon waking. This transcription had its own integral meaning quite apart from any psychoanalytic treatment. In the Theodor W. Adorno Archive there is a collection of Adorno's dreams, which now also exists in English as *Dream Notes* (Cambridge, England: Polity Press, 2007). In this collection of dreams I also found the wonderful sentence with which Adorno paints his own portrait: "I am the martyr of happiness."

Trübner: Wilhelm Trübner (1851–1917) was a German realist painter and member of the Berlin Secession.—Ed.

82

January 9, 1968
[Frankfurt am Main, Kettenhofweg 123]

Dear Elisabeth,

On Thursday in the late afternoon I shall arrive in Paris. Perhaps you will be so kind as to telephone me the same evening, around seven, at the

Hotel Scribe. Perhaps we can have a late meal together—I hope I don't already have the Baudelaire-circus on this evening.

> Warmly, as always,
> your
> [Adorno]

have a late meal together: We did have a late meal together, indeed, at Adorno's specific wish, in a restaurant where the Goncourt jury used to meet but which was yawningly empty on the evening in question. The restaurant was the Drouan.

Adorno uses a rather amusing neologism and pun, *nachtmahlen,* in this invitation to a late dinner. It suggests grinding, a "night mill."—Ed.

Baudelaire-circus: This refers to the "Rencontre Internationale" devoted to the poet, which took place on January 8–13 in Paris, as part of the centenary events marking Beaudelaire's death. The title of the event was "La Découverte du Présent: Hommage à Baudelaire, critique d'art" (The discovery of the present: Homage to Baudelaire, art critic). It was organized by Pierre Schneider. Adorno did not have to give a lecture at the conference but had confirmed his participation "definitively" for the morning of Friday, January 12. At the invitation of Lucien Goldmann, Adorno also gave a lecture at Royaumont. See note to Letter 38.

83

Frankfurt am Main, February 7, 1968
Kettenhofweg 123

Dear Elisabeth,

You will probably have heard that poor Aliette Rohan, with whom we had tea that time in Paris, has been murdered. I enclose an essay about her that my friend Razumovsky published in the *Frankfurter Allgemeine Zeitung* and that may interest you. It is very elegant, if not completely free of cynicism toward the deceased. How entirely nonidentical a fate like this is with the person it has struck down. Despite this, I can recall that when I wanted to have Aliette invited to my Paris circus, and heard that her address was unknown, for a fraction of a second I had a feeling of impending disaster. But naturally something like that can also be a projection after the fact.

How lovely it was with you in Paris. Please let me know when we might be able to count on your being here, or somewhere nearby. It would be really important for you to get in contact soon with Herr Müller, above all in order to work against his increasing irrationality in good time.

I am feeling quite good, if you discount a measure of soulless annoyance, whose quantity does, then, threaten to turn into quality.

As a little token I enclose, in addition to the Aliette-essay, the copy of my Borchardt text.

> As warmly as can be,
> always your
> Teddie Adorno

Aliette Rohan: Descendant of an aristocratic family mentioned in Proust.
an essay ... in the Frankfurter Allgemeine Zeitung: More of a gloss: "Aliette. She was one of half a dozen sisters. Next to the elegance of the others, who served to decorate the Viennese salons of the postwar period prominently enough and not without eccentricity, she, the corpulent one, was somewhat out of the limelight. This, and her ironic intelligence, which set standards above the self-satisfied superficiality of the party life between Kärntner Street and the Eden Bar, later impelled her to Paris, the homeland of her ancestors. Princess Aliette Rohan: daughter of one of the last great aristocrats of our era, the Duke of Bouzillon and Montbazon. She came from a family that was freighted down with history. Castles in Bretagne, splendid Baroque palaces in the Elsass appear in our times like the petrified remains of the ancien régime, from a time before the flood of the revolution. The most arrogant of all sayings on a family crest, 'Dieu ne puis, Roi ne daigne, Rohan suis,' graced the ceiling of the romantically Gothic Lohingrin palace in Northern Bohemia, which the emigrants— loyal to the king despite this challenging motto—had erected amid the most beautiful of all parks at the beginning of the last century. (There, decades later in the chapel of the castle, Anton Dvořák used to pound away on the organ.) ... The last time we met Aliette, by an odd coincidence, was on the Place Rohan in Paris. Diagonally, across this rectangular widening of the rue Royale, past the freshly gold-leafed Maid of Orleans, she came

toward us. The short-sighted eyes with their mocking wit widened into an expression of surprise only when we had almost bumped into each other. No, she replied, it was not true that she walked around all day on this square affiliated with her ancestors. With this she tottered on, on her high heels, as ever rather rotund, still witty, and pleased with herself. Now someone has murdered her, in Paris. Her murder remained within the bounds of nobility. The murderer was a Count. A. R."

How lovely it was with you in Paris: I felt the same way about it and noted: "Adorno was here for a long visit, and I took him around (in the car!), which meant that I got lost every few minutes, but he was very patient. When I missed the highway exit for Royaumont for the second time, he asked politely, referring to a huge administrative complex in contemporary colors, "Didn't we already pass this building once before?"

a measure of soulless annoyance: It was 1968, the year of the student unrest. The turbulent events reached their climax in Germany before they spread to Paris in May. On June 2, 1967, Benno Ohnesorg was murdered in Berlin. Adorno, in his June 6 lecture on aesthetics, had spontaneously expressed his solidarity with the students and declared that Ohnesorg's "fate stands in absolutely no proportion to his participation in a political demonstration." He called for an immediate investigation by an independent authority. On the occasion of his visit to Szondi's seminar in Berlin, however, Adorno refused to provide a letter of recommendation for Fritz Teufel. This led to the student actions that, in Letter 71, he called his "little scandal with the SDS." He also insisted on sticking to his almost provocatively classical topic of Goethe's *Iphigenia*. In February 1968, the student unrest spread to universities throughout West Germany. Adorno found himself in the situation of someone who has shown the way but, to the students' disappointment, isn't marching in the direction he points toward. The situation in Nanterre, which would soon explode, had also just become critical. Shortly after Adorno's departure, there were excited gatherings in Nanterre because a student named Daniel Cohn-Bendit, whom I knew, had been arrested. Suddenly, all manner of slogans appeared on the walls of the University, for example: "Professors, you are old and your culture is old" or "Let us live." An SDS in exile was founded, to prepare for the arrival of Rudi Dutschke, who was expected in Paris. Its members included Uli Preuss, Samuel Schirmbeck, and Ina von Reitzenstein, among others. The attempt to assassinate Dutschke struck like a bomb in Paris too.

84

[138 Bd de la Gare, February 28, 1968, Paris 13e]
...

I should have written long ago, but I have—perhaps utterly inappropriate—faith that you will not begrudge me my long silence, precisely because our time together in Paris was very lovely. In the last little while things have gotten rather chaotic, and everything, even the letter to you, turned out differently from what I wanted. (When it comes to work such circumstances can even be fruitful; one comes up with new, if occasionally crazy thoughts.) Meanwhile, your letter and the enclosure gave me great pleasure. The theory of language, which after all is at the center of the text, excited me, because after all I myself am chewing on similar problems. Borchardt is far away from the world in which I am moving at present, and thus I must first translate for myself all the categories that have emerged for you from this specific work.

In the meanwhile I have also gotten word of the attacks on you. It seems to me that behind them there is more political ambition than love for the matter at hand, for example, Benjamin. For that is what is at stake, after all, and I am of the opinion that the philological truth is more important than any political considerations. I will only hope that in the meanwhile you have been able to return to normal, I mean to your own work.

Now, *une fois de plus* thanks to your mediation, I am in gratifying contact with Minder. He has gathered around himself a few people whom he would like to have as collaborators on the newspaper *Allemagne aujourd'hui* (which, in fact, is in very bad shape). But I am trying to remain free of writing commitments as much as possible because I finally want to get finished with the dissertation.

Unfortunately, there is still no vacation in sight, probably not until Easter, and then, if memory serves me right, unbelievably short. Thus, I will have no other option than to write to Professor Müller, to present the outline of the dissertation to him, and to explain my sins of omission.

Wouldn't that be a first diplomatic step?

I have a funny story about Goldmann. But I must tell it to you when I see you: at some point the *année universitaire* will be over and I can travel wherever I like, for example, to Frankfurt.

Many warm regards
from your
Elisabeth Lenk

theory of language ... at the center of the text: This again refers to the introduction to the Borchardt essay. See note to Letter 78.

the attacks on you: Not only had there been a malicious report in *Der Spiegel,* no. 30 (July 17, 1967) about Adorno's "road to Canossa, to the headquarters of the rebels"; there were also increasing attempts to label Adorno and the editor of Benjamin's works, Rolf Tiedemann, as complicit in the supposed mishandling of Benjamin's legacy. See Heissenbüttel, *Merkur* (see note to Letter 64) and *Alternative 10* 56–57 (October–December 1967).

Minder: The French scholar of German literature Robert Minder, who was teaching at the Collège de France.

85

Frankfurt am Main, May 7, 1968
Kettenhofweg 123

Dear Elisabeth,

Nanterre is constantly in the newspaper, and I am concerned about you. Please be good enough to write me a word about how you are doing, and above all, how the further professional prospects in Nanterre are looking.

I have a guilty conscience that I have not let you hear anything from me for so long. But you have no idea what the last weeks have been like. The Sociology Congress was an indescribable circus. And since I not only bore organizational responsibility but also, at the same time, was involved in the highest degree, and my closest allies—Habermas and Teschner—were absent due to illness, I had to jump into the arena continuously, with, by the way, good success, as it seemed to me; Dahrendorf, at any rate, is foaming at the mouth and projecting. But by the end I was three-quarters dead. Gretel and I traveled to Baden Baden, experienced a splendid burst of springtime there, had ten wonderful days, and came back unexpectedly well restored, so that I was able to plunge into the not exactly peaceful semester in much better shape than I could have expected. The bother is only that I am still prevented from getting to the second phase of the book on aesthetics because I have taken on the introduction to Luchterhand's edited volume on the battle over positivism. But I have applied for leave for the winter semester and hope that they will grant it to me.

Otherwise I am well—better, I would say, than I deserve. But this can only be discussed in person, and I hope that I will see you really soon.

> All warm regards and love
> as ever, your
> Teddie Adorno

the further professional prospects: Adorno's instincts were good when it came to this question. I lost my job in the May uproar. See Letter 89.

The Sociology Congress: The sixteenth German Sociology Congress had taken place in Frankfurt on April 8–11. As president of the German Sociology Society, Adorno, who was about to be succeeded by Dahrendorf, served as chairman. The News and Communications section of the *Kölner Zeitschrift für Soziologie* mentions the unusually high level of public interest aroused by the conference: "In the entire history of the German Sociology Congress there has certainly never been an event marked by as little academic ritual and ceremony as this one." It was reported that Adorno had been quite undogmatic when it came to applying Marxist theory to contemporary society: pauperization and collapse had not occurred as drastically as they would have to be understood without emptying them of all content; he even conceded that capitalism had found within itself the resources for postponing the collapse more or less until the end of time.

Dahrendorf, at any rate, is foaming at the mouth and projecting: Ralf Dahrendorf, who may have been somewhat disconcerted by Adorno's candid comments, took this as an invitation to set aside his prepared remarks. René König, surprisingly, also declined to give his speech. Jacob Taubes, on the other hand, spoke, to applause, on the topic of culture and ideology. Evidently the massive presence of a wide-awake and politically active student body had caused uncertainty among some of the presenters. In contrast to Adorno's more conciliatory remarks, Dahrendorf is reported to have repeatedly expressed his intent to harden the fronts again: "Nachrichten und Mitteilungen" (News and communications), *Kölner Zeitschrift für Soziologie und Sozialphilosopie* 20 (1968): 671–99. When it came to the role of sociology in society, Dahrendorf was Adorno's opponent. However, he wrote a very fair obituary for Adorno, which included the following remarkable sentence: "Even at the core of his activities, where individual and work become inseparable, Adorno was probably one step ahead of his critics, because deep inside he had a readiness for unresolved contradiction, as if in *Negative Dialectics* Kant's antinomies were rediscovered as maxims for action." See: "Nachrufe auf Adorno" (Obituaries for Adorno), *Kölner Zeitschrift für Soziologie* 20 (1968): 671–88.

better . . . than I deserve: The secretive tone leads me to suspect that this concerned an erotic adventure.

86

Paris, May 15, 1968
from June 1, 31, rue Dauphine, 6e

Dear Professor Adorno,

Here we have very beautiful weather today, and one lives in a state of something like intoxication. But I am afraid what has not crossed the borders sufficiently is the night of horrors of May 10 to 11. It became clear then that de Gaulle would be quite prepared to exterminate political opponents (*de les réduire physiquement,* as it was elegantly put). Students, schoolchildren, and a few professors (I was one of them at the beginning) occupied the Latin Quarter during this night, and just in case, and also in order to restrain the nervousness of a few hardliners, built barricades. A group of my students, the most clever and likable, were among them, but also Lefebvre, Touraine, and several "Nobelists." Everything was peaceful, negotiations with the government were underway for the release of the previously arrested students and workers, but no one, not the rector or a single minister, never mind the President, made the slightest concession. Instead, around 2:00 a.m. the order was given from the very top to clear the Quarter. To accomplish this, the police and paramilitary units used not just the usual tear gas but also dangerous poisonous gases and incendiary grenades. Their brutality especially against those who were weaker—children, girls, old people, who could not defend themselves like the young workers and students—according to radio reports that night, and above all according to the eyewitness accounts that were collected later, was dreadful. Five demonstrators have vanished without a trace and are still missing today.

The following morning I attended a meeting of Paris professors and assistants; it had been called for 10:00. The Quarter was still swarming with police, especially around the Sorbonne (for the last few weeks I have had a proper police neurosis; the instant I closed my eyes I would see black columns marching, but when I opened them it was scarcely any different). The professors were made to stand in line in front of the barricades and—to be admitted to the Sorbonne—had to show a piece of paper proving that they are in fact professors. Inside, then, a meeting began that, when it comes to turbulence, passion, and outrage, probably far surpasses anything the Sorbonne's dignitaries have encountered in the last 500 years. I could tell you many encouraging things. The old French university is coming apart at the seams. Innumerable departments and universities have proclaimed their autonomy and are occupied by students and professors. There people sleep, eat, party, and hold discussions day and night; the student cafeterias, swimming pools, and auditoriums are open to workers. It is a truly Fourier-like state of affairs. There are optimists who believe that the workers will also begin to occupy the factories. I am, since I saw the CGT bosses march by on Monday, not among them. But there are already events that just a few days ago no one would have thought possible: yesterday, for example, the official television, which as everyone knows is directly controlled by the state, declared its independence from the government and as proof broadcast an astonishing report on the student protests in Paris, which had been censored.

May 17

The letter remained unfinished, and events are coming thick and fast. In fact, the workers, without waiting for any orders from the unions, have occupied the factories, first at Renault but then almost everywhere in France. Many of them are reporting that they have taken the director prisoner. Some factories, like the Sorbonne, are open to women, children, and curious onlookers; people hold discussions, organize meals, overnights, and even parties. Tonight the railroad workers joined the movement. Numerous train stations are occupied. Trains just come to a stop somewhere.

The Situationists forced their way into the Théâtre de France, at the Odéon. It has been renamed Theater of Rosa Luxemburg, and on the roof there now flutter a black flag and a red one. "The imagination has seized power," they declare. Barrault, the director of the theater, had to step down. Instead, there are actors, curious onlookers, and students discussing the cultural revolution.

The Latin Quarter is one huge wall poster. At the Sorbonne, one can see a manifesto of basic principles that proposes, among other things, doing away with the crisis in education by allowing anyone to teach who feels called to do so and who can stand up to the criticism of the learners, and abolishing all titles, tests, and other educational certification. In Toulouse, they are talking about asking the students to fill their examination booklets with whatever crazy sentences their imaginations can come up with; the professors agree to mark them all equally "adequate."

But quite apart from the sensational doings of the cultural revolution, which attracts thousands of listeners and spectators every night (as a rule, the discussions continue until early morning; night has been abolished, at least for the moment), serious commissions have been established everywhere and are working out the radical reform of the university. The *grandes écoles* are infected, even the military polytechnical academy. de Gaulle is currently in Romania; he is probably preparing to show up on horseback and save the day. The most comical thing—in light of that terrible night tragicomical—is that there are even policemen who are gripped by the deliriuim of anarchy. At least the head of the policemen's union has now uttered a warning, his third, that it was only with the greatest effort that he could prevent his troops from going on strike. On my Boulevard de la Gare I saw a police van in which policemen and workers were fraternizing, with copious amounts of alcohol.

Ach, if only the power of "attraction" would finally also sow confusion in the psychology of the order-loving Germans! In London, Madrid, there are already signs of infection; as for Germany, I have so far heard nothing of the kind (the students are all too isolated!).

I followed the Sociology Congress as best I could, from a distance. It's fortunate, at least, that you have recovered a bit in the meanwhile. I would have so much to tell you; but I have no idea when I will be able to get away from here.

Very warm regards, to your wife as well,

your
Elisabeth Lenk

that De Gaulle would be quite prepared: Today it is known that, to the horror of his cabinet, he had given the order: "Il faut savoir donner l'ordre de tirer" (One must know how to give the order to shoot). But thanks to the prudence of the demonstrators, not a shot was fired. See Alain Peyrefitte, at the time minister of education, *C'était de Gaulle* (That was de Gaulle) (Paris: Gallimard, 2000), 3:479.

around 2:00 a.m. the order was given: The radio was ever-present during that night; even the demonstrators had small transistor radios. When the order was given to clear the Quarter, we heard the "German Jew" Cohn-Bendit make his extraordinary statement: "I call on all France to go on general strike."

Five demonstrators: The five missing people turned up later.

the CGT bosses: The CGT was the Communist trade union. In the end, my skepticism was not entirely unfounded. As Alain Peyrefitte shows, during the May events, for the first time, there was secret collaboration between the Gaullists and the French Communist Party, behind the backs of the strikers. The Communists and their union made sure that despite the general strike there were negotiations going on with the existing regime, i.e., Pompidou. This broke the back of the social movement. Again and again, the strikers shouted, "Ten years are enough." But not long afterward, the same Gaullism that the strikers rejected won an overwhelming victory at the ballot box. Among his closest confidants, Pompidou said, "When the Communists are with us, we have nothing to fear" (Peyrefitte, *C'était de Gaulle*, 461).

Barrault: As Jean-Louis Barrault's memoirs reveal, Gaullist circles considered him a weakling because he had allowed the Situationists to enter. André Malraux fired him as the director of the theater.

87

Frankfurt am Main, July 15, 1968
Kettenhofweg 123

My dear Elisabeth,

A thousand thanks for your letter of May 15. This time I really have a bad conscience on account of my silence. I believe if you had been part of the last months, in which an unusually turbulent life came together with work and the student business, you would grant me absolution.

Your letter was a kind of diary, filled with your Elisabethan élan—how you must have felt, after it all came to such a depressing end! That I judged it pessimistically from the start is no comfort at all. Only it is extraordinarily difficult, in the midst of the movement of a certain sector, which seems to have a mass base, to retain one's awareness of how small this base is, even in France; although there, thanks to the reactionary wage policy, things looked different for a while than they did here. I did, at least, succeed in engineering a joint declaration by opposition intellectuals and the I. G. Metall union; not much, and also too late, just like the demonstration Unseld pulled together against the Emergency Law. That I received small thanks and was even attacked for this, because my friends and I were attempting to handle the matter from above instead of going into the factories—in Germany utterly without any promise of success—you can imagine. The entire situation is somewhat paradoxical; Habermas, Friedeburg, Mitscherlich, and I, plus one or two others, represent a disappearingly small minority in the academic committees but are simultaneously attacked by the students in the sense of the "actionism" with which you are no doubt also acquainted. One has absolutely no backing, but on the other hand this is also how it should be.

I must also tell you a story that seems to be out of Proust. In the German reports on the death of poor Aliette Rohan her name was constantly being confused with Arlette, which, however, is the name of the female friend of mine whom I mentioned at Dhaun, who had meanwhile married, is now recently divorced, and with whom I have been able to spend a lot of time in recent months, partly in consequence of the student protests. I hope you will meet her soon.

And since we are talking about Proust—an acquaintance of mine, Prince Rudolf zur Lippe, is in Paris at the moment. You should absolutely get to know him; I am writing to him simultaneously. His address is 15e, 6 rue Jules-Simon c/o Mme Eric Germain. He could have served as the model for Saint-Loup, is a truly charming human being, politically extremely progressive, out of pure decency, while he is approximately as inclined to rhythmic Ho Chi Minh chants and the like as I am. I would be glad if the two of you were to be in contact.

On Thursday we are leaving for Zermatt for five weeks. Our address there: Hotel Bristol; I expect we will also meet Herbert [Marcuse].

It would be lovely to hear a word from you soon, if you are not all-too angry at your old and faithful

Teddie

came to such a depressing end: See note to Letter 59.
Arlette: Evidently a love affair.

Dhaun: During the conference on "Enlightenment and Myth in Contemporary Thought." See Letter 59.

88

Frankfurt am Main, July 18, 1968
Kettenhofweg 123

Dear Elisabeth,

Today, you will not believe it, a business question, as it were. Could Herr Cahn possibly let me have a sense of how much a complete copy of the *Années Sociologiques* would cost, used? I would be grateful if I could receive this information at the end of August, for before that, *procul negotiis,* I cannot attend to all these things. But there is a certain possibility that the Sociology Department might receive a special fund for this purchase, and I would be happy if I could try to follow on up this possibility immediately after my return.

Please forgive this so un-Elisabethan but also not at all Teddistical business.

> Most warmly, as always,
> Your
> Teddie

In the lower left margin of this letter there is a note: "for Prof. Adorno, who has already left on vacation, with the very best wishes: / Your / Elfriede Olbrich."

Herr Cahn: Adorno meant to refer to the antiquarian book dealer Fritz Meyer, who was my partner.

89

Samoreau, July 26, 1968
17, Grande avenue / chez M. de la Mur

Dear Professor Adorno,

I must prove to you that even in depressing times I do not lose my pleasure in writing. The great steamroller is blanketing the streets of

Paris. In May, it was *sous les pavés la plage*, and today *sous l'asphalte les pavés*.

At any event, I have concrete proof of the fact that the days of May were reality: a few days before the end of the semester I was summarily fired, no reasons given, by the very same Sagave who in late April had still assured me that my contract would "self-evidently" be renewed. To date, he has not answered a letter in which I asked him for some sort of explanation.

The period of transition that has followed the failed revolution has its charms after all: a profusion of very noteworthy communes, in one of which I, initially with the distance of a participant observer, finally was caught up with almost no distance at all. It began when three of us, two of my students and I, settled near the Mediterranean (more or less out of necessity, since the eye of the law is particularly sharp in Paris). Soon we were joined by others: an actor and a girl who was destined from then on to play the role of the femme fatale. Thus a proper group came together. There was a rumor that there was a hiding place of "Katangais" nearby, and a few members of the "March 22" group. I don't know whether the myth of the Katangais has reached Germany? I had refused to believe in their existence until the very end, while the Sorbonne was still occupied and the students were lowering their voices whenever their name came up. Supposedly, they had found a spot for themselves under the roof of the Sorbonne: members of the Foreign Legion, fabulously tall, strong, and furthermore armed. The fact is that when the student committee wanted to leave the Sorbonne of their own volition, a few individuals resisted. But the actual hour of the Katangais only struck during the reaction that set in after. Suddenly they had names; the press speculated on their numbers, their leader, etc. One of them, finally, was found murdered in the woods. You must not think that *I* am crazy; rather, it appears, for some time the French public has gone crazy.

You can therefore imagine that we were very curious about this hiding place, where supposedly several Katangais were living together with some *gauchistes* from Nanterre who were undoubtedly known to us. So we put together an expedition and went looking for them, based on the information we had. In fact, we found the cloister-like house in the wild, lonely, mountainous landscape that had been described to us. We then learned that this house had once served the Cathars, and then the persecuted Protestants, as a hiding place; today it belongs to a sect of psychiatrists, the FGÉRI. Here, once again running the risk of having you believe that I am simply making things up, please note that we, the participants in the expedition, had just read *Justine* together. No wonder we noticed the similarity between the lonesome house and the cloister where Justine vainly sought shelter. "Dear solitude," Justine had sighed, "how I long for your asylum, you must be the refuge of some gentle recluses who think of nothing but God," etc.

A child, who was evidently mentally ill, sat on a swing uttering meaningless sounds. A couple of other disturbed people lived there, but we didn't see them immediately. The "normal" people were having dinner: students, a few former workers whom we knew, a few strangers. Seeing them did not make us feel better. One of them, who had evidently not found anything to eat—the pickings proved to be slim—was incessantly ringing the cloister bells. Another was asking for his *coupe-tête*. He finally found it, a kind of double ax, and went after the others, half seriously, half in jest. None of the psychiatrists was in evidence, only a rather elderly girl who seemed to be a member of the FGÉRI. She was treated with respect. What was especially remarkable was the lack of restraint and politeness. All the animosity that one swallows in ordinary life, or at most doles out in sublimated doses, here—so it seemed—had been given free rein. Scarcely had I shyly taken a seat at one corner of the table, when the person opposite screamed at me: "I can't stand anyone across from me!" Much more remarkable, however, were the erotic quarrels, which were fought out in full public view here.

We arrived on a burning hot day. How great was our astonishment, when in one corner of the labyrinthine house we saw a group sitting in front of a blazing fireplace. Others were smoking hashish. Still others were celebrating orgies in rooms that had no doors that could be shut.

There could be no thought of sleep, and gradually, since they had offered us a little hashish (a great favor!), the distinction between day and night became blurred—especially since the moon was shining and the rooms are dark even in daytime. The crickets created pandemonium, and there were endless complications, as in a tragicomedy. The Katangais—one of whom already had a criminal record; he was called (a comical detail) "the surrealist"—played the main role, since he was the strongest. Only one of the intellectuals, who, by the way, was simultaneously passing the hashish around, had any influence over them. The gender balance was provided by Anik, a giantess, whom I knew as a well-behaved philosophy student from Nanterre. Here, she went by "the Spider," and, in fact, in these surroundings she had about her something of the malicious insect lying in wait for its prey.

In the morning I was not quite awake yet (because I hadn't slept) and wanted to take a walk, but I discovered that there were no paths around the house, only the one by which we had arrived. A few hours later we fled. Two students, both very young, above all an eighteen-year-old girl, were frightfully depressed: So those are our brothers (and sisters) from the barricades, the heroes of the month of May; is it worth all that trouble for *such a life*? (Brigitte had been on the barricades and subsequently spent two days in jail.) I reacted differently, but I will not let this letter grow unnecessarily long. Only very briefly: who knows whether something new might not be more likely to come from that quarter than from those who are brilliantly, smoothly, repeating the old boring commonplaces?

Admittedly, the smoking is dangerous; there are even people who claim that the hashish is smuggled in by police informers (another sign of this transition period: the collective paranoia, but unfortunately with a rational core).

I hope you will be able to make sense of my letter. I have the feeling that I no longer write German, but a frightful nomad's language. Do you think I can meet you in Frankfurt at the end of September or the beginning of October? I wish you both a very good vacation.

Very warmly,
Your Elisabeth Lenk

P.S. As regards my work, of which I have once again not written a single word, I don't believe I have strayed very far from surrealism. Example: a slogan on the Sorbonne, "Be realists. Take your dreams for reality."
P.S. 2 I have passed your request on to Meyer. As soon as I have heard something specific I will write.

sous les pavés la plage: under cobblestones, the beach.—Ed.
sous l'asphalte les paves: under asphalt, the cobblestones.—Ed.
no reasons given: Through Julien Graque, who knew Dean Grappin, I later learned that I had become impossible for him to support because I had given the students, who wanted to found a "critical university" on the German model, a copy of the university memorandum written by SDS in

Germany and a typewriter on which to type their translation. Like many others, Grappin was convinced at the time that "the Germans" had caused the protests. I narrowly escaped the spectacular removal of the Paris SDS, whom the police deported, transporting them straight to Germany from the apartment where the SDS de Paris regularly gathered. Noticing some strange figures looking out the window, I went to the top floor of the building, as if I was looking for someone there, and was able to leave the house unimpeded.

   members of the "March 22" group: On March 22, 1968, the council chamber of the University of Nanterre was occupied by about 150 students and decorated with slogans. The name was an homage to Fidel Castro's "July 26 Movement." One of the students' demands was a critical university on the German model.

   FGÉRI: The *Féderation des Groupes d'Études et de Recherches Institionelles* (Federation of Groups for Institutional Study and Research) was founded by Félix Guattari in 1965.—Ed.

   Meyer: See note to Letter 88.

90

Findeln ob Zermatt
August 14, 1968

My dear Elisabeth,

This is merely intended, in the midst of the stress of doing nothing, to confirm with many thanks the receipt of your letter, which is truly a document! At the end of next week we will return, then we must talk about everything. I will basically be in Frankfurt but with breaks; let us, however, agree on something in good time so we don't end up missing each other or getting caught in a maelstrom. We are recuperating unusually well; the miserable weather is working to the advantage of a little book on Berg that I recklessly took on.

> All imaginable love your
> Teddie Adorno
> Most warmly, Gretel Adorno

Postcard with view of the Matterhorn. Lenk collection.

book on Berg: *Berg: Der Meister des kleinsten Übergangs (Alban Berg: Master of the Smallest Link)*. The book, which appeared in German in 1968, was translated into English by Christopher Hailey and Juliane Brand (New York: Cambridge University Press, 1994).

91

Paris 6e, September 1968
31, rue Dauphine

MANY CORDIAL BIRTHDAY GREETINGS. SOON I WILL LAY THE DISSERTATION AT YOUR FEET YOUR ELISABETH LENK

92

Frankfurt am Main, September 13, 1968

Dear Elisabeth,

A thousand thanks for your telegram. I was terribly glad to get it, and I am very eager to receive your manuscript.

Today only this much: Taubes, who one must admit is a person who is very willing to help, has immediately come up with a lot of things in response to my inquiry. Would you at all consider accepting a position in Germany, in Berlin? I believe that there would be a few things open to you there. Since I do not wish to write to Taubes before I have your reaction, at least in principle, I would be grateful to you for a very quick word about that, or at least if you would let me know immediately, and as far as possible exactly, when you might be here.

I have actually completed my book on Alban Berg, a very reckless undertaking, on time; in the process a lot of new things occurred to me, and altogether, although it was a lot more work than I had imagined, it was work that gave me much more joy than I had any right to expect. Now I am rampaging through my aesthetic manuscript in order to make it into something respectable. I have a research leave that is meant to be entirely devoted to completing this task.

All warm regards,
always your
Teddie Adorno

93

Paris, September 14
[6e, 31 rue Dauphine]

Dear Professor Adorno,

I just wanted to tell you very quickly that, as far as my situation is concerned, everything is once again in order. The German Academic Exchange Service has given me a scholarship, as recompense, without my really having made any effort to get it. It isn't very much, but at least I am once again *à l'abri du travail*.

I admire your élan, that even on vacation you are productive, and am looking forward very much to your Berg book. My dissertation is already able to beat with one wing, but I would like to show it to you only after it is finished. As for the protests, for the protests have still not come to an end, I am observing them from the sidelines. This time they are starting up among the medical students, of all things. Odd, that people's political perspective is completely irrelevant. For this reason I expected little from the well-meaning little leftist groups (including the SDS) and much from spontaneity. Even if Lenin, Glucksmann, and other strategists have long since disproved it.

Is it all right with you if I come to Germany in the last week of October? By then the dissertation will be perhaps not finished but, I hope, far enough along that it can look out for itself.

I am looking forward to you very much.

Warm regards to both of you,

your Elisabeth Lenk

beating with one wing: A reference to Breton's "castle," to which he alludes in the *Surrealist Manifesto*, where he writes that it beats with only one wing.

94

Frankfurt am Main, September 18
Kettenhofweg 123

Dear Elisabeth,

Many thanks for your letter.

I am very glad that you have no acute problems and assume that you plan to remain in France for the foreseeable future.

As far as your visit to Frankfurt is concerned, things are somewhat complicated by the fact that my own plans for October are by no means clear. What is certain is only that I will be in Austria for at least one week around October 20. Whether I then go for vacation to southern Steiermark for another two weeks or spend early October somewhere in Southern Germany is not yet certain—specifically because it does not depend only on me. Perfectly safe would be the first days of October, or November. I am sorry that I have to be so vague, but you know that it is not vanity on my part.

I am moving ahead quite well with the work, am preparing a thorough edit of the aesthetics book with the help of detailed annotations, and am treating myself like a not very gifted schoolboy. Perhaps this schoolboy will learn it after all.

Naturally I am extremely curious about your dissertation, but I would not like to press in the slightest.

> All warm regards, as always,
> your
> Teddie Adorno

95

Paris 6e, November 3, 1968
31, rue Dauphine

Dear Professor Adorno,

Thanks to your wife's friendly reminder, I have meanwhile been to see Professor Müller. Please thank her very much for that! Our conversation was very short but enjoyable. He started off by saying that he had never seen me before. I said that was no surprise, because I had never visited him before. Then he remembered that you had spoken to him about a "surrealism lady." On Breton, to my amazement, he immediately made an association with the *Poisson soluble* (Soluble fish), one of my favorite texts. As a result, I allowed myself to be carried away, although I had intended to talk only about sociology, with a comment that my main work consists in decoding Breton's language of images. He asked whether I had taken any courses in the department of Romance languages and literature. To which I replied (I thought and still think that the question was not meant so very seriously): not exactly, but I had been living in Paris for quite a long time. He: I am glad to hear that you live in Paris, but unfortunately that has nothing to do with philology.

Have I behaved very stupidly? I am, perhaps unjustifiably, quite optimistic.

I envy you the mysterious trip.

I am still writing, and what I would most like is to turn up when the first draft is completely finished. Is that all right with you?

Many warm regards to you two,

your Elisabeth Lenk

Professor Müller: He stands for one of the constant themes in this correspondence, namely, the difficulty that the outsider Adorno encountered within the department—and that consequently his students did too. His protest against departmentalization was quite enough in itself and was perceived by the specialists as a permanent breach of academic rules.

96

Frankfurt am Main, November 18, 1968
Kettenhofweg 123

Dear Elisabeth,

It is truly a pity that we missed each other, but I wash my hands in innocence, whatever that may be symbolically; I had told you ahead of time when I would most likely be absent from here. I am very sad, not only because I have missed you, but also because I have a somewhat uncanny feeling about your meeting with Herr Müller, whom, by the way,

I have not spoken to since. Had I been there, or if I had telephoned him beforehand, I would have been able to guide things in such a way that he would not have spouted any nonsense about philology. But I think I can still direct him to some extent, although at the moment, precisely on account of the student protests, he is out of control in a sense that is not very pleasing to me.

My trip, by the way, was not at all mysterious—I was in Vienna for the so-called vernissage of my book on Alban Berg—written against great resistance—then in Graz, where I gave a lecture aimed at the situation surrounding the Vienna Opera, and then with my female friend in Munich. Everything was very lovely, but I can scarcely afford to be away from my book for so long now. I am making quite good progress with the editing, it is true, but much more slowly than I had imagined. It seems virtually impossible to me that it should appear already in 1969; instead I will toss Unseld something else—something shorter.

Today Roditi telephoned me and wanted to make a date, but I simply couldn't do it timewise. As you probably know, he is very well informed about surrealism, from old times, and without exaggerating his value I could imagine that you would gain something from a meeting with him. You need fear no advances, on Proustian grounds.

When will you be here again, then? Please let us arrange something in good time, so we don't miss each other. No Royaumont plans have surfaced that I am aware of, and thus I don't really know when I will show up in Paris. It would be more certain here. How curious I am about your dissertation I need not tell you, but I am even more interested in you yourself.

All love, as always,
your
Teddie Adorno

Roditi: Edouard Roditi (1910–1992) was a surrealist author, poet, and translator. He published the first surealist manifesto in English, "The New Reality" (*The Oxford Outlook*, 10, June, 1929), and wrote extensively on surrealist and modernist artists.—Ed.

97

Paris, July 9, 1969
31, rue Dauphine

Dear Professor Adorno,

It seems very strange to me to send a manuscript out into the world without your having seen it. You see that I am only half emancipated and very curious as to what you will say about the little text.

The nomadic life in Italy was very lovely, but in the supposedly gleaming cities—Venice, Florence, etc.—it poured rain.

With many good wishes for your vacation!

Your Elisabeth Lenk

the little text: "Sinn und Sinnlichkeit" (Sense and Sensibility), the afterword to the German edition of *Paysan de Paris (Paris Peasant)* by Louis Aragon, which I included in typescript. It is reprinted in Elisabeth Lenk, *Kritische Phantasie* (Critical imagination). A translation of the essay is included in this volume.

98

Frankfurt am Main, July 18, 1969
Kettenhofweg 123

Dear Elisabeth,

A thousand thanks for your lines and the manuscript. That I have meanwhile blown fanfares for you with Rogner publishers is probably already known to you; I hope that I will succeed in advertising the *Paysan de Paris* in *Der Spiegel*. Literarily, your introduction is a masterpiece, of a simultaneous density and lightness that only the greatest talent is able to combine. The text goes right to the heart of the things about which Benjamin and I had the most intensive conversations over many years. You can imagine how much your text moved me. Some things in it—the way cities, precisely in connection with erotic experience, start, with a shock, to become allegorical—reminded me of my own experiences in a way that was again shocking; the location, it is true, was San Francisco and not Paris. Traces can be found in the third part of *Minima Moralia*.

If I had anything critical to say, it would have to do with the somewhat dogmatic adoption of the theses about the obsolescence of modernity and, implicitly, of art itself. These things will be the subject of a whole chapter in my *work of progress [sic]*, whose second draft is now complete, so that in September I can finally start work on the last, final version. Perhaps a couple of sentences could be added in which the reason for the aging of surrealism itself is identified somewhat less summarily, and above all more sharply delineated from Aragon's own apologetic conversion to the Commuist Party. I must confess to you that I am as little persuaded of the decline of the arts today as I was during the surrealist heyday. It was surely forty-five years ago that I came up with the title "Falscher Untergang der Regenschirme" (Erroneous disappearance of the umbrellas) for an essay by Kracauer. It seems to me as if art were such an umbrella.

Hopefully we can talk soon about all that. On Tuesday we are leaving for Zermatt; at the end of August I will be back, then go for a few days to Venice, but after September 10 or thereabouts I will move from Frankfurt as little as possible in order to be able to devote all energies to the book. On the whole, I am feeling much better than I would have hoped only a few weeks ago.

Stichworte is now almost finished in the first corrected galleys. It is going to be an odd little book.

The address in Zermatt, once again, is Hotel Bristol. Let me hear from you. Most warmly, as always,

Your
Teddie Adorno

I have . . . blown fanfares for you: Adorno enclosed these "fanfares" in the form of a letter to Herr Rogner. As the letter reveals, he was involved in negotiations with Rogner & Bernhard publishers about the "film music book," *Komposition für den Film* (Composing for the cinema), which he wrote together with Hanns Eister and which appeared in 1969. At the same time, he points out that he has advocated with Suhrkamp for years on behalf of the *Paysan*.

your introduction: See note to Letter 97.

in the third part of Minima Moralia: See, for example, aphorism 104, "Golden Gate."

work of progress: English in original.—Ed.
Stichworte: Keywords. See note to Letter 1.

99

Dear Professor Adorno,

Many thanks for your letter! I am very happy to hear your praise. You know how much your opinion matters to me.

By no means do I have a new manifesto to add to the already stereotypical ones on the decline of art; instead I wanted to defend the "obsolete" Aragon against the Communist one. Politics is not meant to be presented as the inheritor of art. What we have, rather, is a parallel, that corresponding to Aragon's surrealist phase there was an instinctive anarchism: the rejection of every police state, including the socialist one. That Aragon's path to realism, viewed artistically, was a step backward— the return of the classically French style, of Alexandrines, and, even worse, a descent into the false simplicity and sentimentality of the *chanson*—about this there can be no doubt!

Moreover, in the new phase in which he sacrificed art to politics, in politics a rigid conservatism also makes itself felt. To this extent, my talk of the aging of surrealism, the regression of youth, hence also my reference to Habermas, was meant more ironically.

This letter is an incomplete draft, without a date or a signature. I received the news of Adorno's death before completing it.

100

Paris 6e, August 8, 1969
31, rue Dauphine

I am still quite numb from the news. As you know, I had been toying with the idea of coming to Frankfurt for the coming semester. But without Adorno Germany seems sad and lacking in brilliance. My first feeling is that I, who owe my intellectual existence to Adorno, am much more emotionally affected. The simultaneously personal and objective, unique relationship in which the most difficult problems became easy, is lost to me.

Like many others, certainly, I experience it as especially painful that the *Aesthetics* has now remained a fragment. The thought that in the hysterical shouting about the decline of art Adorno's voice is no longer heard is unbearable to me. I would gladly do whatever is in my power to contribute.

Please accept, dear Frau Adorno, my sympathy and sadness at a moment when for all those who love and revere Adorno the world has become somewhat smaller.

Your Elisabeth Lenk

Paris 6e: *6e* added in Gretel Adorno's handwriting.

101

Frankfurt, August 1969

Dear Elisabeth,

Perhaps the moment will come in which I need your help with the *Aesthetics*; then I shall certainly turn to you. One could publish it as a work in progress, since the third edit is lacking.

What plans do you have now, and how are things going with your dissertation?

Always,
your Gretel Adorno

Card, handwritten, with a printed message on the back: "To all those who have expressed to me their sympathy on the death of Theodor W. Adorno, my warmest thanks."

Sense and Sensibility:
Afterword to Louis Aragon's *Paris Peasant*

Elisabeth Lenk

S URREALISM IS A LATECOMER. It has become obsolete, like modernism, as whose tail end it wanted to be perceived. While the surrealist paintings are still passed around like fetishes, the publication of a work of literature may seem more like an exhumation. Aragon himself has let Marxist grass grow over his *Paris Peasant*.[1] But history sometimes moves in a crabwalk. Among young people, who to the dismay of their critics are regressing,[2] there are symptoms that hark back to surrealism. The formula for this, if one wanted to find one, would be the systematic de-civilizing of culture. At first, a tendency of this kind was noticeable only indirectly, in art. But imagination, which takes the stage in *Paris Peasant* as an allegorical figure, has foretold its possible social consequences: the intellect will fall into disuse. "The Faculties will be deserted, the laboratories closed down."[3]

In *Paris Peasant*, poetic production and philosophical reflection inform each other. The principle of their alternation is distraction. Yet their relation to each other is not arbitrary. Reflective passages are pursued to the point of allegory, while the narrative passages, which range from sudden insights to novelistic fragments and factual reports, are way stations for thoughts that are "inscribed with figures."[4] The mixture proves to be thoroughly artificial. The geographer of myth surrounds and intersperses his two landscapes with commentaries. This introductory and accompanying material is not merely external.

To found his modern mythology, Aragon begins at the beginning, with Descartes. He discovers that without evidence not only can there be no truth, there can be no error either. Truth and error are seen as equivalent and hence indifferent. From now on, the content of thinking is to be measured solely by its effect. This effect, an indicator of the fact that thought is encountering its own projections, Aragon calls a *frisson,* or shudder. Thought, denuded of its logical function, confronts the object immediately. The frisson can only occur where thought runs up against its limit, in sensual perception. But perception, as Aragon sees it, is neither simple nor positive; it is surreal perception. The senses think. They store objects, form images, add something to their objects. Sensual-figurative thought is thought that is actually productive. It does not merely reflect what is given, but itself creates ideal facts.[5] In the struggle among our faculties, intelligence is forced into retirement. Everything is image, or memory in the image. Imagination, the "madwoman in the attic," has been sitting in the house of Western philosophy ever since Plato's *Phaedo* (to which Aragon discretely refers). This has endowed her with many strange features. At once a physician and the servile factotum charged with transporting the sensual material, she—or rather he, the incorruptible master with the beard of the Hapsburgs—becomes an absolute monarch. "And for man there awaits discovery of the particular image that is capable of annihilating the entire Universe."[6] Aragon deploys the concept of modernity as a way of giving an objective definition to the field in which ideal facts, the ones that cause a frisson, are inscribed. This is the field of the indifferent (of the *superflua,* Augustine would have said, as distinguished from the *utilia* and the *perniciosa*). Freud observed that dream thoughts often seize on words and incidents that seemed insignificant during the day; that suppressed desires show up with remarkable frequency in actions, incidents, or words that do not warrant any particular significance. These "recent and indifferent elements," he writes in *Interpretation of Dreams,* figure "as substitutes for the most ancient of all the dream thoughts."[7] Modern poetry, like dreams, loves to dissimulate. Through the back door of the indifferent, a mythical moment sneaks into the rationalized world. Benjamin, who incorporated motifs from modern French lyric poetry into his thought, said of the nineteenth century "that it is precisely in this century, the most parched and imagination-starved, that the collective dream energy of a society has taken refuge with redoubled vehemence in the mute impenetrable nebula of fashion, where the understanding cannot follow."[8]

Aragon's definition of modernism is indebted to Baudelaire, Rimbaud, and Apollinaire. For him, as well, the ephemeral[9] is modern. Modern is the epitome of everything the cultivated bourgeois philistine rejects as tasteless.[10] Modern, finally, is the element of surprise that attaches to chance.[11]

In synthesizing all the individual motifs of the modern, Aragon goes a step further. No longer does the modern consist only of things that assert their novelty in opposition to the old, or that, as ephemera, elude the comprehension of the classically minded. It is whatever emerges when a sensuality that has become completely subjective comes in contact with the world.

What Aragon seeks to uncover in everything specifically modern is an objective process: the concretization of ideas. The frisson that takes the place of surprise is not evidence of a psychic state; instead, like evidence itself, it is an index of reality. Poetry stretches beyond its own limits, toward myth. Pan, "this thrill-exciting being,"[12] returns, and with him the feeling for nature that Hegel, in his *Philosophy of History*, described as that of the Greeks. It is not only in the frisson, shudder, or shiver that Aragon's modern mythology coincides with Hegel's definition, but in its concept of nature as well. "The Natural holds its place in their minds only after undergoing some transformation by Spirit—not immediately," says Hegel. "Man regards Nature only as an excitement to his faculties, and only the Spiritual which he has evolved from it can have any influence over him."[13] Aragon rediscovers this type of pagan nature in the metropolis. He mounts a polemic against the monotheistic, Christian concept of nature, which reserves the realm of the objective for a nature that is untouched by man and reduces everything else to a mere artifact. Our nature is the city. The countryside is denuded of gods. The peasants, one-time creators of myth, have moved their fields to Paris.

Paris Peasant is nothing less than the attempt to show where, in the interstices of the contemporary world, mythical elements reside. Aragon does not claim to be creating myths himself; he merely describes the mental and physical spaces on which a modern mythology is virtually fixated.

The "Passage de l'Opéra" that Aragon described in 1924 no longer exists. The greedy Boulevard Haussmann has devoured this refuge for the dreams of a world metropolis. The changes "modify the ways of thought of a whole district, perhaps of a whole world."[14] The Surrealists had an instinct for places where social storms were brewing. These are the "strategic points"[15] of a city, where historical events can be observed *in statu nascendi*. The researcher has to make haste, for the law of modern myths is acceleration. In "Passage de l'Opéra," Aragon describes a constellation: here love, commerce, and death have forged a unique alliance. The former glitter of bourgeois culture, as it streamed out from the opera, has retreated to the arcade, where it flits about like a will-o'-the-wisp. The microcosm of the arcade, with its hairdressers, tailors, its bordello and honky-tonk theater, is the realm of involuntary poetry. Here, as in the opera, semblance is produced, but it no longer serves to ennoble. This theater is modern in the truest sense of the word. The members of the audience are actors, the street has become a stage on which a dying world gives its final performance.

The central location of Aragon's surreal mythology inspired Benjamin's *One-Way Street* and his *Arcades Project*. The modern charm of *One-Way Street* lies in the fact that in it thought is constantly refracted by things that are exterior, unimportant, ephemeral. Benjamin seeks the sense of what is happening *at this very moment* neither in himself nor in the external world, but at the spot where the two worlds intersect. The bits of dreams that float up and the things that strike the eye work together to pave a pathway to cognition. At the same time, Benjamin's philosophical tradition does not permit any surrealistically carefree oscillation between dreaming and waking. The street is one-way. In the *Arcades Project,* he explicitly distances himself from Aragon: "Whereas Aragon persists within the realm of dream, here the concern is to find the constellation of awakening."[16]

Aragon is intrigued by the moment in time when the arcade has already been condemned to demolition. The love with which he describes the window displays and impotent complaints of the shop owners, emphasizes the names of the hairdresser's seven employees with CAPITAL LETTERS, and even inserts a copy of the drinks menu of the Café Certa into his book as the document of a long-lost era has something necrophiliac about it. Literary convention would have it that novelists have the gift of bringing the dead back to life or rescuing the disappearing. In Aragon, we find something more like the reverse transaction. He consigns an actually living world of boutique owners, cashiers, bartenders, call girls, and down-at-the-heel dandies, all stubbornly clinging to life, to an early coffin. He himself does not feel all that well in the performance of his macabre task: "I feel the ground tremble beneath me. . . . Everything signifies havoc. Everything is crumbling under my gaze."[17] As he writes, the arcade is transformed into a *nature morte,* a still life.[18] And as if it had been conceived from the first as its own death mask, as if it were summing itself up in the greenish light that in the evening hours turns walking sticks into algae, Aragon makes god himself, not the Christian God, but the thousand-armed god of the city, responsible for this state of affairs. "It looks rather as though for God the world simply provides the occasion for a few attempts at still lifes.

He has two or three little stage props which he uses assiduously: the absurd, the bazaar, the banal . . . impossible to get him to change his script."[19]

Aragon, who anticipates the end of the arcade, the victory of the big department stores, banks, and companies, emerges from it onto the big boulevards. Business and pleasure, which in the half-light of the glass-covered passage had formed an apparent unity, break apart. Where consciousness no longer finds its interest piqued, its object inspires a feeling of unending boredom. "Boredom watches people pass by on the street. He goes into a café: he comes out of it. He goes to a girl's place: he leaves her."[20] The soul contracts. Its mirror is the tiny private garden. "Sheepish fellows, if you have not abandoned all claim to human dignity already, the hour of your death is upon you, for you are too fond of sowing seeds of discord, of planting suspicion in people's minds, of pruning your opinions."[21] At the end of his walk through the garden plots, from which his own boredom grins sardonically out at him, the fata morgana of the group appears to him. To her he flees, to escape the idea of suicide.[22]

Freud describes the case of a young man whose psychotic symptom took the form of the exclamation "Nature! Nature!" Something of this state of excitement characterizes the bizarre excursion to Buttes-Chaumont. It is nighttime. Three friends, each alone with his boredom, follow a sudden impulse, and instead of going to a bar they go to nature, as it blooms on the metropolitan garbage heap. (It is well known that the Buttes Chaumont owe their creation, not least, to public garbage removal.) The night is no night of magical romance. It is the neutral darkness of the metropolis, sprinkled with brilliant vices in place of stars. The three strollers do not talk to one other. Each one engages in a monologue. Their complicity consists only in the fact that each of them attaches an inexplicable expectation to the indifferent location. The location, for its part, does not respond but only offers itself up. Aragon patiently deciphers the hieroglyphics of their expectation and finds nothing but the banal plan of the park, which he reproduces at great length in its geographical coordinates and architectonic details. "Nothing will have taken place but the place."[23]

The new feeling for nature that lends the chapter its title does not originate with the park. Aragon is having some fun at the expense of his readers. "They have followed me, the idiots."[24] For as long as it has existed, philosophy has viewed nature as the realm of the unconscious, in opposition to the conscious I. In modernism, the conscious I weakens, and it is the unconscious, as a psychological unconscious, that becomes the counterbalance to external nature. From this, Aragon draws his surrealist conclusion: nature communicates with itself over the heads of mankind. This does not mean that the I is subjugated, once again, to all-powerful, blind fate. The I grows beyond the bounds of individuality. In the phenomenon that the surrealists called automatism, the unconscious, which up until then has been cut off from expression, usurps control of language. It does not sink back into an archaic collective unconscious in the manner of Jung, but expresses itself at the level of the "current state of the artistic forces of production." From the intercommunication of a multitude of unconsciousnesses, surrealist dialogue is born. It differs from prosaic communication in that it represents not the search for a common language, but the pleasure that results from the separate, finally communicable awareness of unbridgeable difference.[25] The lukewarm sense of togetherness that is the unacknowledged precondition of even casual dialogue is cut off. The energies that this liberates within the group—here the group of surrealists—turn into aggression and coldness. The three men's walk in the park has more in common with Kafka's "An Excursion into the Mountains" than with a Boy Scout outing.[26]

Anticipating Dalí's critical paranoia, Aragon projects the newly acquired insight into the nature of the unconscious onto the unconscious of external nature. Nature once again takes on human traits. The old myth of nature returns as a chain-rattling ghost that, to top it all off, is wearing a pince-nez. On the Surrealist Judgment Day, it will appear in the form of the "concrete woman."

One could imagine an expanded version of *Paris Peasant* as a kind of Baedecker to the secrets of Paris.[27] Aragon leads and seduces in the name of imagination. His imagination is sovereign. It tends to create a constant stream of false perspectives and then leave the perplexed reader standing in front of a wall. Such rude awakenings are intentional.

That poetry takes its nourishment from images is nothing new. But the imagination had remained under the sway of a law that was alien to it and was oriented to taste. Now, for the first time, the images become autonomous. They become gods, in the pagan sense of the word. Ideas, scarcely hatched, become petrified. They populate the city as statues. The abstract becomes sensually perceptible. The most insignificant notion can accost the passerby like a stone giant. Wherever the spark of the unconscious jumps over to perception, the merely descriptive takes on suggestive power. Burgeoning details obscure essence. Thought, which wants to live in relationships, is paralyzed. In his description of the Café Certa, Aragon omits not a single chair, not a flowerpot. Precisely in his surrealist phase, he is a thoroughgoing naturalist. Here naturalism, whose intent had been to take seriously the description of milieu, flips over into its opposite; it becomes a means of de-realization.

Georg Lukács sensed the threat that naturalism posed for realism. True, he writes, naturalism also mirrors reality, but it lacks all "hierarchy" of significance in the selection of the facts to be depicted. [28] Details are "reduced to the level of mere particularity." Realism, by contrast, is characterized by its perspective, which "enables the artist to choose between the important and the superficial, the crucial and the episodic."[29] Here the detail is no longer a particularity that can be arbitrarily replaced; it is given meaning by perspective. It becomes *typical*. Lukács quite correctly recognized Walter Benjamin as his theoretical adversary on this question. For Benjamin, the modernity of Baroque allegory lay in the way it freed the details from their duty to mean something and reproduced them as naked, forsaken by god and meaning. The detail gains its sensual power precisely from the fact that it ceases to be typical of a preexisting whole—Lukács admits this himself. But he attempts to avoid the implications of this suggestion; he accuses all art that is characterized by this kind of autonomy of detail of being naturalistic. For him, accordingly, naturalism is not just the type of writing that literary historians have designated as such; all avant-garde art tends in this direction, from the first, milieu-oriented naturalism to impressionism, symbolism, and surrealism.[30]

In his later novels, Aragon applied the recipe of socialist realism. Even the arcade is affected by the new perspective. It turns up again in *Residential Quarter* under the title "Arcades Club."[31] But now its mask has been torn off. The arcade is no longer anything but a site of capitalist decay, replete with loitering gamblers, international speculators, and criminals. In response, the "healthy proletarian" Armand says, "Here France ends." Aragon abandons naturalism. Of the once powerful imagination that set out to demolish reality there remains only the slightly bland pleasure of spinning a good yarn. Reading *Paris Peasant* with the consciousness of a subsequent "avant-garde," one might already glimpse the realist worm in the golden apple of the imagination. With the surrealists, Aragon shared a horror of novels, which they all saw as the refuge of spiritual kitchen gardeners. And yet from childhood on—as he later confessed—he was irresistibly drawn to the novel. [32] In *Paris Peasant,* he approaches it via the technique of montage. The book swarms with beginnings of novels that seem to have been suffocated at birth. No sooner does Aragon launch into a narrative than he suddenly stops short and calls himself back to surrealist order. He is secretly laughing—Rameau's grand-nephew[33]—at the censor and at himself. Someone calls out to him with the insistence of capital letters: "LOUIS." Another time, he finds Conscience (or is it Death?) waiting for him like a housewife with her soup, while he tramps around without a care in the world. The imagination is not allowed to say everything it wants to. "Time to settle up," one seems to hear Breton saying, "back to business."

The excursion into nature remains a fragment. The search for images breaks off, the modernist mixture of word and landscape grows flat. "Lazarus will never leave his tomb. *He never left his tomb.*"[34] The intoxication induced by the group mechanism dissipates.[35] What remains is a profound nihilism. What grips him now is now neither the gentle melancholy of the pessimist nor the elegant *languers* of the doubter, but despair. It condenses in the parable of the acephalous. The uncanny line between the body and the head, which first appeared in Mallarmé's "Hérodiade" as the principle and curse of modern poetry, becomes visible. The peasant of Paris is not a whole human being, but a monster whose extremities have become independent of each other. Body and head each posit the other as existing alongside itself; each seeks to achieve a self-sufficient indifference. Thus, sense and sensuality appear twice, each time under a different sign.[36] Aragon's abstruse parable summarizes this process. The head's wanderings prove to be inconsistent in its juxtaposition with reality. Dreaming passivity alone cannot abolish the gravity of the real. Only a passionate decision, one that incorporates waking consciousness as well, can make the separation definitive. Only now, after dream has become a principle of action, does the head gain the bodily concreteness for which it longs. Surreality—in Benjamin's words a "profane epiphany"—becomes possible. Liberated from all conventional relationships, individuality relates directly to absolute nature. In it, it loves its own diaphanous corporeality. "The limbs, in the throes of an incomprehensible gesture, grew rigid. And the man was no longer anything but a sign among the constellations."[37]

Aragon represents the relationship of poetry to its object, of the word-soul to the image-form, as an erotic one. The stages of poetic cognition correspond to the stages of the erotic. In the world of the arcades, the erotic is a fleeting intoxication of the senses. It is ignited by the glitter of the displays in the shop windows, by makeup, by semblance. In *Anicet,* this becomes even more evident than in *Paris Peasant.* The youthful protagonist is seduced by the perfume salesgirl Lulu into doing a wild cancan, and in the end they make love in full view of the public. Not until Anicet awakens from his intoxication does he realize that the girl he thought was sixteen is a heavily made-up ruin of a woman.[38] For the last time, he has allowed himself to be swept away by the perfume that at one time, in Baudelaire's poetry, was exuded by prostitutes. In *Paris Peasant,* he has lost this kind of naïveté. The ruin is described as a ruin, the arcade as a glass coffin.

Out of the decaying architecture of the nineteenth century, whose entire beauty consisted in reflection, emerges—displaced into the park—a new figure of poetry: poetry of the unconscious. Again, it is incarnated in a woman, whose body is the universe.[39] She no longer merely intoxicates the senses but awakens a crippled nature: passions that initially appear only in negative form, as aggression, as pleasure in criminality. It is the night side of the city, the goddess of violent death.[40]

The wanderings are meant to come to an end; the inconstant imagination is meant to be reduced to its concept. In "The Peasant's Dream," Aragon, once again following in the footsteps of Descartes, tries to find his primal certainty. From chattering, schoolmasterly syllogisms such as "Disorder is unthinkable—the unthinkable is the limit of imagination— therefore God is disorder," a metaphysics springs up; it is unclear how. It is a metaphysics of the concrete. Whereas Aragon had once declared that images were not, in themselves, the concrete but were, instead, that in which the concrete is reflected, "the possible consciousness, the greatest possible consciousness of the concrete";[41] now he asserts that he has found immediate access to the concrete. The route there is not via logic, nor is it via the detour through poetry: it is through love. Love is not a poetic search, but the presence of the concrete. It is stylized as an absolute situation in which poetry no longer merely imagines its object but touches it. Whereas the erotic had previously only referred allegorically to poetry, here all boundaries blur. The hymn to love, which is meant to be the *summum* of the concrete, remains empty and abstract.

Not long after the appearance of *Paris Peasant,* in the essay "Introduction to 1930," Aragon came to terms with his own concept of modernity, which is saturated with reminiscences.[42] The era in which a poet's greatest ambition was to compete with perfume labels,[43] when Baby Cadum neglected its duty to sell soap and haunted the heads of poets,[44] when the inscription "Texaco motor oil"[45] wrote itself, hieroglyphic-like, into poetry—is over. The surprise effect of headlines, of "readymade" and splendidly meaningless advertising slogans, is worn out. Things that were once expressions of protest are now savored as modern art by a public whose senses have become dulled. "In the year 1929, the greatest surprise in the world, if only it had been a surprise, would not have surprised us: the snobs are among us."[46] What is modern today? asks Aragon. And then he gives a truly surprising answer: The symbol to which "today" turns its attention, the newest of the new, in which the archaic aspect of society is also revealed, is the policeman. "I went to the movies, I walked the streets, I have read the newspapers of my contemporaries. In all that I saw only the signs of new violence. The modern, nowadays, no longer belongs to the poets. It belongs to the cops. The transformation is occurring everywhere: the poster becomes a flaming Eiffel Tower with the word Citroen; at the movies, America's unlimited possibilities are at the service of an apotheosis of the police; in the street no one can feel secure anymore, for the official bullies carry weapons; the chief of police pokes his face into every column of the newspaper. Everywhere the ghost of repression is haunting us."[47] From the vantage point of 1969, there is probably no more prophetic text by Aragon, a last document of what his official biographer Garaudy called his idealistic-individualistic phase.

Introduction to the German Edition of Charles Fourier's *The Theory of the Four Movements and the General Destinies*

Elisabeth Lenk

While sociology, with a self-important mien and a slightly overstated emphasis, may pronounce that it has now reached maturity, I don't see with what justification it stamps works like yours as inconsistent and ridiculous—works in which a boldness that as yet knows no limits serves true humanity.

—André Breton, *Ode to Charles Fourier*

The Sunday Sociologist

For the first time, a central text of Fourier's is available in a complete edition in German translation.[1] It reveals a work of whose richness the previously available schoolmasterly "selections" gave no sense. Fourier's work drew contradictory reactions from his contemporaries. He was, by turns, accused of being fantastical, celebrated as a genius and inventor, and ridiculed as a petit-bourgeois utopian. Even today, precisely categorizing his theory—this tissue of realistic observation, fantasy, and calculation—is awkward. Should we relegate Fourier's books, like many a work that we decline to take seriously, to so-called belles letters? This would seem to be supported by the fact that it was writers and poets like Stendahl, Sainte-Beuve, and Balzac who first publicly recognized him, and that today, once again, it is a poet, André Breton, who with his "Ode to Charles Fourier" has brought him to the attention of postwar France. But if the works of Charles Fourier were of "only" literary value, how should we explain the fact that academic-analytic thinkers like Marx and Engels took him quite seriously—Marx ranks him among the ancestors of scientific socialism, and Engels writes that Fourier applies dialectics with the same mastery as Hegel?

In his book *Utopia and Utopias,* sociologist Raymond Ruyer[2] compares Fourier's contribution to the social sciences with customs officer Émil Rousseau's contribution to painting. Like Rousseau, who was an outsider and part-time painter, Fourier, Ruyer says, was a *sociologue du dimanche*—a Sunday sociologist. Like Rousseau, Fourier was an autodidact for whom the necessity of his unfamiliarity with academic techniques became a virtue that helped him explode their limitations. The genius of both men lies in a naïveté that elicited equal measures of derision and admiration from the members of the guild. In academic circles, including those of the Marxists, one often encounters a tendency to neutralize the clashing emotions, the mixture of sarcasm and admiration that overcomes the reader of a Fourier text, by splitting him into a rational, observant, sharply critical thinker, on one hand, and an abstruse one on the other. But this very tendency forecloses insight into the fundamental structure of Fourier's thought, in which boundless optimism and an incorruptibly critical eye are fused in a dialectical unity. Fourier's often-derided remarks about stars, comma rules, or cabbage heads, no less than his insights into social situations, obey a *single* inner logic. Everything in this system springs from one principle: the claim that human happiness is not only possible but is the providential destiny of man according to the plan of creation. "The passions are proportional to the destinies" is the sibylline sentence in which Fourier summarizes his thought.[3] This, so to speak, is the law of identity in practical form. As, in identity philosophy, the dichotomy of subject and object is transcended in absolute unity, so, for Fourier, the highest happiness is the bliss of passion fulfilled. Happiness, in its unity, takes the subjective form of *attractions,* which here must be translated as passions, and the objective form of destiny. Fourier's principle, based on this correspondence of attraction and destiny, may be loosely described as follows: A passionate desire cannot be directed at something that is in principle unachievable. Every passionate desire is, from its inception, destined to be fulfilled.

Fourier maintains—and in this he is entirely a child of the eighteenth century—that the infinitely large universe is constructed to support the happiness of tiny humanity. This pronouncement, which is contradicted by a millennium's worth of evidence, seems absurd today. But it contains an unfathomably humoristic moment insofar as the craziness of placing human happiness at the center of the universe is the unacknowledged craziness of all human beings, including those who greet Fourier's methodical madness with a tolerant smile. Fourier, consequently, has asked the opposite question, whether it is not precisely the others who are crazy—all those people who are always immediately prepared to act as an advocate for the necessities that are inimical to happiness and who, all the same, never stop striving for the fulfillment of their wishes. Isn't their rational, grown-up "insight into necessity" mere hypocrisy, as absurd as would be a "love of self-loathing"?[4]

Fourier's system is the boldness of demanding the fulfillment of human wishes, not just from human society but from the universe and ultimately from God himself. Although it may be difficult to follow Fourier's explanations with the seriousness and naïveté that undoubtedly inspired their author, the reader who will profit from their study is the one whose experience resembles the reaction of one of Fourier's first reviewers, who wrote in the *Mercure de France* on January 9, 1830, that while reading Fourier's book, which had just appeared, he had doubted his own reason at least as much as Fourier's.[5]

Unrequited Love of Praxis

The Theory of the Four Movements, published in 1808 at its author's expense, is a first book by an unknown writer who claims to be an inventor endowed with genius. Fourier believes that he has rediscovered the secret of social happiness, which has been lost over the centuries. It lies in the ordering of human community by associations, or, as he says, by "series" founded on passionate attraction.[6] He calls this the discovery of the "social compass" and writes, "This name is extremely appropriate for the *progressive series* because this simple operation resolves all conceivable problems of social happiness, and is enough on its own to guide human politics through the labyrinth of the passions, just as a compass needle is enough on its own to guide ships through the darkness of storms and the vastness of the seas."[7] He himself feels that he has been chosen by God to redeem humanity. "It is a shop-sergeant who is going to confound all the voluminous writings of the politicians and moralists, the shameful products of ancient and modern quackery. And this is not the first time that God has made use of the humble to put down the proud and mighty, nor the first time that he has chosen the most obscure man to bring the most important message to the world."[8]

The theory of the four movements, which already contains all the elements of Fourierist thought, is borne along by the momentum of his conviction that contemporaries will receive the new discovery with enthusiasm and will put it into practice without delay. The book is written with a practical intent. Fourier calls it a "prospectus," or proposal, which is intended to lead to the founding of a new venture—a venture, however, that differs from all previous foundings inasmuch as it will introduce a new phase of civilization: social harmony. He invites subscriptions and does not tire of providing proofs of the profitability of the planned attempt, which, moreover, will guarantee a place in posterity for those individuals who are courageous enough to finance it. The organization that is to be founded is a phalanstery *(phalanstère)*, which consists of 1,600 to 1,800 individuals of all classes, generations, and character types and is based primarily on agriculture and domestic work but in its concrete form is more like a *cité future*. Fourier, with characteristic pedantry, drafts a detailed plan for the phalanstery he wants to found, from the 2,300 hectares that the experimental canton is to occupy, to the architectural details of the buildings that are needed for the life of the *harmoniens*, their celebrations, labors, pleasures in love, and gastronomy. They are meant to be linked by glass-roofed, gallery-like streets, a construction that recalls the Paris passages that a hundred years later would enter into the mythology of modernism. Fourier believes that the completed phalanstery will emit such powers of attraction that within a few years there will be a worldwide expansion of the principle of passionate series. Social metamorphosis can proceed without a single violent blow having to be struck. Kings, clerics, brutes, capitalists, traders, and criminals, with all their vices, will all fit harmoniously into the new order. Even bloodthirsty Nero, without any need to change his nature, would have become a useful member of the "harmony," namely, the best of all possible butchers.

Fourier is so possessed by the idea of an immediate realization of his plan that in this, his first book, he neglects to include a systematic description of his thoughts. The *Theory of the Four Movements* appeals not to reason, but to readers' passions; it offers diverse examples, each calculated to appeal to a different type of reader. Readers who thirst for knowledge receive an excerpt from the theory; for those who are sensual and interested in practical consequences, there are descriptions of the advantages of the new order for their private life; and finally, there is a third section aimed at virtual critics of his theory, whose combative instincts are meant to be absorbed by diverting their attention to a more worthwhile object: the critique of civilization. He also attempts to ensnare them for his plan with the prospect of a prestige similar to that enjoyed by today's sociologists. The degree to which Fourier relied on practical experiment as the sole possible verification of his theory is demonstrated by a detail from his life that is mentioned by his biographer Charles Pellarin. Fourier, who spent his whole life working as the low-level employee of a merchant, made it a rule during his last decade to return home every day at the stroke of noon. This was the hour that he had advertised in his publications for meeting "the rich man who might want to entrust to him a million" for an experiment with the passionate series, as Pellarin reports.[9] The inventor appeared every day at the appointed hour, but the rich man never showed up. Only once in Fourier's lifetime was an attempt made to set up a phalanstery. The parliamentarian Baudet-Dulary founded a stock company for this purpose and, together with the Devay brothers, made available a piece of property in Condé-sur-Vègres. But during the preparatory period it became clear that the funds were insufficient to support the planned venture. The attempt was broken off, to Fourier's boundless disappointment, before it had arrived at the decisive stage of introducing the principle of passionate series.

Fourier's failure at the practice toward which his thought constantly strove is more than a mere misfortune. As if his ideas had thorns, they resist all immediate practical application, perhaps precisely because they want to be more than mere ideas. From the perspective of the future harmonious order, in which Fourier believed as firmly as in his own existence, he derived what he called "absolute separation" from his time. The methodological principle of absolute separation is then transformed, for him, into a satirical gaze that turns millennia of culture into mere farce. Fourier, who—not without coquetry—calls himself an uncultivated person, heaps scorn on the concept of civilization, the concept that for his contemporaries denotes "triumph and . . . the most elevated development of reason." In this, he resembles Jean-Jacques Rousseau.[10]

"Where does one see reason, justice, and truth flourishing?" he quips. "In the books, for I see nowhere else where one could find them. Our scientific progress can be reduced to creating wisdom and happiness in theory, but in practice corruption and unhappiness."[11] The arrogant speechifiers of civilization, who preach its unlimited perfectibility—"perfectibilarians," as he calls them—have not lessened the sufferings of the majority, but only pasted them over with the mask of progress. Their 400,000 volumes, preaching the love of "gentle and pure morality"[12] to deaf ears, have contributed nothing to the happiness of mankind. The illustrious works, from Plato and Seneca to the French Enlightenment—from whose number he excepts Voltaire and Rousseau as "aspirants" who have not yet been entirely spoiled for the truth—can serve no better purpose in the new order than, after being properly glossed, to amuse the lovers of "social and burlesque archaeology."

As for philosophy and its stillborn child economics, as for the market with its twenty-four types and subtypes of bankruptcy, as for the bourgeois customs surrounding love—all these things inspire in Fourier a laughter that is already the liberated laughter of someone who has made his escape from the old world.

Against the barrenness of pure philosophy, Fourier does not mobilize the world of facts in the manner of positivism. His criticism is more basic. He boils it down, with a self-confidence that can only be called philosophical, to the formulas of "absolute distance" and "absolute doubt." If "absolute distance" characterizes the distance that separates him, the seer of a new order, from his time and its views, his notion of "absolute doubt," in an act that reenacts the Cartesian method, also proclaims the necessity of deriving all theory from first principles. These two methodological principles of the philosopher contradict the pragmatism of the social reformer at every step, for from them there follows not only the uncompromising critique of the present but also the conclusion that the transition to the new world must be not gradual but a qualitative leap. When Fourier, occasionally, condescends to point to concrete, transitional solutions that coincide with the short-term perspectives of the citizen, for example, the founding of a communal bank, which he incorporates under the catchword "guaranteeism," he does so only halfheartedly and with a yawn that the reader cannot help noticing.[13] Basically, he is convinced that these kinds of isolated reforms are a patchwork, and that the new, in trying to make itself commensurable with the old, will lose its irresistible power of attraction. This very power to fascinate adheres, today, precisely to those insights of Fourier's that are not immediately amenable to practice.

Fourier's thinking about this power, which transcends the given realities, has justly been called utopian. However, the notion of what we should understand by "utopian" must be challenged in the light of his self-understanding. The principled questions that must be asked, although we can only touch on them here, are, How is utopia related to science? Does utopian thought really, of necessity, burst the framework of the sciences? And, *ex contrario*, is scientific thought, and sociological thought in particular, even possible without the utopian? For his part, Fourier feels himself to be a practical man and would also like to be seen as an empirical scientist. What he shares with pragmatism is that he starts from facts and remains focused on facts; just like Comte, and later Saint-Simon, he mistrusts the battles of philosophers over mere ideas. He, too, would like to see the human sciences replace the deductive-speculative method with the inductive-empirical one. Thus he distinguishes between the "inexact" and the "exact" sciences and counts his own among the latter. But for him the concept of the empirical has a breadth that is unknown to positivism. Empirical, for him, is not just the scientifically confirming observation of what is, but also the concrete representation, in exact imagination, of what might be. Fourier's manner of proceeding in the realm of the imaginary makes his comments sometimes seem like a parody of positivist exactitude. From the fact that Fourier utilizes the imagination as a means of cognition, people have concluded that his thought is fantastical, not scientific. This presumes that, like Comte, we want to banish imagination from the scientific method. Fourier, to the contrary, is of the opinion that a science that limits itself to what is known, to its observation and analysis, is impoverished and tends to be unscientific. He utilizes imagination with the same self-evident confidence as observation. He also attempts to arm himself against the objection that he has merely been fantasizing: "Superficial minds, when they think they are flattering an inventor by saying that he has a lot of imagination, are making a very stupid compliment. Undoubtedly, men like Kepler and myself, who have an eminent instinct for a particular branch of the sciences, first receive and cultivate every new idea that instinct inspires in us without testing it; but such men would rank far below the writers of novels if they were to adopt such ideas without sufficient proofs. For a novelist, it is permitted to abandon himself to his imagination . . . but the exact sciences are subject to rules and proofs."[14]

If, nevertheless, his constructions go beyond empirical reality and make an impression that is fantastical and occasionally comical, this is not because they are irrational but precisely because they are excessively rational, because here a self-invented sociological-mathematical method, observation, and common sense are applied, with eccentric pedantry, to what is not yet known, not yet real.

Cosmic Rationalism

Fourier believes that with his discovery of the social compass he has found the key that unfailingly unlocks the secrets of nature. He launches his cosmic speculation at the point where he believes science has come to a standstill. What interests him is not so much the "what" of creation; instead, he asks the child's question, Why? Why do giraffes have such a long neck; why does the zebra have stripes; what was God thinking when he distributed the stars? For Fourier, as for the rationalist Enlightenment philosopher Christian Wolff, the rationality of the world is a given. God is merely the emphatic expression of this thoroughgoing lawfulness of all natural things. What is more, God's existence is the explanatory hypothesis for the fate of humanity. The lawfulness that is revealed in the human world is hypostatized as the nature of God. Fourier equips God with the full range of the passions. This rational and passionate god is, for him, the guarantor of the rightness of the universe, which he wants not merely to explain but also to *understand*. He undertakes to decipher God's intentions and motives based on his work. In the process, Fourier presumes that in creating the world God has been guided by three fundamental principles: the "unity of system," the "universality of providence," and the "economy of forces."[15] Unity of system ranks first among the divine attributes. It is guaranteed by the universal law of movement of attraction. Fourier's theory of the four movements states that not only is material movement subject to the law of attraction, but organic, animal, and social movement are too. This tendency to universalize Newton's law was already evident in the thought of the eighteenth century. But while previously the attempt had been to grasp psychic and social life in *analogy* to the material world, Fourier turns this relationship on its head and declares that social movement is the fundamental phenomenon of the universe and that the other orders have been constructed in analogy with it. Humankind—this is Fourier's optimistic thesis—is not only for itself but also for God, the "foyer," or center, of creation. Thus God's second attribute, the "universality of providence," means that creation, in all its details, is organized for the good of humanity. The creator is not a god of sternness and morality, but a god of pleasure. "His [human] creatures' enjoyment occupies the most important place in God's calculations."[16] The third attribute, the "economy of forces," means that to accomplish his aims God never uses a large number of tools; he always uses only one. Thus, he has built the passions into human beings as their *principium mobile*. The passions alone are designed to be the sole

motor of social movement. God did not make humankind dualistic. He
wants humans to obey their nature, and it alone. Human nature does not
need to be corrected by philosophical or policing measures. Like everything God has created, it is good, or, better, good for something, for Fourier
never argues morally but always from the standpoint of purposefulness.

But if God, true to his three attributes, could create only the best of all
possible worlds, how can we explain the fact that there are many forces and
creatures in the world that contradict these three principles? Like Leibniz,
the optimistic Fourier necessarily comes up against the question of where
evil in the world comes from. His answer to this question is odd: the hostility or at best indifference of many natural things toward humanity can
be explained by the fact that the universe is dependent on the state of the
social world. The latter, however, stands on its head as long as reason
claims to be the ruler of human nature. The universe, for Fourier, is a universal system of relations that corresponds to society, a system in which
nothing is accidental or meaningless—a cryptogram that humankind must
learn to decipher with philological exactitude. "The different kingdoms
of Nature are, in all their details, so many mirrors of some effect of our
passions; they form an immense museum of allegorical pictures, in which
are depicted the crimes and the virtues of Humanity."[17] Fourier's cosmic
system of social analogies is extremely complicated. Only those things he
terms "furnishings" of planet Earth are immediately dependent on earthly
societies; the universe that surrounds the planets is dependent on them
in a mediated way. However, he also assumes, besides planet Earth, other
heavenly bodies that are inhabited by human beings, each of which, like
Earth, is the center of a world. Thus, there is not only a universe but a
biniverse, triniverse, etc., up to the octaverse, as the loftiest harmony of all
the worlds. The harmoniousness of all these spheres is assumed to be foreseen by providence, but it does not come about automatically; rather, the
cosmos has a history, just like human societies. Since, in Fourier's weltanschauung, the big revolves around the small, it is human beings who are
responsible for the state of their universe. As long as human beings rudely
oppose the universal law of attraction and take refuge in violence as their
social *ultima ratio,* God has no choice but to adapt the furnishings of the
planet to this sad state of affairs. Our spiders, toads, and 130 species of
snakes, even the annually worsening weather, are mirrors that God holds
up to mankind so that humans will finally realize that they are on the
wrong path with their prisons and hangmen. The remaining planets, which

Fourier views as bisexual, body-and-soulful beings, have turned away from Earth like the neighbors who avoid an unhappy person. "A planet in a subversive condition is for the others what for us a person is who is infected with leprosy or the plague—one avoids contact."[18]

The planets, and God himself, share in the sufferings and joys of human beings. And although the effect on them is immeasurably less, still they must react to human history, from case to case, in keeping with the law of analogy. Thus, for example, Fourier firmly believes that the joy of creation, which he conceives as a copulation of the planets, can be slowed down or stimulated by the social conditions of humanity. Our Earth, to date, has brought forth only two creations: a first, experimental creation, which God wiped away by means of a flood after it became too large, with its mammoths and fossils; and the present-day, stagnating and very inadequate creation. Fourier expects that the introduction of social harmony will result in a decisive stimulation of our planet's creativity. During the period of harmony he foresees no less than fourteen new creations—"creations whose annunciation is not surprising, since the earth, which has brought forth two, can also very well bring forth four, or nine. Anyone who can theoretically explain the present creation can equally well deduce from it the theory of future ones."[19] Fourier predicts that the future creations will include 549 new species of animals, of which seven-eighths will be domesticable, along with anti-crocodiles, anti-rats, and innumerable additional innovations that your average philosophy has never dreamed of. The atmosphere is to be purified by the return of five stars that join in friendly cooperation with the earth and provide the services of well-disposed neighbors.[20]

From Fourier's consciousness of having solved the previously hidden riddles of creation, there emerges, for him, a peculiar relationship to God, on the one hand, and the philosophy that represents human reason, on the other. The exploration of the origins of creation by no means springs from blind faith in God but rather from a rationalism that is indebted to the Enlightenment. Fourier distances himself completely from theology and calls himself an atheist, but he opts for a "combinatorial," one might almost say dialectical, atheism, which is equidistant from blind faith and from the philosophical tendency to put self-founding reason in place of the divine order. The dialectical atheist begins by negating the existence of a wise, providential God in consideration of the shortcomings of creation. In this, he is no different from the simple atheist. But at the same time, the dialectical atheist negates this negation, with the result that the prosecutor—autonomous reason—becomes the defendant. The dialectical atheist is both more and less modest than the simple one. More modest, because he doesn't arbitrarily assume the competence to legislate social laws but merely seeks to decipher the social "code" that is implicit in the cosmic plan; less modest to the extent that he feels confident of finding the traces of nature's secrets, which philosophy had claimed were hidden behind an "iron veil." This is the source of Fourier's characteristic duality. He continuously plays God's wisdom, as revealed in nature, against the false reason of the philosophers. But at the same time, as the first person to have fully grasped God's plans, he feels called on to exercise an immanent "rational critique of God's works." The critique is immanent because Fourier applies to creation the standard that he firmly believes is also God's standard: the welfare of humankind. From this vantage point, following the motto of Alphonse de Castille, "If God had asked my advice in matters of creation, I would have given him many a useful pointer,"[21] he has quite a bit to criticize in regard to "actual and provisional creation." Fourier notes critically that the earth's axis is several degrees too acute, that innumerable animals are neither edible nor useful for labor, and much more of this ilk. The last objection makes clear the limitations of Fourier's anthropomorphism—animals do not belong to the society of harmonic beings. Like everything natural that surrounds humankind, they are mere furnishings, at best distortions of human characteristics. In the harmonic order, too, animals are at the mercy of human violence and arbitrariness. Consequently, to salvage the universal principle of attraction, there remains for Fourier no option but to equip oxen with a passion for the slaughterhouse.[22]

From the double trial that Fourier conducts against God and human reason, God, with his three attributes, emerges unscathed. The guilty party is human reason, which, instead of modestly searching for God's laws, puts itself in the position of lawgiver. God, who remains true to his three principles and renounces the use of authoritarian means to achieve his aims, is dependent on the voluntary cooperation of human beings. "If he had opted for force, it would have been easy for him to create much more powerful police thugs than ours, amphibious giants ten feet tall, with scales, impervious to harm and initiated into our military arts. They would have climbed out of the oceans unsuspected, would have destroyed our harbors, fleets, and armies, set them afire and in the blink of an eye forced the recalcitrant rich to abandon philosophy and swear allegiance to the divine laws of attraction. If God has chosen not to arm himself with giants like this, who would be just as easy to create as the great whales, then one must conclude from this that he was thinking only of attraction and that attraction should be the sole object of scientific inquiry for a century that wants to ally itself with God by studying nature and its destiny."[23]

The source of the problem is not human nature itself. It lies in the fact that this nature does not unfold in keeping with its destiny, but instead—led astray by philosophers and theologians—it has gotten lost in the labyrinth of history. Fourier feels called to bring an end to the sufferings and meanderings of human beings, in which the universe and even God himself are enmeshed. Anthropology and history, sociology and morality are joined, for him, in a system that is meant to provide the theoretical key to the new world.

The Theory of the Passions

The passions form an orchestra of 1,620 instruments; our philosophers, who want to conduct it, are like a legion of children who break into the opera, seize the instruments, and make a frightful caterwauling music. Should we conclude from this that music is inimical to man and that we should suppress the violins, force the basses to be silent, and suffocate the flutes? No; we should chase the little oafs out and give the instruments back to experts.

—Fourier, *The Passions of the Human Soul, and Their Influence on Society and Civilization*

The basis for understanding the law of social movement, for Fourier, is humanitarian science. In explicit opposition to the philosophical tradition, however, he does not locate the nature of humanity in reason. The latter is only the shell; the key is to delve deeper, to the passions as the real motors of the soul.

Fourier groups the passions under the unifying concept of attraction, which is fundamental for him. The cosmic power of attraction expresses itself in social movement as an "inner impulse" and "motor" of human beings.[24] It is responsible for the spontaneity of the passions, which are so many modifications of that fundamental force. Empirically, the passions are never pure; we always encounter them already in their relation to reason and morality. Hence they are initially to be defined negatively, in human beings, as that which, resists all attempts at control, as stubbornly resistant nature.[25] And yet they are not blind, anarchic forces that must first be moderated by reason and led along cultivated paths. Rather, the passions, as emanations of attraction, are designed to be the seat of the autonomy and self-affirmation of human beings. They are impulses that don't just have the character of drives and instincts; they are already material/sensual and intellectual/soulful at the same time, and as this kind of "combined" impulses they are capable of infinite intensification and unfolding. They need no complement of rational or ethical purpose, for they are already teleological in themselves. According to the goals toward which they strive, Fourier distinguishes five sensual passions, which aim at voluptuousness *(luxe)*; four affective, or group, passions; and finally three still almost unknown social passions. If we refer, here, to the aims of the passions, this should not be misunderstood. For the passions to unfold their teleology, what is required is not the purposefulness of an individual person; rather, what is at work in the passions is something like Hegel's "cunning of reason." While the individual has his eye on this woman, this beautiful object, this pleasure, he is simultaneously, by dint of his participation in the system of the passions, serving the general purpose. Precisely by following his highly individual impulses, he is implementing the law of attraction.

Fourier initially talks about drives that are rather well known, although the names may vary. These are the five senses and the four group passions: friendship, ambition, love, and the paternal or family drive. Together, these nine can be correctly seen as the motor of all previous social movement. Yet focusing on them alone produces a foreshortened, false picture of humanity and its destiny. These simple passions assume their actual, that is, societal meaning only with the addition of the final group of *social* passions, which represent the crowning elements in Fourier's system. The three social passions are "cabalist," associated with the formation of combinations and with struggle, intrigue, and calculation; the "butterfly" or change drive, linked to variety and the desire for transition; and "composite," which includes rapturous enthusiasm and love.[26] They are meant to play the leading role in the society of the future, when they will lend rhythm and harmony to a social movement that, until now, has found expression in periodic catastrophes. Unlike the other passions, these social passions are purely formal. They are principles of movement that are anchored in human nature, and in Fourier's universe their various moments are attuned as precisely as dissonance, rhythm, and consonance are in a musical work.

Sociologically, one can describe the two poles of cabalist and composite, between which the life of the new society is meant to oscillate in ever-changing variations, as group competition and group solidarity. Social antagonisms and their opposite—the boredom that results from enforced equality—are both supposed to be banished, not by bringing social movement to a standstill but by reconciling them with human nature through the medium of the three social passions.

The social passions, in other words, are what first conduct the remaining, seemingly unchanging and natural passions to their true destiny.[27] At present, the latter are in a deplorable state. While the five senses, in most people, are crude and unrefined, the affective passions tend to congeal into tiny groups that stymie all movement. Only the unfolding of the social passions will release the elementary passions from this gelid state. In the future, the five senses will not be passive instruments that merely register the world but will press forward, actively and critically, in the direction of continuous refinement, steadily improving quality and gradually perfecting their objects. At the same time, the private and so often sterile groups (series) will expand, in constant fluctuations, to form larger groups.

When Fourier, like Saint-Simon and Owen, writes about the organization of work and about passionate association representing the future relations of production, he derives the necessity of this economic reform from the principles and laws inherent in his theory of the passions. For him, the fundamental problem of all economy is the economy of the passions. The passions, as the organs through which man relates to external nature and to his fellow human beings, are the real forces of production. From them spring economic categories such as production, consumption, and distribution. Let us examine the connections among them, as presented by Fourier.

Quite often, theorists of Marxist persuasion have had a problem with the fact that Fourier's critique of capitalism focuses so exclusively on commerce.[28] And, in fact, his denunciation of the scurrilous behavior and betrayals of the marketplace, his scarcely veiled anti-Semitism (it is always Judas Iscariot who unleashes the avalanche of bankruptcies) bring him uncomfortably close to the Fascist distinction between productive and rapacious capital. But his sociological outlook shields him from the consequences. It is not individuals who bear the blame for rapaciousness and betrayal, much less a race that would be characterized by certain exclusive traits; rather, it is the organization of society, which for Fourier is synonymous with the organization of the passions, that is to blame. The fact that the sphere of circulation has been able to become so autonomous is for Fourier merely a symptom of a fundamental distortion between consumption and production. The true, passionate-productive relationship of human beings to things is disturbed. This is expressed in the fact that work, as something forced and as a punishment, is radically separated from the enjoyment of life.

If association is to bring about a truly qualitative change in social relations, it must be capable of undoing this dichotomy, which splits human beings into two warring parts. Production and consumption should achieve a balance that makes them merely two poles of the same movement, namely, a manifestation of the passions. Fourier defined the relationship of production and consumption concretely using the example of gastronomy. Only the person whose tongue is fine and cultivated enough to really enjoy a wine in its specific nuances, which are different from those of all other wines, could produce a bottle of wine that meets all expectations. In fact, he can do it only if he is passionately devoted to these nuances. At the same time, the connoisseur who consumes this particular wine will benefit from knowing how it was produced. What is true of cuisine also applies to the whole of culture. True consumption cannot take place in separation from production, and vice versa. In the phalanstery, enjoyment is pursued with the same seriousness as work, and work with the same seriousness as enjoyment. Work is simultaneously production-oriented consumption and consumption-oriented production. The concept of attractive work, which is at the center of Fourier's theory of association, embraces viniculture no less than love, the planting of a forest no less than an extended, varied, and sophisticated repast.

This kind of metamorphosis of work is admittedly only possible if association is grounded in attraction, that is, when it consists in the very sophisticated, intentional social constellation in which all the passions can have their spontaneous effect without endangering the order of the whole. In this case, association is the artful order of human relations, such that every action takes on a threefold meaning. First, it is the spontaneous manifestation of an individual passion, a desire. Second, because this desire is always socially mediated, it is productive, since it stimulates the creation of the desired object. And third, since every individual passion

simultaneously belongs to the objective system of the passions, it is an act
that builds society and builds relationships. That this complicated system
can only function because human beings relate primarily to objects, and
it is only through the mediation of these objects that they relate to their
fellow human beings, is something that Fourier specifically emphasized.
No moralistic exhortations or consensus derived from a common weltanschauung are needed to guarantee social cohesion; instead, the latter is
continuously guaranteed behind the backs of individuals who are merely
pursuing their passions by means of the cunning of attraction. There is
only one relation in which the social mechanism threatens to come to
a standstill, because it is short-circuited, so to speak, and that is the love
relationship. Fourier's plea on behalf of free love appears diametrically
opposed to the attitudes of the Philistines. This attitude is actually progressive, even revolutionary, because it aims at the destruction of the insti-
tution of the family. Fourier's description of the two "republican savages,"[29]
who know and love only each other, recalls what Bloch correctly denounced
as petty-bourgeois pairs of cooing turtle doves. And yet in Fourier's dis-
taste for exclusive love there is something else that reverberates along with
antibourgeois scorn—his fear of the anarchic, completely asocial aspect
of love. What if the passions diverge from the paths in which the general
and the particular are scrupulously attuned to each other in order to fall for
a specific and extremely accidental being, to become crystallized in a point
beyond which the real world disappears like a dream? At this point, the law
of attraction, which was originally conceived as a law of nature, is transformed into an ethical law. Fourier, who has always advocated for freedom
and against duty, paradoxically elevates free, nonexclusive love to a duty.
At least he promises to award it the highest honors.

In the phalanstery, love will assume an entirely public character. Liberated from the fetters of monogamy, it will develop novel, socially constructive characteristics. There will be a *noblesse galante,* a gallant nobility,
which will be outranked only by the saints. This nobility will include all
those individuals who, through their numerous love relationships, have
formed many new social bonds. "Vices, according to the law of attraction,
are anything that diminishes the number of relationships; virtue anything
that multiplies them. . . . Among the 'polygynous,' who are by nature inclined to allow love to turn into friendship, the lack of constancy only benefits virtue, for a polygynous woman who has changed her lovers a dozen
times and remains friends with all twelve of them, while reserving her love

for a thirteenth, has formed twelve bonds of friendship that would not have existed if she had remained faithful."[30]

The directionality of the passions dictates that they are not able to unfold within the rigid form of the family. They push beyond this form, which fetters them, to the series made up of rival groups, for which association is only another name. The precondition for a series to function is not the equality of its members, as one might suppose, but precisely the most extreme differentiation of passions and characters. Every passion, be it the oddest one imaginable, for example, a preference for tough chickens, has its irreplaceable spot in the economy of this universe. The passions that Fourier describes as the motors of the new order have almost fetishistic qualities—they seize on details. The fanatical lover of soft pears is the sworn enemy of the devotee of firm pears. In this passion for the unique, this sensitivity to nuance, the men and women of Fourier's community of the future resemble the aristocratic dandy—a figure that had emerged in his era as a living protest against the banality and mediocrity of the bourgeois lifestyle.

The series that is to be constantly reconstituted under the direction of the three social passions is the "compass needle" of the social world. It points toward the wonderland that mankind has dreamed of ever since the expulsion from paradise. Once the proper hierarchy of passions has been established, allowing people to multiply and differentiate their human capacities ad infinitum, then—Fourier believes—humans will discover the fundamental drive that they all share: the unifying drive, which defines the fully and completely individualized person as a part of humanity. "Unityism" (unitéisme) is the loftiest realization of all destinies, the harmonious interplay of all the passions, as white is the color that unifies all the others. Fourier calls it the "pivot," the hinge of harmonious order. The unifying drive will take the place of false, of (one could say, with Herbert Marcuse) de-sensualized reason, which is the axis of all perverted societies. It will lead not only the passions but reason as well to their true destiny. For as long as reason remains the enemy of the passions, it is also at war with itself. And despite all its vaunted authority, it always achieves the opposite of what it wants. "Unique result of the *perfectionnement* of reason. It leads to its banishment from all relationships."[31] The rule of reason will become superfluous when society is reconciled with human nature in the divine *code social*. Then, and only then, will reason reach its true positive destiny, which is nothing other than the refinement of desire.

Dark Horizons

If it is true—and Fourier's theory of the passions claims that it is—that humankind only needs to follow its nature in order to be happy, why have people not listened to the voice of nature, which is simultaneously God's voice? In the answer to this question lies the germ of Fourier's theory of history. History, here, is no longer, as it still was in Condorcet, the process of reason's continuous upward development, culminating in the present. Fourier's philosophy could more properly be called cyclical. Like his cosmology, his thinking about history embraces great expanses of time, a perspective in which the past history of humankind appears as a brief, failed foretaste. But he undertakes to examine this foretaste with microscopic precision.

Human history begins with the divergence of two originally unified aspects: the human desire for happiness, on the one hand, and the conditions for its realization, on the other. It is the history of industry and of the passions, of the always repeated and always failed attempt to bring the two into harmony. There is a state of prehistory, in which humans were unconsciously unified in a state of mere nature. This is Edenism, of which humans of all subsequent epochs retain a vague and happy memory. The memory is imprecise and therefore unfruitful, for the real secret of the state of paradise, the social form of the passionate series, was lost. Along with this, however, mankind lost the thread, as it were: the history of mankind's fall from its destiny begins. Fourier explains the expulsion from paradise not morally but economically by an increase in population accompanied by the fundamental evil of poverty. "Poverty is radical evil, the fundamental principle of our social misery."[32] Need impelled human beings to all the vices and emergency measures; among these the end of the freedom of love relationships, institutionalized in the form of the family, had the most serious consequences. For Fourier, the replacement of the series as the fundamental form of society by the family is the beginning of what he calls "social fragmentation." At the same time, the family, as institutionalized repression of women, was at the root of the brutal dominance that mankind henceforth imposed on itself. For Fourier, the position of women is the touchstone of every social order. In the relationship between the sexes, one can see the relationship of mankind to itself, to its own nature. Thus the liberation of women is the measure of human emancipation.

In keeping with the form of the family, which is always accompanied by a specific, corresponding form of labor, Fourier distinguishes four social orders: primitivism, savagery, the patriarchate, and civilization. The historical sequence of these forms by no means indicates a gradual improvement of society. Thus, for example, civilization differs from savagery only in that it "gives each of the vices that savagery practices in simple form a combined existence, and lends them a dual, ambiguous, hypocritical character."[33] Measured against the sole valid criterion, the state of the passions, all four social orders are perverted (subversive), because mankind's natural inclinations, instead of reaching their goal, are a source of ceaselessly proliferating unhappiness. The fate of the passions, in these four false societies, is like that of bees who are transported to a desert island covered with rocky cliffs: "They will not find a flower there, nevertheless they will constantly be in search of flowers, because their essential destiny is to live from the pollen of flowers. . . . Thus, God has conceived the human passions in light of the state of wealth and voluptuousness that is their true destiny."[34] In the four barren societies founded on poverty and coercion, a constant, painful surplus of wishes points beyond the possibilities for their fulfillment.

The only progress of civilization, as opposed to the three previous forms of society, is the development of industry as the objective precondition of a harmonious society. But this very material progress sheds a harsh light on its social backwardness. In an image that recalls that of Brecht's "palace," Fourier compares civilization to a peacock, which, for all its splendid plumage, stands on ugly feet. Its ugly feet are the barbaric relics of domination. In the same way in which passions, which are good in themselves, turn into vices in civilization, the progress of industry has only heightened the misery of the masses. Civilization is the perfect image of the perverted world. But this very fact, that civilization and all its ugly traits are already developed, gives Fourier hope that it has already outlasted itself. When a reviewer wrote praising him for lashing out justifiably at the imperfection of our civilization, Fourier responded scornfully: Imperfect? On the contrary, he had proven that, of its kind, it was utterly perfect. Except that the civilized critics, who were evidently suffering from cataracts, couldn't comprehend this. He sketches the outline of a dynamic sociology: "Every society has the capacity to generate from within itself the society that will succeed it. It arrives at the crisis of birth when it has developed all its essential traits."[35] The metamorphosis of the caterpillar into a harmonious butterfly is immanent.

In the conviction that the transition from bourgeois society—for this is precisely what civilization means—to harmony must be a qualitative leap, Fourier is no less radical and uncompromising than Marx. However, this leap, for him, consists not in the insurgency of an oppressed class that is historically in the right, but in the insurgency of the passions, which are always—independent of all historical and social conditions—in the right. The history of mankind is embedded in the natural history that surrounds it. Thus, Fourier's philosophy of history does not stop at the liberation of society, for which humankind longs and which is its objective destiny. He may estimate the period of harmony that will follow civilization as enduring for 70,000 years, or seven-eighths of all of human history. But then the unhappy childhood of the human race will repeat itself in reverse, until the history of our planet comes to an end in a less than comfortable phase that resembles its beginning. For Fourier there is no progress, only very extended happy high points in history, all of which can be identified by the sociological characteristic of the series. History is basically nothing but a progression from the confused series (hordes) of the primitive state; through the development of industry, which was enforced by poverty and took the form of the family; to the consciously constructed series of harmony combined with social wealth. The series is the leitmotif of history, with which history begins, toward which it presses as its high point, and with which it ends.

> *The Absolute Lover must exist, since women can conceive of him, just as there is but one proof of the immortality of the soul, which is that man, through fear of nothingness, aspires to it!* ... Ipsissima verba sancti Thomas.
>
> —Alfred Jarry, *The Supermale* (1902)

The Construction of Happiness

Happiness—as St. Just said in the first French National Assembly—was a new idea for Europe. It probably did not take the Enlightenment and its political apogee, the French Revolution, to arrive at the insight that the spur to all human action is the pursuit of happiness. What was new in the idea of happiness, however, was that happiness, specifically its earthly variety, was publicly proclaimed as a legitimate claim of every human being and was declared to be the actual content and goal of all human life.

The philosophical optimists, who, in their initial intoxication with the new idea, interpreted all of nature in the light of happiness, would soon be disappointed. In their search for happiness, they everywhere bumped up against necessities that were inimical to happiness and that only fanatical obstinacy could simply deny. To the question of what optimism is, Voltaire has Candide respond: "Alas! It's the madness of maintaining that everything is all right when everything is going wrong!"[36] And while, on the one hand, people fell back on time-tested recipes of moderation as a means of avoiding distress, on the other hand, the idea arose that happiness was something that was yet to be realized. It was the postrevolutionary social reformers who first put forth the inquiry into the "possible objectivity of happiness . . . extended to the structure of the social organization of humanity."[37] In their search for objective criteria of happiness they—Saint-Simon no less than Fourier[38]—return to Bentham's ideal of the greatest happiness of the greatest number, made quantifiable by their participation in the wealth of society. But while for Saint-Simon, and above all for the Saint-Simonists, happiness then becomes a problem in the form of the question of how the happiness of the individual can coexist with the happiness of all, Fourier regards this problem as having already been resolved once and for all. His fundamental principle that "the attractions are proportional to the destinies" means the happiness equation comes out even. Every possible imaginable passion is destined to be fulfilled. Fourier, who, like Saint-Simon, battles against liberalism, holds fast to egoism as the driving force behind all social movement. The desire for wealth and personal ambition are not, as Adam Smith himself had already preached, to be constrained by morality. On the contrary, they are to be intensified. For the law of social harmony works most harmoniously when people follow their natural inclinations, and only them, without any ethical reservations.

Like Marx, Fourier emphasizes the material and sensual moment of happiness. He, too, is of the opinion that in a world in which the majority of people are condemned to poverty the higher spiritual joys are mere ideology or, as he says, "illusions and foolishness." In formulations that recall Brecht, he scoffs that the person who is hungry will not be sated by having the good fortune to live in a republic. But while Marx intentionally confines himself to the question of how to create the objective conditions for happiness, Fourier attempts to resolve not only the elementary problem of the elimination of poverty, but something closer to the heart of the matter:

the elimination of boredom. The young Marx also considers this question when he speaks of the alienating quality of property, of the fact that even the capitalist has a perverted, less than happy relationship to his possessions. Fourier places humankind's proper relation to its riches—one that will produce happiness, not boredom—at the center of his reflections. He attempts to construct happiness not only from its objective side, industrial production, but from its subjective side as well. The possession of material goods will neither lead automatically to happiness, nor is the latter to be found in moderation and wise resignation. Happiness is created only when the wealth that inheres in objects is touched by the magic wand of the unfettered passions. Fourier explains the strange disconnect between human beings and the world around them, which today is on everyone's lips as alienation, by the shackles that reason imposes on the passions. Moral, civilized man is anguished; he is constantly in a state of war with himself, and thus he tends to be at war with other human beings. He is an "absurd mechanism and would be the shame of the creator, if the latter had not provided the means with which to replace this war with a double harmony."[39] As long as this state has not been reached, human beings are thwarted. They are usually dominated by a despotic passion that cannot be satisfied. This awkward condition can continue even though the objective elements and preconditions for happiness are present. Fourier explains the fact that in civilization even the rich cannot be entirely happy by observing that they, too, necessarily participate in the false social state of the passions. Even if all their elementary passions are satisfied, the *social* passions still cannot unfold. But happiness, for Fourier, is the real, not the merely apparent and playful satisfaction of *all* the passions. "God has given us twelve passions; we can be happy only when we satisfy all twelve."[40] Since the passions can unfold fully only in a social manner, happiness cannot be left to the individual. Happiness itself, not merely its objective preconditions, is social by nature. As long as the passions are banished from the decisive social relationships and confined to private life, there can be no real happiness.[41] The paradox of happiness is that we have knowledge of it only as private individuals, but the happiness of which we are aware is only a reflection. It has—at least to Fourier's way of thinking—no real existence. Real happiness, for him, is something objective. It will surround the properly constructed society like an aura, the way charm is the inevitable result of a successful work of art. In fact, Fourier regards the right society as analogous to aesthetic situations. The new art, *l'art social*, consists in no longer leaving the interplay of the passions to chance, but in finding their proper proportions and combining them in such a way that a social work of art results.

When all the domination and coercion that civilized humanity imposes on itself have been lifted, this will set free forces that were unknown to all previous societies. Then the dynamic of the passions will correspond to a dynamic of happiness whose extent cannot be imagined based on the few guest appearances that happiness has made in history until now and that is suggested only by the extent of the misfortune and unhappiness that periodically wash over civilization. For Fourier, happiness and unhappiness are dynamic categories. Nothing is more false than the principle of counterbalance, which the philosophers call justice—that every good can be counterbalanced and neutralized by an opposite evil, and vice versa. Not only does this law prove to be empirically false, but as an ideal it is also the dumbest thing the theologians and philosophers could have thought up. For mediocrity, tepidness, and monotony, which are the end result of such a counterbalancing law, are the archenemies of happiness. Fourier proves that in civilization unhappiness does not appear singly or occasionally in the company of something good, but instead, as a rule, gains momentum like an avalanche. From the growth of unhappiness in civilization, as it becomes constantly more intense and refined, Fourier derives the possibility of a happiness that grows constantly more fervent and sophisticated. Civilization, for him, is the polar opposite of the right state of affairs. As such, he attempts to interpret it in all its details, right down to the tapeworm, which is a perverted hieroglyphic for the immense appetite that human beings will develop in the harmonious order.

Why, if a society is capable of multiplying the unhappiness of the individual, shouldn't another, countervailing one succeed in creating an opposite result—guaranteeing and multiplying the happiness of every individual? Fourier names some of the guarantees of the harmonious order. For example, in every phalanstery there will be a happiness exchange, where every evening the pleasures corresponding to each wish and character will be listed and exchanged. Besides that, every inhabitant of a phalanstery, including the most impoverished (Fourier wants to retain class differences, on account of the differentiations that are necessary for a series), will experience at least one run of good luck per day. The run of good luck is something Fourier developed in opposition to the idea of a run of bad luck. It does not need to be consciously implemented, any more than a run of bad luck does, but at the same time it is not just a fleeting accident; it is exuded, as it were, as the daily byproduct of a society founded on series. It is described by Fourier, with a claim to mathematical exactitude, as the sevenfold multiplication of happiness, occurring over the space of several hours, with one happy event giving rise to six more that follow. "Leander has been successful with the woman he has been wooing. This is a combined, equally sensual and soulful pleasure. Immediately thereafter, she hands him the letter promoting him to a lucrative position that she has procured for him: second pleasure. A quarter of an hour later, she leads him to a salon where he encounters happy surprises—he meets a friend whom he had believed dead: third pleasure. Soon after this, a famous man arrives, Buffon or Corneille, whom Leander has long wanted to meet, and who stays for dinner: fourth pleasure. There follows an exquisite meal: fifth pleasure. At dinner, Leander finds himself seated next to a powerful man who declares that he is ready to help him by giving him a loan: sixth pleasure. Finally, during the meal, he receives the news that he has won a lawsuit:[42] seventh pleasure."[43] Such runs of good luck, as they are also described, by the way, in Balzac's *Illusions perdues,* are, to Fourier's mind, completely unknown in civilization. Not even kings could manage to experience them. Even if one is tempted to suppose that the pleasures of civilized kings are as great or greater than Leander's, still, the concrete picture of such a *parcours* makes one thing clear: in the harmonious order, happiness sheds its character as something exceptional, an event that flashes up only momentarily; it belongs to the lives of those who share in its social construction like the very air they breathe.

Fourier, as a passionate devotee of systems, cannot rest content with this kind of description of social happiness. Happiness, if it is to be worth talking about, must be something absolute. For this, however, there is a nasty barrier: death. Fourier, who negates all necessities and duties, consequently negates death, as the darkest of all necessities, too. God, who has determined that all our inclinations never reach for something that is unattainable, cannot have refused to grant the most tenacious of all human wishes, the wish for immortality. "The happiness that is the lot of humankind on this planet would be imperfect, were they unable to return to this life."[44] Fourier, in the pose of the strict scientist, is not satisfied with this deduction of immortality from the fundamental principle of his system. He names an entire spectrum of proofs, whose demonstration he postpones, however, since there is still too much to do for the welfare of this world. Immortality, removed from its Christian context of reward for past sufferings, becomes a guarantor of the eternity of desire. "It is not through fear, but through love that the creator will win us over to himself; through the guarantee of pleasures that, in eternity as in this life, are varied in infinite degree."[45] Heaven, which he paints here as the golden ground of harmony, has nothing to do with the pallid beyond of the theologians and philosophers, "these Elysian fields where the souls of the just arrive for monotonous walks and sterile conversations on virtue; this Olympus where gods and demigods always eat the same thing, always ambrosia, and the other ascetic domains in which the most important senses, the senses of taste und touch, are not satisfied at all."[46] In Fourier's heaven, all the senses and all the passions receive their due, even the butterfly drive, for the departed souls, living in a body of fire and air, are permitted to flutter around however they wish, to visit other planets, or, now and again, to be reborn on earth. Only a person who has had little enjoyment in this world can be satisfied with another world that offers such impoverished, theological delights. Man's mistake until now was not, as the moralists aver, to have demanded too much but rather to have demanded too little. The souls of the departed, which are more alive and wiser than earthly ones, know that the destiny of man is harmony. More closely linked to the soul of the planet than we are, they suffer with it from the sickness known as "civilization" that has befallen it. They wait impatiently to be reborn into a better-organized world. "The best service that could be provided to the departed, as to the living, is therefore to bring about social harmony, without delay."[47]

Modes of Freedom

Fourier's theory of destiny is no determinism. Man is free to follow the divine *code social* or not. Even societies based on coercion are the result of freedom. So it is important to distinguish between formal and substantive freedom. Human beings have formal freedom because, from the very beginning, God has granted them *libre arbitre*, freedom of choice.[48] But they can only achieve real, that is, substantive freedom, if they are reconciled to their own nature and have brought their own will into harmony with God's. In history, formal and substantive freedoms have become divorced.

The form that freedom has assumed in the post-revolutionary era, according to Fourier, is that of a mere phrase. It has entered into the liberal constitutions, "whose nominal content is freedom, equality, fraternity, but whose actual content is coercion, hangmen, and gallows."[49] While equality and fraternity, even as ideals, are just philosophical nonsense, which—if it should ever be possible to realize them—would only produce mediocrity and deathly boredom, he would like to establish criteria for freedom that would finally make it possible to distinguish between nominal and real liberty. The advancement of industry, for him, also meant the decay of freedom. The stage of savagery, for example, although it was very imperfect in regard to industry and the pitiable position of woman, was nevertheless, in terms of substantive freedom, far superior to a civilization that is constantly chattering about it. The primitive human being possessed "complex" freedom. He had corporeally active freedom, for he could live and act freely according to his impulses, and at the same time he had socially active freedom, for he had a voice in deciding the concerns of his horde. The great mass of civilized people, on the other hand, do not wholly possess even one of these freedoms. The wage earner, as opposed to the slave, may nominally control his body, but during the workweek this bodily freedom is merely passive, since need forces him to work. The price of modern industry has been the elimination of those elementary rights of freedom that even primitive men enjoyed. "Every wage-earner would consider himself lucky if he could eat according to his appetite, live happily and without cares, hunt, fish, fight, and steal like the primitive."[50] To offer him the Magna Carta in place of the seven elementary rights, whose loss is identical with the forfeit of spontaneity, is pure scorn and ridicule.

And yet, Fourier does not conclude, from this supposed superiority of the savage over seven-eighths of civilized humanity, that the goal is to return to the state of savagery. First, as he argues against Rousseau, there is no such thing as nature in the singular; rather, there are as many natures as there are forms of social organization. In the first phase of human history alone, he believes he can count nine different natures, and no one can say to which one the "friends of pure nature" are actually referring. Second, the nature of the savage, compared with that of a civilized human being, is a simple one and therefore wrong for us because the element of industry, which mediates nature, is lacking. Industry belongs essentially to the destiny of mankind. True freedom, therefore, must be "doubly constituted." In it, the savage's elementary rights to freedom must be combined with modern industry. The first right that should be reinstated in modern form is the right to be carefree. *Post equitem sedet atra cura*[51] applies to the tormented *pater familias* of civilization. To be carefree is something that one group of people cannot afford because they would die of hunger; others, because they would be subject to social opprobrium. "A less wealthy father of a family who made the attempt to devote himself entirely to pleasure, without attending to his business, without setting something aside for taxes, rent, and future expenditures, would soon be reminded by evil rumors and the tax authorities that he does not have the right to live in a carefree manner reminiscent of savages and animals, that he must suffocate the natural inclination in himself to be carefree."[52] To create an equivalent to the natural right to be carefree, Fourier demands that everyone, from the worker to the rich man, should have a "minimum," a share of social wealth, always distributed a year in advance, as a kind of lifelong stipend that is intended to do away with forced labor once and for all. He knows that such a radical innovation—for him the absolute prerequisite of true freedom—would necessarily destroy the fundamental law of civilization.

Civilization is a perverted world, because in it freedom can only be realized in a destructive way, against the existing order of things. While actually productive work is founded on need and coercion, only the negative work called theft is pursued with a passion. Theft takes place either in a simple form or as trading in the marketplace. In the pleasure the trader takes in lying and cheating there survives something of the freedom of the savage, who hunts, fishes, steals, and fights with delight. "One should not believe that a merchant feels physical discomfort after, in a single morning, he has unloaded a hundred bolts of fabric, told countless lies, and sold innumerable pairs of trousers. This effort is pleasure, appealing work, physical freedom; and as proof our merchant, who is very satisfied today, will be in a bad mood and cranky tomorrow when he sees no customers walking in, and can neither lie nor sell."[53] While the honest person is condemned to mediocrity and the passionlessness of a boring Sunday morning, something of what freedom once was, and what it could be, survives paradoxically in vice, in perversions, and even in crime. Here, Fourier agrees with the insights of Sade and Nietzsche, except that he does not, like them, arrive at the conception of the "libertine," or "free spirit," who alone realizes freedom and bursts the bonds of social lawfulness. Instead, he envisions a societal order in which the freedoms of *all* individuals fit together like the pieces of a jigsaw puzzle. If theft and criminality are not indestructible traits that must constantly be combated, but merely false modes of freedom, and if the passions manifested in them are rehabilitated as socially useful and divinely ordained, it then becomes possible to do without repression of any kind. The state, as an apparatus for imposing force, can disappear. "Every use of power is only the complement of justice, and if justice could be realized otherwise, all that[54] would be superfluous." The dynamics of Fourier's anti-ascetic system will—he is convinced— gradually undermine all political/state institutions, because the order they are attempting to impose through the use of violence will appear all by itself through attraction.

Surrealist Readings

Castor Zwieback (Theodor W. Adorno and Carl Dreyfus)

Editorial Note

A strange mixture of an association with Thomas Mann and a reference to twice-baked bread (highlighting the number two) as literary pseudonym! The following short texts were written in the early 1930s by Theodor W. Adorno in collaboration with his friend Carl Dreyfus. Four of them appeared on November 17, 1931, in the *Frankfurter Zeitung* under the collective title "Surrealist Readings" *(Surrealistische Lesestücke).*[1] Without offering any explanation of the pseudonym, the literary journal *Akzente* published an expanded series in 1963, with the laconic note, "The 'Readings' of Castor Zwieback were written before 1933."

Dreyfus, who was born in 1898, had worked at the Institute for Social Research since 1930 and, like Adorno, was a trusted friend of Max Horkheimer, Siegfried Kracauer, and Alfred Sohn-Rethel. Dreyfus had spent the 1920s working on a novel but abandoned it and poured his literary energies into a study of the profession and ideology of white-collar workers, which he managed to have published just before the Nazi takeover.[2] This suggests reading the jointly composed Zwieback prose as "covert sociology" and situating it in corresponding contexts.

But another avenue for interpreting Castor Zwieback's prose pieces opens up if we look at them from a literary perspective, as freestanding experiments. The merger of philosophy with sociology and of both with literature—and vice versa—was in the air. In 1928, Walter Benjamin had published his prose volume *One-Way Street*; in 1930, Ernst Bloch followed with a volume of parables titled *Traces (Spuren)*; and that same year Siegfried Kracauer acquired the pseudonym Ginster (Broom), under which he also wrote fiction. Since 1913–14, all three had published critiques and essays in literary journals like *Die Aktion* (Action), *Die Erhebung* (The rising), *Die weissen Blätter* (The white pages), and *Die Argonauten* (The Argonauts). Since the early 1920s, Benjamin and Kracauer had been staff writers of the *Frankfurter Zeitung*.

We know little about the nature of the collaboration in whose course Adorno and Dreyfus carried out their pseudonymous intention, but the fact itself is significant enough. Evidently, as was usual in this type of coproduction, each contributed his share—and they most likely stimulated each other. We may assume that their plan, from the very start, was to get their products published in a newspaper—which they did. Thus, the individual pieces fell well short of the length required for a short novella of the type that abounds, for example, in the early work of Thomas Mann. In fact, the pieces have precisely the length that predominates in a newspaper's arts and culture section. Robert Walser's short prose might serve as a literary pendant.

Publication in the *Frankfurter Zeitung* was accompanied by the motto, "Knock on the door, cry 'Enter!' and don't enter" (André Breton and Paul Éluard). Later, in a letter to Walter Höllerer, Adorno, in a somewhat different vein, recalled that in this work he had "reproduced the feeling that assails someone who is climbing a flight of stairs and thinks he has another step ahead of him, when in fact he is already at the top. In other words the translation of a bodily response into a written text." With Breton and Éluard, Adorno thus pointed to the two principal representatives of French surrealism, which after its start in Dada-Zurich went on to make its reputation in Paris in the 1920s and become the mainstream of modernism. There is a direct link between Castor Zwieback and the Adorno quote, since most of these prose texts end with an odd omission of their *pointe*. This makes the reader spin his wheels and leaves him in suspense. It recalls the recent "cut-up"[3] prose of Helmut Heissenbüttel or Ror Wolf, for whom related prose pieces of the French surrealists or Russian futurists provided inspiration. The omissions lead directly toward something dreamlike and refer to circumstances buried more deeply than those on the surface of the texts.

The program of literary surrealism called for collective creativity only to push it in the direction of "automatic writing." This does not seem relevant to the Adorno-Dreyfus texts, whose narrative tone, at times, resembles the sort of anecdote that, in a conversation, can suddenly pop up to illustrate an abstract topic.

The immediate occasion for *Akzente*'s publication of the pieces, after the Second World War, was most likely the return of Adorno's friend Dreyfus from exile in South America. This is indicated in the letter with which Adorno offered the pieces to Walter Höllerer for publication. Among other things, Adorno wrote, "This is, after all, a perhaps not uninteresting experiment, from which I would not want to distance myself, although I did not continue it later; certain developments during the last thirty years have shown that the intention was not so far-fetched, or perhaps that the far-fetched is precisely what is not far-fetched. . . . I ask you to please understand correctly why I would like to see the thing published. I have developed a special fondness for certain things that, for me, crystallize a possibility that was never realized in my own development."

The present edition of Castor Zwieback's prose pieces has been enriched by the inclusion of two previously unpublished texts, which appeared neither in the *Frankfurter Zeitung* nor in *Akzente*: "Harpsichord" and "Funerary Monument." This addition appears to complete the literary oeuvre of this interesting literary pseudonym. Special thanks are due to the Theodor W. Adorno Archive in Frankfurt and to Rolf Tiedemann, as well as to Suhrkamp Publishers for making these manuscripts available and giving permission for their publication.

—*Karl Riha*

Harpsichord

When the choral concert began, the light was already burning fitfully. Once, when the stuffy hall fell dark, an astonished murmur ran through the listening audience before suddenly ceasing. The lights had come on again, and the performance of the first part of the work continued to the end. In keeping with the serious occasion, there was no applause. When the second movement began, the flickering of the lights immediately recommenced. This time the disturbance was not temporary. The lights burned more and more faintly. The audience remained calm, even when the bulbs burned red. Then darkness fell. The conductor put down the baton and turned toward the hall. The emergency lighting over the doors did its work. The musicians in the orchestra ceased playing. Only the chorus sang on. As the voices gradually became fewer, the thin tone of an old-fashioned keyboard instrument could be heard, which accompanied the entire work almost imperceptibly. It played a few more measures. Soon afterward the concert could be continued.

Funerary Monument

Due to the lovely weather the tourist excursion was at capacity. They had already visited the poet's house, the gardens, and the remains of the fortress, when the big car stopped in front of a dense copse of trees. That is the evangelical church, the guide said. It was built in 1855 in the Gothic style. Since 1905 it is no longer in use but serves as a shelter for the famous English funerary monument with Amor and Psyche. Visitation is free two days a month; today the church is closed. Then the car drove on.

Railroad

A merchant had spent all morning busy with activities in the capital and got on the express train at two o'clock. It left the station punctually at seven minutes after two. On the table in front of his seat by the window lay a scrap of paper with the trilingual message: This train contains a dining car. Immediately an employee of the Dining Car Association appeared and invited the passengers to take their places for coffee. Was it still possible to get something to eat? Certainly, but only à la carte. The merchant stood up; the next car was the dining car. There he took a seat in the nonsmoking section; other than himself, there was only a young married couple. The headwaiter asked whether he would like coffee or tea. Can I still have something to eat? Of course, sir, even the daily special, which is particularly nice today. Of course, very fresh. It was served at once, and the server uncorked the bottle of red wine that already stood on the table. On the way back to the compartment, he met the maid, in apron and bonnet. She was shining the bronze handrails with a leather cloth; in her other arm she held a package of fresh towels. In the compartment he read a magazine with the printed notice: Dedicated to our guests. It had been placed on the seats by the Dining Car Association. Soon the conductor arrived and, without entering the compartment, asked for the tickets. Are we running late? No, replied the official, we are on schedule. On this route there is absolutely never any delay. When he descended from the train, the other traveler assisted him.

Complaint

At the start of the business day, after the big front doors were swung open, a carefully dressed woman entered the main hall of the bank building and walked quickly up to the currency exchange window on the opposite side. Asked what she was seeking, she said she wanted to speak with the director general. Then she was in the wrong place; the director general's office was on the second floor. They should please announce her. Unfortunately, there was no point in doing so, since the director general was most likely not in the office yet and appointments had been made for the entire morning. Now the woman, who until then had been calm, began to cry; it was urgent that she see the director general. They were truly sorry. It's because of this, she cried out very loudly, he no longer wants to have anything to do with my son, which is sad for him. The doorman and a page, who had been rung for, removed the complaining woman; the office of the director general was informed.

Encounter

In lively conversation, four young girls entered the streetcar and sat down in pairs opposite each other, their schoolbags on their laps. Without a pause they continued to chat. Then one of them pointed to the street and interrupted herself: My mother. They all turned their heads and looked out. A gray, open truck passed the streetcar. There were several people in it, with blankets, perhaps three gentlemen and a lady. The girl's greeting did not reach the mother. But she knew that the streetcar and the truck would meet again at the next stop. Indeed, the truck waited there until the streetcar passengers had gotten off and on. Now the girl's waving could not be overlooked. The mother gave her a friendly nod.

Expectation

After their evening meal together, while the diners were still in the dining room, a Herr Dr. Kuntzel took from his notebook a clipping cut from an illustrated magazine: Isn't this a beautiful woman? The men passed the clipping around. I will be picked up at nine, so we gentlemen won't be all by ourselves. By this woman? No, by her friend, who had also been employed at the municipal theater in Chemnitz but was now working here. Soon afterward they repaired to the hotel lobby. The gentlemen took their places at various smoking tables, for coffee and liqueurs, while Herr Dr. Kuntzel paced back and forth in the vestibule, his eye on the revolving door. From time to time one of the gentleman glanced up: had the lady they were awaiting appeared yet? A quarter of an hour after the appointed time, the gentlemen paid and began to leave, not without conferring with Herr Dr. Kuntzel on the continuation of the evening. He remained uneasily behind. The gentlemen, meanwhile, fanned out in a group across the large square, which had already become quieter. Intending to save time and be of assistance to their friend, they greeted various unknown ladies and asked them whether perchance they had an appointment with Herr Dr. Kuntzel. In the process, they selected ladies whose appearance and clothing seemed to suggest an artistic character, but to no avail. Only a short distance from the agreed-on location, the gentlemen noticed a slim woman in a wide fur coat and an evening scarf that left her temples bare. Yes, she knew him. It was the lady from the clipping.

The Connecting Trams

A young working girl said to her colleague: The streetcar is no fun. If I leave five minutes earlier than necessary in the morning, it doesn't help much. I can make the connecting tram, which has fewer passengers than the crowded main streetcar, but I hardly ever arrive at my destination any earlier. The connecting trams, you see, don't habitually run in the middle of the interval between two main streetcars, but rather immediately before the next one, because the engineers and conductors of the connecting trams talk to the officials from the main streetcars at the station where they originate. So at the transfer stop I can't make the connection with the scheduled streetcar, only the one after that. And that is not all. Sometimes on account of the long wait I arrive at my destination later than if I had taken the next main streetcar, which goes farther than the connecting tram and so arrives at a second, larger transfer stop, where there are several connections. From there it may be a greater distance to the destination as the crow flies, but thanks to the many lines one never has to wait.

The Morning

A youth spent his holiday in a southern spa hotel. In the morning, when he went to the washroom, still in his pajamas, he found an elderly lady there.

Although he hastened to close the door immediately, he could not help seeing the lady. She wore a black dress with embroidery; under the hitched-up skirt she wore long white knickers and black boots. The lady began to murmur. At noon, when she entered the veranda in the black dress, the youth bowed.

Regent

The summer palace of the deceased regent, with its beautiful setting, was much visited. Tours were given in groups of thirty people. The participants waited by the revolving door. When there were thirty, they were admitted. In the stairwell only the five statues were deserving of attention; they were larger than life-size and ranged up the staircase. These were allegorical representations of the five continents, with Europe at the center. The statues were plaster, but were to have been marble. Ceilings and walls of the hunting room were decorated with carvings of hunting scenes: hunters, hounds in pursuit, and much dead quarry in valleys. The crowning glory, a hunt with the Kaiser, was also of plaster; it was to have been ivory. In the regent's office a large desk abutted the glass French doors to the terrace and park. It bore a clock of fine craftsmanship from the high period, in bronze. The parquet floor under the carpet runner had been created by Italian woodworkers in the form of a labyrinth. The ceiling painting was also Italian. Through the death room one entered the ornate bathroom. The frescoes had been damaged by rising steam and were therefore covered; fortunately their artistic value was not great. The numerous other rooms were not available for visitation. They were occupied by the living ladies and gentlemen.

Incognito

An Aunt Anna complained: Ever since I turned seventy, I have been having a hard time of it. To escape the onslaught of honors, I traveled to Wiesbaden with my best friend. Now I must stay home for two weeks to receive felicitations. I cannot expect the bearers of congratulations, who knew of my absence, to come in vain. I am expecting still more visitors.

The Murder

A girl told the following story: I was in a better house in Cologne. One evening a fine gentleman arrived in a long coat and top hat. Good evening, said the gentleman and touched his hand to the top hat. Then he asked Madame for Hilda. She was upstairs. He went up and stayed a good hour. When he came back, alone, he again touched the top hat and said only: Good evening. Not much later a policeman appeared, also raised his hand in greeting, and asked for Madame. If the girl didn't leave the window, he would have to close the house. Which window? On the second floor. Madame went to look for her herself, then we heard how she screamed, and we all ran to the second floor. In the bed Hilda lay naked without a head. The head stood on the round table by the window, its face turned to the street. Next to the head lay a long knife and a thousand-mark note. Since that evening every girl must accompany her gentleman to the door when he leaves.

The Trip

The pharmacy assistant rang the bell at the home of a pharmacist's son: Was he acquainted with Herr Baumann? Because Herr Baumann wanted to take exactly the same trip to the Mediterranean as the assistant would take, and was a classmate of the young gentleman. He was thinking of taking the very same route, starting from Genoa: Malta, Gibraltar, Spain, ultimately Marseille. He supposed he must be very well off; he had made specific inquiries about all the prices. Herr Baumann, too, was planning to be away for three weeks, including round-trip travel. He had sat for his *Abitur* together with the young gentleman. But the young gentleman had entered middle school a year later. He had compared his plan in detail with the one the assistant had described, all the hotels. By the way, he had occasionally made music together with the young gentleman. He was a tall, well-built young man. The young gentleman must be able to remember him. Unfortunately they had almost completely lost touch in recent years. He just wanted him to know that. Many thanks.

Visit

A boss came into the room where correspondence was done. On the desk of the first employee, a man, lay two equally tall stacks of correspondence. One was completed, the other was yet to be completed. Between the telephone and the telephone meter was a stand hung with numerous stamps.

At the desk of the second employee, a man who also had an armchair and was smoking, assignments were being given out. There a longish row of handbooks was arrayed, their spines facing outward. Four women sat at their desks. The first woman ruffled the steno pad noisily. The second hammered with all her fingers on the typewriter, while the third woman was scarcely visible behind her typewriter and rang a bell. Many cardboard files filled with papers lay on the desk and were stacked under the desk of the fourth woman; the girl worked busily at her typewriter. It was difficult for the boss to ascertain what work was being done. He left the room without a word.

Evening Seminar

A young lady, herself matriculated, attended a seminar with other male and female students. She appeared shortly before the beginning of the session, punctually enough to greet her closer acquaintances. After the second bell the seminar leader arrived and soon proffered a few theses for discussion. First, the two assistants spoke and defended their differing opinions for some time. Then substantive objections to the opinion of the second assistant were raised by a young man who would soon stand for his examination. The claim of the second assistant seemed to him altogether too obscure, without achieving the profundity of the initial thesis. The seminar leader wanted to take the side of the talented young man, but still held back. The young lady listened to all the opinions. She decided to intervene and chose the opinion of the second assistant. "If I have understood Herr Doctor properly," she explained, "his view was by no means as was claimed. Understanding what is known in this sphere unquestionably faces great difficulties. Only a thorough examination reveals that, in truth, the starting point and the end point are identical." "Very good," said the seminar leader. "I am only afraid that not all those present have fully grasped the sense of what Fraulein N. has said. She wanted to say: Here it is not by accident that the solution is identical with the problem; the subject itself demands this, to be fully absorbed. Have I restated your view correctly, Fraulein N.?" The young lady assented, without saying anything further. She had been invited to dinner after the seminar. Although she was wearing only a little evening dress, she hid it under her coat, so as not to distinguish herself from the other students. As the only one in a coat and hat, she nevertheless attracted the others' gaze. A half hour before the end of the seminar it was time to go. She rose softly, nodded to the leader of the seminar, and left the seminar room.

Suicide

Fräulein Lucie was able to report the following concerning the death: After three o'clock in the morning, when Madame had returned from the visit to Herr Director, we were talking as we got ready for bed. Not since the divorce, she said, had he been as nice as he was that evening. Good liqueurs had contributed to the good mood. He had inquired about details of Madame's life. Also, he had not been at all tired. Then when I was in the adjoining room looking after the little one, I heard Madame. I went in and found her on the bed with the telephone. She cried: Berti, my Berti, and hung up. The servant had announced the death. She was deeply shaken by the news.

Laughing Louder

When the farce was over, the theater employee came to the dressing room and looked for one of the actresses. She had played the role of a wealthy young girl from a distinguished family who was working as a secretary in the office of her future husband in order to observe him. Now she was called to the office of the director. The director asked her to take a seat and said: "Dear child, why are you not more cheerful? In a farce, in the summertime, one must above all be happy. Is something wrong? Why don't you laugh more loudly? Why don't you move about more? This is a charming role. The best part is lost. When one is young and as beautiful as you are, it can't be difficult. Tomorrow it will surely all be fine."

Clarifying Conversation

The friends had agreed to have a clarifying conversation with Frau Hegemann. When they entered the apartment dusk was already falling. They found Frau Hegemann in the music room; she was resting on the divan. Apparently startled out of her reverie, she arose; she was wearing a little pale blue dress. The older friend collected himself and began, "We have come to discuss something very grave." "So," responded Frau Hegemann.

"He maintains that what occurred between the two of you did not happen exactly as you described it. You must see that whether the friendship can continue depends on the outcome of this discussion." "Indeed," she responded, and held out a jade cigarette case. "Dear madam," the younger man began his explanation, "I regret profoundly that I must speak of things that are doubtless embarrassing to you, as they are to me as well. May I ask you a few questions?" Frau Hegemann crouched over the Chinese taboret stool. After her vague nod, he continued. "I had to assume that you were already inwardly separated from my friend. On that evening, when we accompanied you to the little dinner at Professor Georgi's, you whispered something to me in the car that admittedly I did not quite understand. Further, I recall a conversation, several days later, here at your place. You explained to me that a man is actually finished for you at the moment when you have given yourself to him. The reference to my friend was unmistakable. I won't, certainly, mention the letter to Gladys. But think of the afternoon on which you played a series of new dance records for me. You didn't believe in faithfulness. You told me abruptly that you had a relationship with Dr. Tsian." "That's a lie," interrupted Frau Hegemann. She jumped up and bent over the smoking table; her face was unrecognizable. "And all the things you said about your friend." "What I said about him was merely provoked by your comment, my dear lady. Or do you perhaps want to deny that you showed me over and over, through repeated unconcealed remarks, that he is actually ridiculous in your eyes? Even when during the move a marble ashtray fell on his head, you found nothing but an occasion for mirth. You decribed the wound to me on the telephone. Do you deny all this?" Frau Hegemann was incapable of lying. "No," she said. Her face had regained its composure. She leaned against the window and gazed into the allée, whose trees still held the last traces of light. "That is enough for me," said the older gentleman, rising. The two gentlemen kissed her hand, one after the other, and departed together.

Return Visit

Two friends had agreed to go together to a burial. One of the two was a frequent social caller at the home of the daughter of the deceased. The other had mainly professional reasons for attending the burial, especially since after it he had a second one to attend at the same cemetery. The company car belonging to the second friend came to fetch the first one at his apartment, which was in a suburb. When they met at the office, a business acquaintance from another city unexpectedly appeared. The gentlemen drove on together, through the allée of poplars that wound around the periphery. All three had taken off their top hats so they would not be damaged in the low-roofed car. "I find it touching," the first friend said to his business acquaintance, that you have made a special trip from Pirmasens, all the more since, as far as I know, you are said to have had only an extremely slight business connection with the deceased." "That is not quite true," responded the person thus addressed, "for the families were friendly. After all, the deceased came personally to my late father's burial in Pirmasens. For this reason I must also pay him my final respects."

Memory

The powerful representative of a large enterprise once made the following remarks: When it comes to women I have a secure sense of judgment. I am very sensitive in this area; fancy-dress balls are something I never attend. In Baden Baden I met an American artist and spent a week with her, in the same hotel. The days flew by like hours. No one asked about names and essentials. When we separated, we knew nothing about each other. Thus the experience became a beautiful memory and has remained one.

Meeting

Not all the members of the board appeared, only five, because it was six in the afternoon. They discussed the business plan for the next six months. Coming up with the plan presented difficulties, because some of the gentlemen board members also sat on the boards of other firms of a similar kind. One of those firms would have to be merged into this one, otherwise the competition would make it impossible for the two separate firms to work fruitfully. Allow me to refer to our sister firm in Hamburg, objected a gentleman who sat on two boards. Its six-month plan is much more extensive than the combined plan of the two firms we are discussing, although it is significantly younger than both. From this it follows that here, under changed circumstances, both firms can safely exist alongside each other. I do not agree with that, came a rejoinder; the fundamentals are completely different. In Hamburg the potential is far less exhausted than here. I would like to recount for you an incident that may not be on the agenda, but that is nevertheless relevant. A man from Hamburg, whom we all know, happened to be conversing with someone else: "I had bought myself a new suitcase at a time when difficult circumstances made every such purchase a sacrifice. One day, I took it along on a trip. I left the compartment for a few moments. When I returned, the case had disappeared. In desperation I searched for it everywhere, without success. Days later I went to the lost-and-found office. There I found my suitcase again. It was the happiest day of my life."

Notes

Editor's Note

1. Thanks to Jennifer Kapczynski for this observation.
2. The phrase translates as "Knock on the door, cry 'Enter!' and don't enter."

Departures

1. Alexander Mitscherlich played a decisive role in ensuring that the involvement of German doctors in the crimes of the National Socialists was made public. In 1947, he published his documentation *Medizin ohne Menschlichkeit: Dokumente des Nürnberger Ärzteprozesses* [Medicine without humanity: Documents of the Nuremberg doctors' trial] (Heldelberg: Fischer, 1960), which mercilessly exposed the crimes of German medical personnel in the concentration camps. Later, he directed the Sigmund Freud Institute in Frankfurt am Main and became the author of much-discussed books, most famously *The Inability to Mourn: Principles of Collective Behavior.*

2. From Elisabeth Lenk's introduction to the correspondence, included in this volume.—Ed.

3. In a conversation with a journalist, Lenk had evidently placed the Situationists in the surrealist tradition and argued for collaboration with them. Jean Schuster, who served as the leader of the group after Breton's death, was of a different opinion and organized her expulsion. A few years later he thought better of it and changed his position. See also Lenk's introduction to the correspondence.

4. "Critical Theory and Surreal Practice" is included in this volume.—Ed.

5. Roberto Calasso, "Theodor W. Adorno, il surrealismo e il 'mana,'" in *Paragone* 138 (1961). See also Letter 5.

6. The Miller photographs were also exhibited at dOKUMENTA 13.

7. Carolyn Christov-Bakargiev in conversation with Heinz-Norbert Jocks, in *Kunstforum,* no. 217 (August–September 2012): 299.

8. It was published at the suggestion of Rolf Tiedemann as part of the series *Dialektische Studien* [Dialectical studies], which he edited. Tiedemann was Adorno's student and later the editor of his *Collected Works.*—Ed.

9. Compare, on this subject, Letters 18 and 19.

10. *The Correspondence of Walter Benjamin, 1910–1940,* ed. Gershom Scholem and Theodor W. Adorno, trans. Manfred R. Jacobson and Evelyn M. Jacobson (Chicago: University of Chicago Press, 1994), 488.

11. For a fuller discussion of this theme, compare the chapter "Plädoyer für eine Theorie des dialektischen Bildes" [Plea for a theory of the dialectical image], in Rita Bischof, *Teleskopagen, wahlweise: Der literarische Surrealismus und das Bild* [Telescopages, or Literary surrealism and the image] (Frankfurt: Vittorio Klostermann, 2001).

12. Benjamin, "Surrealism," in this volume.—Ed.

13. The term *Jetztzeit,* especially in Benjamin, also has unmistakable overtones of revelation.—Ed.

14. French in original.—Ed.

15. See Adorno, "Surrealism Reconsidered," in this volume.—Ed.

16. The literal translation of the title of the essay in question, "Looking Back on Surrealism," makes quite clear this sense that surrealism is over and done with. This is the title given to the essay in the translation by Shierry Weber Nicholsen, in Adorno, *Notes to Literature,* vol. 1 (New York: Columbia University Press, 1991).—Ed.

17. See Adorno, "Surrealism Reconsidered," in this volume.—Ed.

18. An exception was Julien Gracq, who in his 1945 monograph *André Breton* had already emphasized Hegel's importance for Breton.

19. For additional information on Breton's relationship to Hegel, see Rita Bischof, *Nadja Revisited: Studien zu André Breton* [Nadja revisited: Studies on André Breton] (Berlin: Matthes & Seitz, 2013).

20. Georg Wilhelm Friedrich Hegel, *Phenomenology of Spirit,* trans. A. V. Miller (Oxford: Oxford University Press, 1977), §525, 319. Translation modified. "Spirit," here, should be taken in a sense that also includes the intellect.—Ed.

21. Ibid., §590, 360. Translation modified.—Ed.

22. Karl Riha, "Editor's Note," in *Castor Zwieback, Lesestücke* [Castor Zwieback, readings](Cologne: Édition Fundamental, 1994), 28 (the first complete edition).

23. Ibid., 29.

24. In Adorno's *Collected Works,* ed. Rolf Tiedemann, the Castor Zwieback pieces are included among the posthumous works, in volume 20.2. Two items, "Harpsichord" and "Funerary Monument" are missing. Both are included in this volume.—Ed.

25. Carl Dreyfuss, *Beruf und Ideologie der Angestellten* (Berlin: Duncker and Humblot, 1933); published in English as *Occupation and Ideology of the Salaried Employee,* trans. Eva Abramovitch and Ernst E. Warburg (New York: Arno Press, 1977). In connection with the book, Dreyfuss had given up the long-planned project of writing a novel about white-collar employees.

26. The book was published in English as *The Salaried Masses: Duty and Distraction in Weimar Germany,* trans. Quintin Hoare (London: Verso, 1998).

27. André Breton, *Essais et témoinages* [Essays and testimony], ed. Marc Eigeldinger (Neuchâtel: Éditions de la Baconnière, 1950), 28.

28. André Breton, *Oeuvres Complètes,* ed. Marguerite Bonnet (Paris: Éditions de la Pleiade, 1976), 1:187.

29. He tried unsuccessfully to get in touch with them. Unlike Georges Bataille and Pierre Klossowski, the surrealists were not aware of Benjamin.

30. André Breton, *Ode à Charles Fourier, avec une Introduction et des notes par J. Gaulmier* [Ode to Charles Fourier, with an introduction and notes by J. Gaulmier] (Paris: Librarie C. Klinksieck, 1961), 9.

31. André Breton, *Arcane 17,* trans. Zack Rogow (Los Angeles: Green Integer, 2004), 69. Emphasis in original; translation modified.—Ed.

32. Adorno refers here to the countries of Central and Eastern Europe then under the domination of the Soviet Union.—Ed.

33. Theodor W. Adorno, *Gesammelte Schriften* [Collected works], ed. Rolf Tiedemann, vol. 20.2 (Frankfurt: Suhrkamp, 1986), 699.

34. See Letter 31.

35. Ibid.

36. Adorno's handwriting was not only difficult to decipher; he also wrote in the German script known as Sütterlin, which was taught in schools there in the 1920s and 1930s.

37. The dissertation was submitted shortly after Adorno's death and published under the title *Der springende Narziß: André Bretons poetischer Materialismus* [Leaping Narcissus: André Breton's poetic materialism] (Munich: Rogner & Bernhard, 1971).

Surrealism

1. Emphasis in original. The more familiar translation of this phrase, "profane illumination," fails to reflect the sudden, sometimes violent nature of the experience as well as its theological connotations.—Ed.

2. "Good News Boulevard."—Ed.

3. Massachusetts governor Alvan Fuller could have pardoned Sacco and Vanzetti, thus preventing their execution, but did not.—Ed.

4. Erich Auerbach, *Dante, Poet of the Secular World,* trans. Ralph Manheim, 2nd ed. (Chicago: University of Chicago Press, 1969), 60. Translation modified.—Ed.

5. André Breton, *Nadja,* trans. Margaret Cohen, who points out that Benjamin slightly misquotes the sentence, which in the original French reads "all that is mine." Margaret Cohen, *Profane Illumination: Walter Benjamin and the Paris of Socialist Revolution* (Berkeley and Los Angeles: University of California Press, 1993), 191n.—Ed.

6. Guillaume Apollinaire, "The New Spirit and the Poets," in *Selected Writings,* trans. Roger Shattuck (New York: New Directions, 1971), 229.—Ed.

7. Ibid., 234.—Ed.

8. Paul Karl Wilhelm Scheerbart (1863–1915) was an author of fantastic literature and drawings. He also published under the pseudonym Kuno Küfer.—Ed.

9. The *Songs of Maldoror,* written between 1868 and 1869 by Idisore Ducasse under the pen name of Lautréamont, Comte de Maldoror, is an extraordinary work in six cantos that served as an inspiration to the surrealists.—Ed.

10. Author of the *Songs of Maldoror.* See above.—Ed.

11. French in original.—Ed.

12. French in original.—Ed.

13. French in original.—Ed.

Surrealism Reconsidered

1. French in original.—Ed.

2. The reference is to a book by Alan Bott, *Our Fathers (1870–1900): Manners and Customs of the Ancient Victorians* (London: W. Heinemann, 1931).—Ed.

3. G. W. F. Hegel, *Phenomenology of Spirit,* trans. A. V. Miller (Oxford: Oxford University Press, 1977), 360. Translation modified.—Ed.

4. From Kurt Weill and Bertolt Brecht, "Happy End," American adaptation and lyrics by Michael Feingold (Vienna, Universal Edition UE 17243), 13.

Critical Theory and Surreal Practice

1. The essay is based on a speech given in Frankfurt am Main in 1996.—Ed.

2. Elisabeth Lenk, *Der springende Narziß: André Bretons poetischer Materialismus* [Leaping Narcissus: André Breton's poetic materialism] (Munich: Rogner & Bernhard, 1971).

3. Julien Gracq, "Revenir à Breton" [Coming back to Breton], in *Le Monde des Livres,* February 16, 1996.

4. Elisabeth Lenk, "Adorno gegen seine Liebhaber verteidigt" [Adorno defended against his admirers], in *Das unerhört Moderne: Berliner Adorno-Tagung* [Outrageous modernity: Berlin Adorno conference], ed. Frithjof Hager and Hermann Pfütze (Lüneburg: zu Klampen, 1990), 10–27.

5. Max Horkheimer, "Traditional and Critical Theory," in *Critical Theory: Selected Essays,* trans. Matthew J. O'Connell (New York: Continuum, 2002), 212.

6. Ibid., 241. Translation modified.—Ed.

7. Both quotations are taken from an article by Ignacio Ramonet in *Le Monde Diplomatique* (German), supplement to *TAZ,* March 15, 1996, 1.

8. Quoted in *Der Spiegel,* no. 8 (February 19, 1996).

9. Horkheimer, "Traditional and Critical Theory," 206n. Translation modified.—Ed.

10. Alfred Kerr (1867–1948), German Jewish theater critic and essayist.—Ed.

11. Heinrich Böll, "Frankfurter Vorlesungen" [Frankfurt lectures], in *Werke,* ed. Bernd Balzer (Cologne: Kiepenhauer & Witsch, 1964–1972), 2:42.

12. The Treuhandanstalt, or German Trust Agency, was formed on June 17, 1990, to oversee the restructuring of East German industries that at one time employed four million people.—Ed.

13. Theodor W. Adorno, *Aesthetic Theory,* ed. Gretel Adorno and Rolf Tiedemann. Newly translated, edited, and with a translator's introduction by Robert Hullot-Kentor (Minneapolis: University of Minnesota Press, 1997), 318. The quote within the quote is from Johann Huizinga, *Homo Ludens.*—Ed.

14. Friedrich Schiller, *On the Aesthetic Education of Man,* trans. Reginald Snell (Mineola, N.Y.: Dover Publications, 2004), twenty-second letter, 107.

15. Letter of August 21, 1941, cited by Gunzelin Schmid Noerr, in "Gesten aus Begriffen" [Gestures from concepts], *Zeitschrift für Kritische Theorie* [Journal of critical theory] 1, no. 1 (1995): 73.

16. Hugo Ball, *Flight out of Time,* trans. Ann Raimes (Berkeley and Los Angeles: University of California Press, 1996), 117. Emphasis added by Elisabeth Lenk.

17. Georges Bataille, "Max Ernst Philosopher!," in *The Absence of Myth: Writings on Surrealism,* trans. Michael Richardson (London: Verso, 1994), 134–36.

18. Ibid., 135.

19. André Breton, "Max Ernst," in *The Lost Steps,* trans. Mark Polizzotti (Lincoln: University of Nebraska Press, 1996), 61.

20. The essay is included in this volume.—Ed.

21. See Castor Zwieback (Theodor W. Adorno and Carl Dreyfus), "Surrealist Readings," in this volume.—Ed.

22. Max Ernst, "Histoire d'une histoire naturelle," in *Écritures* [Writings] (Paris: Gallimard, 1970), 244.

23. Ibid., 250. The Breton quote is from "Le Château étoilé," *Minotaure* 8 (1936).

24. Max Ernst, "Die Naktheit der Frau ist weiser als die Lehre der Philosophen" [Woman's nudity is wiser than the philosopher's teachings]. (Cologne: Galerie der Spiegel, 1970).

25. Ibid., Max Ernst, "Beyond Painting," in: *Max Ernst and Others: Beyond Painting,* trans. Dorothea Tanning and Ralph Mannheim (Chicago: Solar Books, 2009), 18.

26. Ibid., 16. Emphasis in original (Ernst).—Ed.

27. Max Ernst, *Femme 100 têtes* (Paris: Éditions du Carrefour, 1929). The English edition, trans. Dorothea Tanning, cleverly reproduces the homophonic pun on French *cent* (100) and *sans* (without), by titling the book *The 100 Headless Woman* (New York: George Braziller, 1981)—Ed.

28. Georges Bataille, "The Sorcerer's Apprentice," in *Oeuvres Complètes* (Paris: Gallimard, 1970), 1:523–37. Originally appeared as "Pour un collège sociologique," *Nouvelle Revue Française*, no. 298 (July 1, 1938).

29. Adorno's literary estate has preserved the compositions of several songs and a complete libretto. See *Frankfurt Opernhefte* [Frankfurt Opera brochures] 5, no. 3 (December 15, 1976); and Adorno, *Der Schatz des Indianer-Joe: Singspiel nach Mark Twain* [The treasure of Indian Joe: Singspiel after Mark Twain], ed. and with a postscript by Rolf Tiedemann (Frankfurt: Suhrkamp, 1979).—Ed.

30. *Critique: Revue Générale des Publications Françaises et Étrangères* [Critique: General review of French and foreign publications], ed. Georges Bataille, no. 1 (June 1946): 2.

31. *Die Demokratie lebt vom Streit und auch von der Ungewissheit* [Democracy lives on struggle and also on uncertainty]. From the taped record of the conference. Documentation in the *Frankfurter Rundschau,* October 28, 1978, 14.

32. Compare Rita Bischof, *Souveränität und Subversion: Georges Batailles Theorie der Moderne* [Sovereignty and subversion: Georges Bataille's theory of modernism] (Berlin: Matthes & Seitz, 1984), particularly the chapter "Heterology," 138ff.

33. Georges Bataille, *Inner Experience,* trans. Leslie Anne Boldt (New York: State University of New York Press, 1988), 28. The translation reads, in full, "of the universe [present-day man] is no longer the rational (alleged) master, but the dream."—Ed.

Introduction to the Correspondence

The essay is slightly abridged.—Ed.

1. Walter Benjamin, letter to Ernst Schoen, September 19, 1919. In *Briefe* [Letters], ed. and with notes by Gershom Scholem and Theodor W. Adorno (Frankfurt: Edition Suhrkamp, 1978), 1:220.—Ed.

2. Joachim Perels, "Verteidigung der Erinnerung im Angesicht ihrer Zerstörung—Theodor W. Adorno" [Defense of memory in the face of its destruction—Theodor W. Adorno], in M. Buckmiller, D. Heimann, J. Perels, *Judentum und politische Existenz: Siebzehn Portraits deutsch-jüdischer Intellektueller* [Judaism and political existence: Seventeen portraits of German-Jewish intellectuals] (Hanover: Offizin Verlag, 2000), 274–75.

3. Adorno's maternal grandfather, Giovanni Francesco Calvalli-Adorno, was actually a fencing master.

4. The German title *Stichworte* suggests a stinging, or piercing.—Ed.

5. Adorno himself twice addresses Lenk using the intimate *Du* form, but as Lenk does not respond in kind, he reverts to *Sie.* See Letters 31 and 32.—Ed.

6. José Pierre (1927–1999) was Breton's right-hand man. He became the historian of surrealism, with works like *André Breton et la Peinture* [André Breton and

painting] (1987) and *Le Surrealism d'aujourd'hui* [Today's surrealism] (1973). He also published a comprehensive two-volume collection of surrealist manifestos and tracts.—Ed.

7. "Surrealism: Last Snapshot of the European Intelligentsia." The essay is included in this volume.—Ed.

8. The full title of the journal is *La Brèche: Action Surréaliste* [The breach: Surrealist action]. A total of eight issues appeared between 1961 and 1965.—Ed.

9. The Spanish playwright Fernando Arabal was briefly associated with Breton.—Ed.

10. Christiane Rochefort (1917–1998) was a feminist writer and best-selling author.—Ed.

11. Elisabeth Lenk, *Der springende Narziß: André Bretons poetischer Materialismus* [Leaping Narcissus: André Breton's poetic materialism] (Munich: Rogner and Bernhard, 1971). German *springen* means both to leap and to shatter, as in "glass shatters when broken."—Ed.

12. Jean Schuster (1929–95) became a surrealist after World War II. He was the executor of Breton's will, editor of *Surréalisme même,* and a collaborator of *L'Archibras.*—Ed.

13. Guy Debord (1931–1994) was the editor of the journal *Internationale Situationniste* from 1958 to 1969.—Ed.

14. Danish artist Asger Jorn (1914–73) was a founding member of the avant-garde movement COBRA and the Situationist International.—Ed.

15. The essay was called "The Poverty of the Students." The title is a parody of Karl Marx's *The Poverty of Philosophy,* which itself was a response to Proudhon's *The Philosophy of Poverty.*—Ed.

16. Rudi Dutschke (1940–1979) and Bernd Rabehl (1938–) were activists in the Socialist German Students' Union (SDS). Dutschke suffered an assassination attempt in 1968 that led to widespread student protests and to his death a decade later.—Ed.

17. Rolf Tiedemann rightly placed this essay at the conclusion of the second and final volume of *Notes to Literature,* trans. Shierry Weber Nicholsen (New York: Columbia University Press, 1992).—Ed.

18. Elizabeth Lenk's introduction appears in this volume.—Ed.

19. Herbert Marcuse, "On Hedonism," trans. Jeremy J. Shapiro, in *Negations: Essays in Critical Theory* (Boston: Beacon Press, 1968), 165.—Ed.

20. In a sensational trial, Vera Brühne (1910–2001) was found guilty, on insufficient evidence, of murdering an industrialist and his housekeeper. She was later pardoned.—Ed.

21. Adelheid von Weislingen is a character in Wolfgang von Goethe's 1773 play *Götz von Berlichungen with the Iron Hand,* a role characterized by her beauty, demonic sensuality, and lust for power.—Ed.

22. See the dream protocol included in this volume with Letter 81.—Ed.

23. The "Action Un-expiated Nazi Justice" was organized by the student Reinhard Strecker and the SDS, based primarily on the criminal and civil files of 105 judges who had served under the Third Reich. The German parliament had invited citizens to write petitions bringing to their attention important questions that had been insufficiently addressed—in this case the possible criminal culpability of the judges. Although the exhibition was developed in response to a call by the Bundestag, and its accuracy was attested by the attorney general of the Federal Republic, it was criticized by the German government and by the Social Democratic Party (SPD). The SPD also joined in a villainous campaign against Strecker based on false accusations. See Michael Kohlstruck, "Reinhard Strecker—'Darf man seinen Kindern wieder ein Leben in Deutschland zumuten?' [Reinhard Strecker— 'Can one again expect one's children to live in Germany?']" in *Engagierte Demokraten: Vergangenheitspolitik in kritischer Absicht* [Engaged Democrats: Politics of the past with critical intent], ed. Claudia Fröhlich and Michael Kohlstruck (Münster: Verlag Westfälisches Dampfboot, 1998), 185–212.

24. Alex Demirović, *Der nonkonformistische Intellektuelle: Die Entwicklung der kritischen Theorie zur Frankfurter Schule* [The nonconformist intellectual: The development of critical theory into the Frankfurt School] (Frankfurt: Suhrkamp, 1999), 890 ff.

25. The Red Army Fraction (Rote Armee Fraktion), or RAF, was a leftist group that used terror in an attempt to unmask and destroy capitalism in Germany. Formed in 1970, it carried out numerous attacks including bank robberies and high-profile kidnappings. The group is sometimes known as the Baader-Meinhof gang, after two of its leaders, Andreas Baader and Ulrike Meinhof. Baader and Meinhof were among five RAF leaders who were arrested in 1972 and sentenced to life imprisonment. In 1979 Baader, Meinhof, and two other RAF leaders were found dead in their prison cells under suspicious circumstances.—Ed.

Sense and Sensibility

1. Originally published in France as *Le Paysan de Paris* (Paris: Éditions Gallimard, 1926, 1953). In English it appeared as *Paris Peasant*, trans. Simon Watson Taylor (Boston: Exact Change, 1994). Cited as *Paris Peasant*.—Ed.

2. See, for example, Jürgen Habermas, *Protestbewegung und Hochschulreform* [Protest movement and university reform] (Frankfurt: Suhrkamp, 1969); and Raymond Aron, *The Elusive Revolution: Anatomy of a Student Revolt*, trans. Gordon Clough (New York: Praeger, 1969).

3. Aragon, *Paris Peasant*, 67.

4. Ibid., 127.

5. Ibid., 111.

6. Ibid., 66.

7. Sigmund Freud, *The Interpretation of Dreams,* trans. James Strachey (New York: Basic Books, 2010), 563.

8. Walter Benjamin, *The Arcades Project,* trans. Howard Eiland and Kevin McLaughlin (Cambridge, Mass.: Belknap Press of Harvard University Press, 1999), 64.

9. Charles Beaudelaire, "to extract from fashion whatever element it may contain of poetry within history, to distill the eternal from the transitory." *The Painter of Modern Life and Other Essays,* trans. and ed. Jonathan Mayne (London: Phaidon, 1964), 12.

10. Rimbaud: "J'aimais les peintures idiotes, dessus de portes, décors, toiles de saltimbanques, enseignes." [I preferred bad paintings, decorated lintels, carnival backdrops, signs.] *Rimbaud Complete,* trans. Wyatt Mason, (New York: Modern Library, 2003), 1:208. Translation modified.

11. See Apollinaire's last manifesto, "The New Spirit and the Poets," 1917: "What is new exists without being progress. Everything is in the effect of surprise. . . . *Surprise is the greatest source of what is new." Selected Writings of Guillaume Apollinaire,* trans. Roger Shattuck (New York: New Directions, 1971), 233.

12. G. W. F. Hegel, *Philosophy of History,* trans. J. Sibree (New York: Colonial Press, 1899), 235.

13. Ibid., 234.

14. Aragon, *Paris Peasant,* 14.

15. Breton speaks of the Boulevard Bonne-Nouvelle as of one of the "major strategic points I am looking for in matters of chaos, points which I persist in believing obscurely provided for me." *Nadja,* trans. Richard Howard (New York: Grove Press, 1960), 153.

16. Walter Benjamin, *Arcades Project,* 458.

17. Aragon, *Paris Peasant,* 48.

18. For Aragon, what Adorno wrote about surrealist montages holds true: "By rigorously composing out things that are obsolete, they create *nature morte."* The literal meaning of *nature morte,* or still life, is "dead nature." The quotation is from "Surrealism Reconsidered," which is included in this volume.—Ed.

19. Aragon, *Paris Peasant,* 48. Translation modified.

20. Ibid., 128. Translation modified.

21. Ibid., 121.

22. Ibid., 130.

23. "Rien n'aura eu lieu que le lieu." [Nothing will have taken place but the place.] The quotation is from Mallarmé, "Un coup de dés jamais n'abolira le hasard" [A roll of the dice will never abolish chance.]—Ed.

24. Aragon, *Paris Peasant,* 182.

25. See Georges Bataille, *Literature and Evil,* trans. Alastair Hamilton (New York: Penguin Books, 2012).

26. Problematic enough that Monnerot, who attempts to bring surrealism into line with the positions of Heidegger and Jaspers, revives the category of the *Bund,* or league, to characterize the surrealist group! *La Poésie moderne et le sacré* [Modern poetry and the sacred] (Paris: Gallimard, 1945), 73, 190n37.

27. Evidently Aragon himself had this idea. See Garaudy, *L'Itinéraire d'Aragon: Du surréalisme au monde réel* [The itinerary of Aragon: From surrealism to the real world] (Paris: Gallimard, 1961), 144.

28. Georg Lukács, *The Meaning of Contemporary Realism,* trans. John and Necke Mander (London: Merlin Press, 1963). The thought is developed systematically in "On Specific Particularity as a Category of Aesthetics," trans. Nicholas Walker, in *The Continental Aesthetics Reader,* ed. Clive Cazeaux (London: Routledge, 2000), 220–33.

29. Lukács, *The Meaning of Contemporary Realism,* 33.

30. Ibid., 34.

31. *Les Beaux Quartiers* (Paris: Gallimard, 1936). The book was published in English as *Residential Quarter,* trans. Haakon M. Chevalier (New York: Houghton Mifflin Harcourt, 1938).

32. See Aragon's notes to the new edition of *Aventures de Télémaque,* published in English as *The Adventures of Telemachus,* trans. Renée Riese Hubert and Judd D. Hubert (Boston: Exact Change, 1974).

33. On the relationship between Aragon's style and that of Diderot, see Dominique Arban, *Aragon parle* [Aragon speaks] (Paris: Seghers, 1968). *Rameau's Nephew* is a novel in the form of a dialogue between a philosopher and his self-satirizing nephew, written by Enlightenment philosopher Denis Diderot but not published in his lifetime.—Ed.

34. Aragon, *Paris Peasant,* 187.

35. Not forever. The theses of the dythrambic final manifesto culminate in the sentence: "The characters have completed their time on earth."

36. Bataille, who chose the programmatic title *Acéphale* [Headless] for a journal that appeared in 1936–37, was the first to take the plunge into a "headless" materialism.

37. Aragon, *Paris Peasant,* 189.

38. *Anicet ou le panorama* [Anicet or the panorama] (Paris: Gallimard, 1921), 33f.

39. Ibid., 207.

40. "The goddess who holds the axe," says Aragon.

41. Aragon, *Paris Peasant,* 201.

42. Louis Aragon, "Introduction à 1930," in *La Révolution surrealiste* [The surrealist revolution], no. 12 (December 15, 1929).

43. Apollinaire, "Rivalise donc poète avec les etiquettes des parfumeurs" [Poet, compete with the perfumers' labels].

44. Aragon, "Introduction à 1930," 60.

45. Aragon, *Paris Peasant*, 117.

46. Aragon, "Introduction à 1930," 62.

47. Ibid., 64.

Introduction to the German Edition of Charles Fourier's *The Theory of the Four Movements and the General Destinies*

1. The book appeared in German in 1966 as *Theorie der vier Bewegungen und der allgemeinen Bestimmungen,* ed. Theodor W. Adorno (Frankfurt: Europäische Verlagsanstalt, 1966). It was published in English as *The Theory of the Four Movements,* ed. Gareth Stedman Jones and Ian Patterson, trans. Ian Patterson (New York: Cambridge University Press, 1996). Cited as *Four Movements.*—Ed.

2. Raymond Ruyer, *L'Utopie et les utopies* [Utopia and Utopias] (Paris: Presses Universitaires de France, 1946). Ruyer is generally described as a philosopher. His theory of pan-psychism influenced Deleuze and Guattari, among others.—Ed.

3. "Les attractions sont proportionelles aux destinées. La série distribue les harmonies." The quotation is inscribed on his tombstone.—Ed.

4. Compare Fourier's satire on "L'amour du mépris de soi-même" [Love of self-contempt], in *Publications des manuscrits de Charles Fourier* [Publications from the manuscripts of Charles Fourier], 4 vols. (Paris: Librarie phalanstérienne, 1851–1858). Cited as *Manuscrits.*

5. Cited in Charles Pellarin, *The Life of Charles Fourier,* trans. Francis George Shaw, 2nd ed. (New York: William H. Graham, 1848), 66. Translation of Pellarin, *Fourier: Sa vie et sa théorie* (Paris, 1849). Cited as *Life of Fourier.*

6. In *The Utopian Vision of Charles Fourier: Selected Texts on Work, Love, and Passionate Attraction* (London: Jonathan Cape, 1972), the editors and translators Jonathan Beecher and Richard Bienvenu sometimes call this "passional attachment," presumably to indicate that not all of Fourier's passions are emotional; for example, they include "passions" based on the five senses. The term is also used in the translation of Charles Pellarin's early, enthusiastic biography of Fourier.—Ed.

7. Fourier, *Four Movements,* 105n.

8. Ibid.

9. Pellarin, *Life of Fourier,* 200.

10. Paul Hazard, *La pensée européenne au XVIIIe siècle de Montesquieu à Lessing* [European thought in the 18th century from Montesquieu to Lessing] (Paris: Boivin, 1946), 2:136.

11. Fourier, *Manuscrits,* 1:321.

12. Pellarin, *Life of Fourier,* 154.

13. See, for example, Fourier, *Four Movements,* 65.

14. Fourier, *Manuscrits,* 1:128.

15. These are the terms employed by Shaw in his translation of Pellarin's early biography of Fourier, cited above. They are closer to the original than those employed in the later translation of the *Four Movements* by Ian Patterson.—Ed.

16. Fourier, *Four Movements*, 15.

17. Quoted by Pellarin, *Life of Fourier*, 81; from Charles Fourier, *Théorie de l'unité universelle* [Theory of universal unity], in *Oeuvres complètes*, 2nd ed. (Paris: Librarie sociétaire, 1841), 3:114ff. Cited as *L'unité universelle*.

18. Fourier, *Manuscrits*, 1:330 and passim. For Fourier, "subversive" means rebelling against the divine law of attraction.

19. Ibid., 329.

20. Ibid., 330, 347.

21. Alphonso X of Castile (thirteenth century). This statement is recorded in Bayle, *Dictionnaire historique et critique* [Historical and critical dictionary] (1730), 2:95.

22. Fourier, "Le nouveau monde industriel et sociétaire, ou Invention du procédé d'índustrie attrayante et naturelle, distribuée en séries passionées" [The new industrial and societal world, or Invention of the process of attractive and natural industry, distributed in passionate series], in *Oeuvres complètes*, 3rd ed. (Paris, 1846), 6:288. Cited as *Nouveau monde*.

23. Ibid., 355f.

24. Compare the analysis of "l'attraction passionée" in ibid., 47ff.

25. "L'attraction passionée est l'impulsion donnée par la nature antérieurement à la reflection, et persistante malgré l'opposition de la raison, du devoir, du prejudice, etc." [Passionate attraction is the impulse that is given by nature prior to reflection, and persists despite the opposition of reason, duty, prejudice, etc.] Fourier, *Nouveau monde*, 47.

26. The explanations here draw on Ian Patterson's translation of the *Four Movements*.—Ed.

27. Fourier, *L'unité universelle*, 3:114.

28. See, for example, Fourier, *Four Movements*, 222ff.

29. Fourier, "Des sympathies puissancielles ou amours polygames et omnigames" [On primal sympathies or polygamous and omnigamous love], published for the first time in the catalogue of the Exposition International du Surréalisme 1959/60 (Paris: Galérie Cordier), 27ff.

30. Ibid., 27.

31. Fourier, *L'unité universelle*, 2:105.

32. Fourier, *Manuscrits*, 1:50.

33. Quoted in F. Armand and R. Maublanc, *Fourier* (Paris: Éditions Sociales Internationales, 1937), 1:181. Cited as *Fourier*.

34. Fourier, *L'unité universelle*, 3:315.

35. Cited in Armand and Maublanc, *Fourier,* 100. The fact that Fourier is anticipating an essential aspect of Marxist historiography probably does not need to be emphasized here.

36. Voltaire (François Marie Arouet), *Candide,* trans. Lowell Blair (Bantam Classics, 1984), 69.

37. Marcuse, Herbert, "On Hedonism," in *Negations: Essays in Critical Theory,* trans. Jeremy J. Shapiro (1938; Boston: Beacon Press, 1968), 159–200, 174.

38. That Saint-Simon also refers expressly to Bentham is shown by Werner Leendertz in his book *Die industrielle Revolution als Ziel und Grundlage der Sozialreform: Eine systematische Darstellung der Ideen Saint-Simons und seiner Schüler* [The industrial revolution as goal and foundation of social reforms: A systematic presentation of the ideas of Saint-Simon and his students] (Emsdetten: Heinr. & J. Lechte, 1938).

39. Fourier, *Pièges et charlatanisme des deux sects Saint-Simon et Owen, qui promettent l'association et le progress* [Traps and charlatanism of the two sects of Saint-Simon and Owen, which promise association and progress] (Paris: Bossange Père, 1831), 57f.

40. Fourier, *Nouveau monde,* 348.

41. On this see also Marcuse, "On Hedonism," 161ff.

42. The *harmoniens,* whose combativeness is much more fully developed than ours, go to court frequently and gladly.

43. Fourier, *Nouveau monde,* 349.

44. Fourier, *L'unité universelle,* 309.

45. Ibid., 343.

46. Ibid., 310.

47. Ibid., 334.

48. Fourier's treatise "Du libre arbitre" [On free will] is revealing in regard to his concept of freedom. In *Oeuvres Complètes,* 2:v–lxviii.

49. Fourier, *L'unité universelle,* 184.

50. Ibid., 170.

51. Behind the rider sits dark care (Horace).—Ed.

52. Fourier, *L'unité universelle,* 167.

53. Ibid., 156.

54. That is, everything that limits human freedom.

Surrealist Readings

1. The four were "Return Visit," "Meeting," "The Connecting Trams," and "Encounter."

2. Carl Dreyfus, *Beruf und Ideologie der Angestellten* (Berlin: Duncker und Humblot, 1933).

3. English in original.—Ed.

Publication History

Walter Benjamin, "Surrealism: Last Snapshot of the European Intelligentsia," was originally published as "Der Surrealismus: Die letzte Momentaufnahme der europäischen Intelligenz," in *Literarische Welt*, February 1929. It is included in *Gesammelte Schriften* (Frankfurt am Main: Suhrkamp, 1991), II.1:295–310. All rights reserved by Suhrkamp Verlag Berlin.

Theodor W. Adorno, "Surrealism Reconsidered," was originally published as "Rückblickend auf den Surrealismus" in *Texte und Zeichen*, no. 6, 1956. It is included in *Gesammelte Schriften* (Frankfurt am Main: Suhrkamp, 1997), 11:101–5. Copyright 1974 Suhrkamp Verlag Frankfurt am Main.

Elisabeth Lenk, "Critical Theory and Surreal Practice," was originally published in *Theodor W. Adorno und Elisabeth Lenk: Briefwechsel, 1962–1969*, ed. Elisabeth Lenk (Munich: edition text + kritik, 2001), 199–219. Copyright 2001 edition text + kritik.

Correspondence between Theodor W. Adorno and Elisabeth Lenk, 1962–1969, was originally published in *Theodor W. Adorno und Elisabeth Lenk: Briefwechsel, 1962–1969*, ed. Elisabeth Lenk (Munich: edition text + kritik, 2001), 23–167; introduction by Elisabeth Lenk, 9–22. Copyright 2001 edition text + kritik.

Elisabeth Lenk, "Sense and Sensibility: Afterword to Louis Aragon's *Paris Peasant*," was originally published as "Sinn und Sinnlichkeit," in Louis Aragon, *Pariser Landleben*, trans. Rudolf Wittkopf (Munich: Rogner & Bernhard, 1969), 257–75. Reprinted by permission of the author.

Elisabeth Lenk, "Introduction to the German Edition of Charles Fourier's *The Theory of the Four Movements and the General Destinies*," was originally published as "Vorwort" (Preface), in Charles Fourier, *Theorie der vier*

Bewegungen und der allgemeinen Bestimmungen, ed. Theodor W. Adorno, trans. Gertrud von Holzhausen (Frankfurt and Vienna: Europäische Verlagsanstalt, 1966), 5–41. Reprinted by permission of the author.

An initial selection of Castor Zwieback (Theodor W. Adorno and Carl Dreyfus), "Surrealist Readings," was published pseudonymously as "Surrealistische Lesestücke" in the *Frankfurter Zeitung,* November 17, 1931. Additional pieces were included in a 1963 publication—also pseudonymous—in *Akzente.* With the exception of "Cembalo" ("Harpsichord") and "Grabmal" ("Funerary Monument"), the short pieces are included in Theodor W. Adorno, *Gesammelte Schriften,* vol. 20.2 (Frankfurt am Main: Suhrkamp, 1997), 587–97. "Cembalo" and "Grabmal" were originally published in Theodor W. Adorno and Carl Dreyfus, *Lesestücke,* ed. Karl Riha (Fulda: Edition Fundamental, n.d.). Copyright 1986 Suhrkamp Verlag Frankfurt am Main. All rights reserved by Suhrkamp Verlag Berlin.

Index

THEODOR W. ADORNO (1903–1969) was a German sociologist, philosopher, and musicologist known for his critical theory of society and his work on aesthetics and philosophy. He was a leading member of the Frankfurt School of critical theory and author of dozens of books. Translations available from the University of Minnesota Press include *Aesthetic Theory* (1998), *Kierkegaard: Construction of the Aesthetic* (1989), and *Philosophy of New Music* (2006).

ELISABETH LENK is a German literary scholar and sociologist. She is professor emeritus of literature at the University of Hanover.

SUSAN H. GILLESPIE is a translator of German philosophy, poetry, memoirs, and fiction. She is founding director of the Institute for International Liberal Education at Bard College, where she is vice president for special global initiatives.

RITA BISCHOF is an author and translator. Her publications focus on the history of French intellectuals between the two World Wars.